T0142018

Scala Design Patterns

John Hunt

Scala Design Patterns

Patterns for Practical Reuse and Design

Dr. John Hunt
Department of Computer Science
and Creative Technologies
University of the West of England
Bristol, United Kingdom

ISBN 978-3-319-34972-5 ISBN 978-3-319-02192-8 (eBook)
DOI 10.1007/978-3-319-02192-8
Springer Cham Heidelberg New York Dordrecht London

Printed on acid-free paper

Springer is part of Springer Science+Business Media (www.springer.com)

This book is dedicated to my children.

Author's Note

I would like to thank several people who have contributed to my understanding and appreciation for Scala. These people helped through discussions, explanations and as sounding boards. They include Paul Storer-Martin, George Ball, Ivan O'Mahony, Theo Mauger and Yan Tordoff.

All the source code examples presented in this book can be found at Springer Extras (http://extras.springer.com) by searching for the book's ISBN (978-3-319-02191-1).

Contents

Part I Introduction

1 Introduction ... 3
1.1 Introduction ... 3
1.2 Introduction to Scala ... 4
1.3 What Is Scala? ... 6
1.4 The Class Person ... 7
1.5 Functional Programming ... 8
1.6 A Hybrid Language ... 9
1.7 Scala Oriented Patterns ... 10
1.8 Resources ... 11
Reference ... 11

2 Design Patterns ... 13
2.1 Introduction ... 13
2.2 Motivation Behind Patterns ... 14
2.3 Design Patterns ... 15
2.3.1 What Are Design Patterns? ... 15
2.3.2 What They Are Not? ... 15
2.3.3 Architectural Patterns ... 16
2.3.4 Documenting Patterns ... 16
2.3.5 When to Use Patterns ... 18
2.3.6 Strengths and Limitations of Design Patterns ... 18
2.4 Fundamental Patterns ... 19
2.5 Code Reuse Patterns ... 19
2.6 GoF Design Patterns ... 19
2.7 Functional Patterns ... 20
2.8 Patterns and Scala ... 20
2.9 Further Reading ... 21
References ... 21

3 UML and Scala 23
3.1 Introduction 23
3.2 The Models 24
3.3 Use Case Diagrams 25
3.4 The Object Model 26
3.4.1 Representing Classes 26
3.4.2 Representing Objects 28
3.4.3 Representing Relationships 28
3.5 Packages 33
3.6 Sequence Diagrams 34
3.7 Collaboration Diagrams 36
3.8 OOD Is Language Independent – Right? 38
3.9 Making UML Work for You 39
3.10 Questions to Consider 39
3.11 The Scala Platform 40
3.12 Classes in UML 41
3.13 Fields in UML 41
3.14 Operations in UML 42
3.15 Constructors 42
3.16 Properties in Scala 43
3.17 Packages in UML 44
3.18 UML Interfaces 45
3.19 Scala Traits as Stereo Types 45
3.20 Templates 46
3.21 Associations 46
3.22 Multiplicity in UML 48
3.23 Aggregation and Composition 48
3.24 Singleton Objects 49
3.25 Synchronous and Asynchronous Messages 50
References 50

Part II Fundamental Patterns

4 Immutability 53
4.1 Introduction 53
4.2 Pattern Classification 53
4.3 Intent 54
4.4 Context 54
4.5 Forces/Motivation 54
4.6 Constituent Parts 55
4.7 Implementation Issues 56
4.8 Concrete Example 56
4.9 Pros and Cons 59
4.10 Related Patterns 59

5 Singleton 61
5.1 Introduction 61
5.2 Pattern Classification 61
5.3 Intent 61
5.4 Context 61
5.5 Forces/Motivation 62
5.6 Constituent Parts 62
5.7 Implementation Issues 62
5.8 Concrete Examples 63
5.8.1 Basic Scala Singleton Implementation 63
5.8.2 Extended Singleton Scenario 63
5.8.3 Extended Singleton Example 64
5.9 Pros and Cons 68
5.10 Related Patterns 69

6 Marker Trait 71
6.1 Introduction 71
6.2 Pattern Classification 71
6.3 Intent 71
6.4 Context 71
6.5 Forces/Motivation 72
6.6 Constituent Parts 72
6.7 Implementation Issues 73
6.8 Concrete Example 73
6.9 Pros and Cons 75

7 Delegation 77
7.1 Introduction 77
7.2 Pattern Classification 78
7.3 Intent 78
7.4 Context 78
7.5 Forces/Motivation 80
7.6 Constituent Parts 80
7.7 Implementation Issues 81
7.8 Concrete Examples 81
7.8.1 Object Based Approach 81
7.8.2 Trait Based Approach 82
7.9 Pros and Cons 82
7.10 Related Patterns 83
References 83

Part III Code Reuse Patterns

8 Lazy Parameters 87
8.1 Introduction 87
8.2 Pattern Classification 87

8.3 Intent ... 87
8.4 Context ... 87
8.5 Forces/Motivation ... 88
8.6 Constituent Parts ... 88
8.7 Implementation Issues ... 88
8.8 Concrete Example ... 90
8.9 Pros and Cons ... 91

9 Partially Applied Functions ... 93
9.1 Introduction ... 93
9.2 Pattern Classification ... 94
9.3 Intent ... 94
9.4 Context ... 94
9.5 Forces/Motivation ... 94
9.6 Constituent Parts ... 94
9.7 Implementation Issues ... 95
9.8 Concrete Example ... 95
9.9 Pros and Cons ... 97
9.10 Related Patterns ... 97

10 Trait Based Template Operation ... 99
10.1 Introduction ... 99
10.2 Pattern Classification ... 99
10.3 Intent ... 99
10.4 Context ... 100
10.5 Forces/Motivation ... 100
10.6 Constituent Parts ... 100
10.7 Implementation Issues ... 100
10.8 Concrete Example ... 101
10.9 Pros and Cons ... 101
10.10 Related Patterns ... 102
Reference ... 102

11 Stackable Traits ... 103
11.1 Introduction ... 103
11.2 Pattern Classification ... 103
11.3 Intent ... 103
11.4 Context ... 103
11.5 Forces/Motivation ... 104
11.6 Constituent Parts ... 104
11.7 Implementation Issues ... 104
11.8 Concrete Example ... 104
11.9 Pros and Cons ... 107
11.10 Related Patterns ... 107
Reference ... 107

12 Currying and Code Reuse ... 109
12.1 Introduction ... 109
12.2 Pattern Classification ... 111
12.3 Intent ... 111
12.4 Context ... 111
12.5 Forces/Motivation ... 112
12.6 Constituent Parts ... 112
12.7 Implementation Issues ... 112
12.8 Concrete Example ... 112
12.9 Pros and Cons ... 114
12.10 Related Patterns ... 114

13 Cake Pattern ... 115
13.1 Introduction ... 115
13.2 Pattern Classification ... 116
13.3 Intent ... 116
13.4 Context ... 116
13.5 Forces/Motivation ... 116
13.6 Constituent Parts ... 117
13.7 Implementation Issues ... 117
13.8 Concrete Example ... 117
13.9 Pros and Cons ... 119
13.10 Related Patterns ... 119
Reference ... 119

14 Structural Injection ... 121
14.1 Introduction ... 121
14.2 Pattern Classification ... 121
14.3 Intent ... 121
14.4 Context ... 121
14.5 Forces/Motivation ... 122
14.6 Constituent Parts ... 122
14.7 Implementation Issues ... 122
14.8 Concrete Example ... 122
14.9 Pros and Cons ... 124
14.10 Related Patterns ... 125

15 Implicit Injection Pattern ... 127
15.1 Introduction ... 127
15.2 Pattern Classification ... 127
15.3 Intent ... 127
15.4 Context ... 128
15.5 Forces/Motivation ... 128
15.6 Constituent Parts ... 128
15.7 Implementation Issues ... 128
15.8 Concrete Example ... 129

15.9 Pros and Cons ... 131
15.10 Related Patterns ... 131

Part IV Gang of Four Patterns

16 Gang of Four Design Patterns ... 135
16.1 Introduction ... 135
16.2 GoF Patterns ... 135

17 GoF Patterns Catalog ... 137
17.1 Introduction ... 137
17.2 Creational Patterns ... 137
17.2.1 Factory Method ... 137
17.2.2 Abstract Factory ... 138
17.2.3 Builder ... 138
17.2.4 Prototype ... 138
17.2.5 Singleton ... 138
17.3 Structural Patterns ... 138
17.3.1 Adapter ... 138
17.3.2 Bridge ... 139
17.3.3 Composite ... 139
17.3.4 Decorator ... 139
17.3.5 Façade ... 140
17.3.6 Flyweight ... 140
17.3.7 Proxy ... 140
17.4 Behavioural Patterns ... 141
17.4.1 Chain of Responsibility ... 141
17.4.2 Command ... 142
17.4.3 Interpreter ... 142
17.4.4 Mediator ... 142
17.4.5 Memento ... 144
17.4.6 Observer ... 144
17.4.7 State ... 144
17.4.8 Strategy ... 144
17.4.9 Template Method ... 145
17.4.10 Visitor ... 146
17.5 Summary ... 146
References ... 146

18 Factory Operation ... 147
18.1 Introduction ... 147
18.2 Pattern Classification ... 147
18.3 Intent ... 147
18.4 Context ... 147
18.5 Forces/Motivation ... 148
18.6 Constituent Parts ... 148

18.7 Concrete Example 150
18.8 Pros and Cons 153
18.9 Related Patterns 154

19 Abstract Factory Pattern 155
19.1 Introduction 155
19.2 Pattern Classification 155
19.3 Intent 155
19.4 Context 155
19.5 Forces/Motivation 156
19.6 Constituent Parts 156
19.7 Implementation Issues 157
19.8 Concrete Example 158
19.9 Pros and Cons 161
19.10 Related Patterns 161

20 Builder 163
20.1 Introduction 163
20.2 Pattern Classification 163
20.3 Intent 163
20.4 Context 163
20.5 Forces/Motivation 164
20.6 Constituent Parts 164
20.7 Implementation Issues 165
20.8 Concrete Example 165
20.9 Pros and Cons 168
20.10 Related Patterns 168

21 Adapter Pattern 169
21.1 Introduction 169
21.2 Pattern Classification 169
21.3 Intent 169
21.4 Context 170
21.5 Forces/Motivation 171
21.6 Constituent Parts 171
21.7 Implementations 171
21.7.1 Object Based Solution 172
21.7.2 Class Based Solution 172
21.7.3 Trait Based Solution 172
21.7.4 Function Based Solution 175
21.8 Concrete Example 178
21.9 Pros and Cons 180
21.10 Related Patterns 181

22 Decorator 183
22.1 Introduction 183
22.2 Pattern Classification 183

22.3 Intent ... 183
22.4 Context ... 183
22.5 Forces/Motivation ... 184
22.6 Constituent Parts ... 184
22.7 Implementation Issues ... 184
22.8 Concrete Example ... 185
22.9 Pros and Cons ... 187
22.10 Related Patterns ... 188

23 Façade ... 189
23.1 Introduction ... 189
23.2 Pattern Classification ... 189
23.3 Intent ... 189
23.4 Context ... 189
23.5 Forces/Motivation ... 190
23.6 Constituent Parts ... 191
23.7 Implementation Issues ... 192
23.8 Concrete Example ... 192
23.9 Pros and Cons ... 194
23.10 Related Patterns ... 194

24 Flyweight ... 195
24.1 Introduction ... 195
24.2 Pattern Classification ... 195
24.3 Intent ... 195
24.4 Context ... 195
24.5 Forces/Motivation ... 196
24.6 Constituent Parts ... 196
24.7 Implementation Issues ... 197
24.8 Concrete Example ... 197
24.9 Pros and Cons ... 199
24.10 Related Patterns ... 200

25 Proxy ... 201
25.1 Introduction ... 201
25.2 Pattern Classification ... 201
25.3 Intent ... 202
25.4 Context ... 202
25.5 Forces/Motivation ... 202
25.6 Constituent Parts ... 202
25.7 Implementation Issues ... 203
25.8 Concrete Example ... 203
25.9 Pros and Cons ... 205
25.10 Related Patterns ... 205

26 Filter ... 207
26.1 Introduction ... 207
26.2 Pattern Classification ... 207
26.3 Intent ... 207
26.4 Context ... 208
26.5 Forces/Motivation ... 208
26.6 Constituent Parts ... 208
26.7 Implementation Issues ... 209
26.8 Concrete Example ... 209
26.9 Pros and Cons ... 212
26.10 Related Patterns ... 213
Reference ... 213

27 Bridge ... 215
27.1 Introduction ... 215
27.2 Pattern Classification ... 215
27.3 Intent ... 215
27.4 Context ... 215
27.5 Forces/Motivation ... 216
27.6 Constituent Parts ... 216
27.7 Implementation Issues ... 217
27.8 Concrete Example ... 217
27.9 Pros and Cons ... 221
27.10 Related Patterns ... 221

28 Chain of Responsibility ... 223
28.1 Introduction ... 223
28.2 Pattern Classification ... 223
28.3 Intent ... 223
28.4 Context ... 223
28.5 Forces/Motivation ... 224
28.6 Constituent Parts ... 224
28.7 Implementation Issues ... 225
28.8 Concrete Example ... 226
28.8.1 Function Chain Approach ... 226
28.8.2 Chain Manager Approach ... 227
28.8.3 Processing Chain Approach ... 229
28.9 Pros and Cons ... 230
28.10 Related Patterns ... 231

29 Command ... 233
29.1 Introduction ... 233
29.2 Pattern Classification ... 233
29.3 Intent ... 233
29.4 Context ... 234

29.5 Forces/Motivation ... 234
29.6 Constituent Parts ... 234
29.7 Implementation Issues ... 235
29.8 Concrete Example ... 236
29.9 Pros and Cons ... 238
29.10 Related Patterns ... 238

30 Strategy ... 239
30.1 Introduction ... 239
30.2 Pattern Classification ... 239
30.3 Intent ... 239
30.4 Context ... 240
30.5 Forces/Motivation ... 240
30.6 Constituent Parts ... 240
30.7 Implementation Issues ... 241
30.8 Concrete Example ... 241
30.9 Pros and Cons ... 243
30.10 Related Patterns ... 243

31 Mediator ... 245
31.1 Introduction ... 245
31.2 Pattern Classification ... 247
31.3 Intent ... 247
31.4 Context ... 248
31.5 Forces/Motivation ... 248
31.6 Constituent Parts ... 248
31.7 Implementation Issues ... 249
31.8 Concrete Example ... 250
31.9 Event Manager Sample Code ... 251
31.10 Pros and Cons ... 254
31.11 Related Patterns ... 255
Reference ... 255

32 Observer ... 257
32.1 Introduction ... 257
32.2 Pattern Classification ... 257
32.3 Intent ... 257
32.4 Context ... 258
32.5 Forces/Motivation ... 258
32.6 Constituent Parts ... 259
32.7 Implementation Issues ... 259
32.8 Concrete Example ... 260
32.9 Pros and Cons ... 261
32.10 Related Patterns ... 262

33 State ... 263
33.1 Introduction ... 263

33.2 Pattern Classification ... 263
33.3 Intent ... 263
33.4 Context ... 263
33.5 Forces/Motivation ... 264
33.6 Constituent Parts ... 264
33.7 Implementation Issues ... 265
33.8 Concrete Example ... 265
33.9 Pros and Cons ... 268
33.10 Related Patterns ... 269

34 Visitor ... 271
34.1 Introduction ... 271
34.2 Pattern Classification ... 271
34.3 Intent ... 271
34.4 Context ... 272
34.5 Forces/Motivation ... 272
34.6 Constituent Parts ... 272
34.7 Implementation Issues ... 273
34.8 Concrete Example ... 273
34.9 Pros and Cons ... 276
34.9.1 Advantages ... 276
34.9.2 Drawbacks ... 276
34.10 Related Patterns ... 276

35 Memento ... 277
35.1 Introduction ... 277
35.2 Pattern Classification ... 277
35.3 Intent ... 277
35.4 Context ... 277
35.5 Forces/Motivation ... 278
35.6 Constituent Parts ... 278
35.7 Implementation Issues ... 278
35.8 Concrete Example ... 279
35.9 Pros and Con ... 281
35.10 Related Patterns ... 282

Part V Functional Design Patterns

36 Functor ... 285
36.1 Introduction ... 285
36.2 Pattern Classification ... 286
36.3 Intent ... 286
36.4 Context ... 286
36.5 Forces/Motivation ... 286
36.6 Constituent Parts ... 287
36.7 Implementation Issues ... 287

36.8 Concrete Example ... 287
36.8.1 Function Based Solution ... 287
36.8.2 Hybrid Solution ... 288
36.9 Pros and Cons ... 289
36.10 Related Patterns ... 289

37 Applicative Functor ... 291
37.1 Introduction ... 291
37.2 Pattern Classification ... 292
37.3 Intent ... 292
37.4 Context ... 292
37.5 Forces/Motivation ... 292
37.6 Constituent Parts ... 292
37.7 Implementation Issues ... 293
37.8 Concrete Example ... 293
37.9 Pros and Cons ... 296
37.10 Related Patterns ... 296

38 Monoid Pattern ... 297
38.1 Introduction ... 297
38.2 Pattern Classification ... 298
38.3 Intent ... 298
38.4 Context ... 298
38.5 Forces/Motivation ... 298
38.6 Constituent Parts ... 298
38.7 Implementation Issues ... 299
38.8 Concrete Example ... 299
38.9 Pros and Cons ... 300
38.10 Related Patterns ... 300

39 Monad Pattern ... 301
39.1 Introduction ... 301
39.2 Pattern Classification ... 302
39.3 Intent ... 302
39.4 Context ... 302
39.5 Forces/Motivation ... 302
39.6 Constituent Parts ... 303
39.7 Implementation Issues ... 303
39.8 Concrete Example ... 303
39.9 Pros and Cons ... 306
39.10 Related Patterns ... 306

40 Foldable ... 307
40.1 Introduction ... 307
40.2 Pattern Classification ... 307
40.3 Intent ... 307
40.4 Context ... 308

40.5 Forces/Motivation ... 308
40.6 Constituent Parts ... 308
40.7 Implementation Issues ... 308
40.8 Concrete Example ... 308
40.9 Pros and Cons ... 310
40.10 Related Patterns ... 310

41 Zipper ... 311
41.1 Introduction ... 311
41.2 Pattern Classification ... 311
41.3 Intent ... 311
41.4 Context ... 311
41.5 Forces/Motivation ... 312
41.6 Constituent Parts ... 312
41.7 Implementation Issues ... 312
41.8 Concrete Example ... 312
41.9 Pros and Cons ... 314
41.10 Related Patterns ... 314

42 Lens Pattern ... 315
42.1 Introduction ... 315
42.2 Pattern Classification ... 315
42.3 Intent ... 316
42.4 Context ... 316
42.5 Forces/Motivation ... 316
42.6 Constituent Parts ... 316
42.7 Implementation Issues ... 316
42.8 Concrete Example ... 317
42.9 Pros and Cons ... 318
42.10 Related Patterns ... 318

43 View Pattern ... 319
43.1 Introduction ... 319
43.2 Pattern Classification ... 319
43.3 Intent ... 319
43.4 Context ... 320
43.5 Forces/Motivation ... 320
43.6 Constituent Parts ... 320
43.7 Implementation Issues ... 321
43.8 Concrete Example ... 321
43.9 Pros and Cons ... 322
43.10 Related Patterns ... 322

44 Arrow Pattern ... 323
44.1 Introduction ... 323
44.2 Pattern Classification ... 324

44.3 Intent 324
44.4 Context 324
44.5 Forces/Motivation 324
44.6 Constituent Parts 324
44.7 Implementation Issues 325
44.8 Concrete Example 325
44.9 Pros and Cons 326
44.10 Related Patterns 327
Reference 327

Part I
Introduction

Chapter 1
Introduction

1.1 Introduction

Scala is an exciting new language that marries Object Oriented Programming concepts with Functional Programming concepts (and results in something that is more than the sum of its parts). However, understanding how to use the features in the language, the way in which these can be combined together and how they relate to concepts with which you are already familiar is a significant next step in learning Scala.

This book explores a variety of themes related to design patterns that can be used with Scala. These range from Fundamental Patterns such as Immutability and Singleton through Code Reuse Patterns such as Currying and the Cake Pattern into Object Oriented patterns from the so-called Gang of Four (Gamma et al. 1995) to Functional patterns such as Functor, Monoids and Monads.

The aim of this book is that it can be read from cover to cover or can be dipped into depending on the readers time, inclination or needs. The intent though is that through the presentation of these patterns the power of Scala can be exposed both in terms of the simplicity of the resulting solutions (compared to Java for example) or the inherit support provided by the language for other patterns (such as the Singleton pattern).

The key here is not that Scala is a functional language nor that it is an object oriented language. Either view is in my opinion limited and misses the point (and much literature available tends to focus on Scala as a functional language) but that it combines eloquently the two paradigms resulting in a richer more sophisticated development environment. It does not negate all that you already know from other languages and environments. For example, some have claimed that the Gang of Four design patterns are not relevant to Scala. That is not true, their implementation may be radically simplified or may be very different in implementation but the concepts still hold and are still valid. However, it does require a shift in perspective and a re-evaluation of well-established concepts.

J. Hunt, *Scala Design Patterns: Patterns for Practical Reuse and Design*,
DOI 10.1007/978-3-319-02192-8_1, © Springer International Publishing Switzerland 2013

This book then considers Scala from the point of view of various types of patterns that can be used and are used in real world systems. It is structured in the following way:

Part 2: Fundamental Patterns

This section considers some basic software development patterns which may be used in Scala applications. For example, concepts such as Immutability, Marker Traits and Delegation are all discussed. The Singleton pattern is also included in this section. It may be claimed that this is not a pattern as Scala incorporates the concept of Singleton in the language. However, it is important to understand when to use a singleton, its purpose, scope and design considerations (such as when to create a singleton and when, if necessary, to kill a singleton etc.).

Part 3: Code Reuse Patterns

Scala has many language constructs that can aid in the development of reusable code. These include constructs such as Traits, partially applied functions, currying and functions themselves. This section considers various different ways in which these features can be used to achieve code reuse. The section also considers the concept of dependency injection (DI) and ways in which Scala inherently supports the generic DI concept. The section therefore introduces the Cake pattern, structural injection and implicit injection.

Part 4: Gang of Four Patterns

This section examines the Gang of Four Patterns (as originally described in (Gamma et al. 1995)). These patterns are often referred to as the Gang Of Four (or GoF) patterns as four authors, Erich Gamma, Richard Helm, Ralph Johnson and John Vlissides wrote the Design Patterns book. This book contains 23 patterns divided into three categories (creational, structural and behavioural). This section considers many of these patterns and adds one or two additional patterns that represent either variations on a theme or a more appropriate Scala view of a pattern.

Part 5: Functional Design Patterns

The final section of the book looks at a range of Functional patterns that are derived from the functional programming world. These functional design patterns consider commonly occurring patterns within many functional languages including Scala. For example, many of the patterns can be observed in the implementation of the data structure oriented classes within Scala. The patterns start with the Functor pattern and extend through Monoid to Monad. They also include a number of other functional patterns such as Lenses, Views and Arrows.

1.2 Introduction to Scala

If you have picked up this book then you are interested in development in Scala. You will have been learning the language and exploring its language constructs. You may be wondering what it is, what it is like and what it is not like, and why we need yet another programming language.

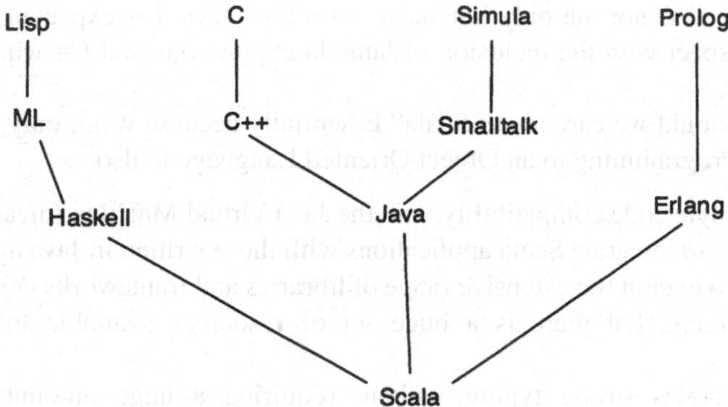

Fig. 1.1 Scala genealogy

Of course the short answer is that we don't need another programming language per se. However, languages such as C++, Java and C# have now been around for some considerable time and much has been learnt about what is both good and bad about them. Based on these experiences new languages may provide new features that make them easier to use when developing today's software systems.

Scala is certainly a language which can trace its ancestry from these (and other) languages (see Fig. 1.1) and which attempts to provide constructs and facilities that make it easier to build software solutions. Whether is succeeds you must judge for yourself; I certainly believe so otherwise I would not have written this book.

It is of course worth considering the goal of those who developed Scala as this can illuminate some of the language design decisions that underpin the constructs you will be using. The primary consideration was the desire to produce:

> A scalable language suitable for the construction of component based software within highly concurrent environments.

The intent was also that the same concepts are used to describe small and large parts of a system, rather than having different primitives for different types of elements (consider the different between JavaBeans and Enterprise JavaBeans). The focus in Scala is therefore on abstraction, composition and decomposition.

However from a programmer's point of view it is not this that marks Scala out as different from (for example) Java, but that fact that it unifies the Object Oriented Programming paradigm with the Functional Programming paradigm. Of course, it is not the first language to do this, back in the 1980's I was working with Lisp Flavours and the Common Lisp Object System (CLOS). Both Flavours and CLOS were languages that married the concepts of Object Orientation with the functional programming facilities of LISP.

The significant difference between Scala and Lisp Flavours or CLOS is that Scala marries the two paradigms in a language which looks more familiar to those used to C, C++, Java or C#. In other words it brings functional programming to the masses using a syntax with which they are familiar (rather than in a LISP based syntax).

Even then it is not the only language to do this. Java 8 is expected to adopt a functional aspect with the inclusion of lambda expressions and C# which already has lambdas.

So why should we care about Scala? Essentially because it not only introduces Functional Programming to an Object Oriented Language it also:

- Provides byte code compatibility with the Java Virtual Machine (meaning that it is possible to integrate Scala applications with those written in Java and it is also possible to exploit the extensive range of libraries and frameworks developed for Java meaning that there is a huge set of resources available to the Scala developer)
- It incorporates strong typing without requiring a huge amount of Thing thing = new Thing(); thanks to extensive use of type inference
- It avoids a large amount of boilerplate code (for example setters and getters in Java).
- A concise language for expressing common concepts.
- A presumption of *immutability* that greatly enhances maintenance and future development.
- In corporates extensive pattern matching features making many conditional situations easier to write.

Of course that combination of Functional Programming and Object Orientation is also a massive plus which results in greatly simplified constructs and code if used judiciously.

1.3 What Is Scala?

So if asked to summarise Scala what might we say?

Scala is a new language originally developed by Martin Odersky and his team at the EPFL (Ecole Polytechnique Federale de Lausanne, Lausanne), Switzerland. The name Scala is derived from Sca(lable) La(nguage) and is a multi-paradigm language, providing:

- Object oriented concepts, such as classes, methods, inheritance, polymorphism, etc.
- That adds in (compared to Java at least) the concepts of traits and mixins.
- Functional concepts, such as functions as first class entities in the language, as well as concepts such as partially applied functions and currying which allow new functions to be constructed from existing functions.
- Static typing with type inference used whether ever possible
- Adopting a concise, but still expressive, syntax.
- With direct support within the language for XML (that is rather than treating XML based facilities as a library to be invoked XML literals can be embedded directly into the Scala code).
- Concurrency based on the Actor/AKKA model.
- Interoperability with the Java/JVM world.

- Results in far fewer null pointer errors than occur in Java. One of the biggest issues in Java is what does the Null Pointer Exception relate to as that actual exception provides very little information.
- Scala allows for operator overloading, an omission from Java intended to keep things simple, but which often results in either more complexity and certainly in less readable code.
- Extensive list processing operations. Java and C# do include some list processing facilities but Scala takes this further and provides extensive support for operations that can be applied to collections of objects.
- Explicit support for the Singleton design pattern, which makes it easy (and natural) to use the Singleton pattern within applications.
- Allows for the creation of new syntax and control structures without using macros and still retaining strong static typing.

Such lists mean little without something to back them up so to illustrate this idea let us compare a sample Java class and the equivalent in Scala.

1.4 The Class Person

The following classes define a simple class Person which has a first name and a last name and an age. A Person is constructed by providing the first and last names and their age and setters and getters are provided for each.
Here is the Java class:

```
class Person {
  private String firstName;
  private String lastName;
  private int    age;

  public Person(String firstName, String lastName, int age) {
    this.firstName = firstName;
    this.lastName  = lastName;
    this.age   = age;
  }

  public void setFirstName(String firstName) { this.first
Name = firstName; }
  public void String getFirstName() { return this.first
Name; }
  public void setLastName(String lastName) { this.last
Name = lastName; }
  public void String getLastName() { return this.last
Name; }
  public void setAge(int age) { this.age = age; }
  public void int getAge() { return this.age; }
}
```

And here is the equivalent Scala class:

```
class Person(var firstName: String, var lastName: String, var age: Int)
```

Certainly the Java class is longer than the Scala class, but look at the Java class "How many times have you written something like that?". Most of this Java class is boilerplate code, In fact it is so common that tools such as Eclipse allow us to create the boiler plate code automatically. Which may mean that we do not have to type much more in the Java case than the Scala case. However, when I look back and have to read this code I may have to wade through a lot of such boilerplate code in order to find the actual functionality of interest. In the Scala case this boilerplate code is handled by the language meaning that I can focus on what the class actually does.

Actually the Object Oriented side of Scala is both more sophisticated than that in either Java or C# and also different in nature. For example, many people have found that distinction between the static side of a class and the instance side of a class confusing. Scala does away with this distinction by not including the static concept. Instead it allows the user to define singleton objects, if these singleton objects have the same name as a class and are in the same course file as the class, then they are referred to as companion objects. Companion objects then have a special relationship with the class that allows them to access the internals of a class and thus provide the Scala equivalent of static behavior.

The class hierarchy in Scala is based on single inheritance of classes but allows multiple traits to be mixed into any given class. A Trait is a structure within the Scala language that is neither a class nor an interface (note Scala does not have interfaces even though it compiles to Java Byte Codes). It can however, be combined with classes to create new types of classes and objects. As such a Trait can contain data, behavior, functions, type declarations, abstract members etc. but cannot be instantiated itself.

The analogy might be that a class is like a flavor of Ice Cream. You can have vanilla as the basic flavor with all the characteristics of ice cream, Chocolate could be a subclass of Vanilla which extends the concept to a chocolate flavor of ice cream. Separated we could have bowls containing chocolate chips, mint chips, M&Ms, sprinkles of various types. We can combine the Vanilla Ice Cream with the mint chips to create Vanilla Mint Chip Ice Cream. This provides a new type of ice cream but that mint chips are not in and of themselves an ice cream. Traits are like the mint and chocolate chips while classes are like the ice cream.

1.5 Functional Programming

So much for the Object Oriented view of Scala, what about this Functional Programming concept? For those of you coming from a Java background this may seem a bit alien, however, functional programming languages have a long history from LISP developed in the late 1950s to more recent functional languages such as ML and Haskell.

However, up until recently functional languages were often regarded as *Ivory tower languages* used only by academics. This was true to a certain extent but is no longer the case; Scala has significantly widened the appeal of Functional Languages. In additional Java and C# have (or will have) functional aspects to them.

This view was not helped thanks to the esoteric syntax of some of the functional languages and this combined with a view that functional languages are hard to learn has meant that *functional languages* have had something of a bad press. However, this last issues is due in part to the fact that so many developers have either grown up with object oriented languages or have worked with them for some considerable time. Back in the 1980s when I was presented with an object oriented language for the first time, it felt very alien and somewhat esoteric in nature. Yet today object oriented languages are mainstream!

Working with functions is *not* that difficult although until you become familiar with the syntax they may seem unwieldy – but the key is to hang in there and keep trying.

The following provides a simple example of a functional literal in Scala that takes two numbers and adds them together:

```
val add = (a: Int, b: Int) => a + b
```

This defines a new function that takes two integers in the parameters a and b and returns the result of adding a to b. The function can be accessed via the variable add. This is a variable of type Function. We can invoke this function as following:

```
add(4, 5)
```

Which should return the value 9. In Scala we can then partially apply this function. This means that we can bind one of the parameters to a value to create a new function that only takes one parameter, for example:

```
val addTwo = (2, _: Int)
```

This function, addTwo, now adds 2 to whatever integer is passed to it, for example:

```
addTwo(5)
```

will return 7.

1.6 A Hybrid Language

If all Scala did was provide the ability to program functionally all that would do is provide yet another functional programming language. However it is the fact that Scala mixes the two paradigms that allows us to create software solutions that are both concise and expressive.

The Object Oriented paradigm has been such a success because it can be used to model concepts and entities within problem domains. When this is combined with the ability to treat functions as first class entities we obtain a very powerful combination.

For example, we can now create classes that will hold data (including other objects) and define behaviours in terms of methods but which can easily and naturally be given functions that can be applied to the members of that object.

```
val numbers = List(1, 2, 3, 4, 5)

numbers: List[Int] = List(1, 2, 3, 4, 5)
```

In this case I have created a list of integers (note that this is a list of Integers as the type has been inferred by Scala) that are stored in the variable numbers.

```
val filtered = numbers.filter((n :Int) => n < 3)

filtered: List[Int] = List(1, 2)
```

I have then applied a function to each of the elements of the list. This function is an anonymous function that takes an Int (and stores that Int in the variable n). It then tests to see if the value of n is less than 3. If it is it returns true otherwise it returns false. The method filter uses the function passed to it to determine whether the value passed it should be included in the result or not. This means that the variable *filtered* will hold a list of integers where each integer is less than the value 3. Again note that this is again a List of Ints as once again Scala has inferred the type.

1.7 Scala Oriented Patterns

Learning the syntax, semantics and constructs in a new language is one thing. However, being able to examine a variety of different examples, based around particular ideas significantly enhances your ability to use a language such as Scala. It is also important to consider how what you already know, applies to a new language and the way in which it changes.

This book explores they ways in which the Scala language supports numerous concepts wither available in a wide range of languages or often implemented in those languages as well as exploring constructs specific to Scala itself.

1.8 Resources

The following are a set of resources that you should consider using as you work with Scala.

The Scala programming language home page
- see http://www.scala-lang.org

The Scala mailing list
- see http://listes.epfl.ch/cgi-bin/doc_en?liste=scala

The Scala wiki
- see http://scala.sygneca.com/

A Scala plug-in for Eclipse
- see http://www.scala-lang.org/downloads/eclipse/index.html

A Scala plug-in for IntelliJ
- http://plugins.intellij.net/plugin/?id=1347

Reference

Gamma, E., Helm, R., Johnson, R., & Vlissades, J. (1995). *Design patterns: Elements of reusable object-oriented software*. Reading: Addison-Wesley.

Chapter 2
Design Patterns

2.1 Introduction

Design patterns have their basis in the work of an architect who designed a language for encoding knowledge of the design and construction of buildings (Alexander et al. 1977; Alexander 1979). The knowledge is described in terms of patterns that capture both a recurring architectural arrangement and a rule for how and when to apply this knowledge. That is, they incorporate knowledge about the design as well as the basic design relations.

This work was picked up by a number of researchers working within the object oriented field. This then led to the exploration of how software frameworks can be documented using (software) design patterns (for example, (Johnson 1992) and (Birrer and Eggenschwiler 1993)). In particular Johnson's paper describes the form that these design patterns take and the problems encountered in applying them.

Since 1995 and the publication of the "Patterns" book by the Gang of Four (Gamma et al. 1995), interest in patterns has mushroomed. Patterns are now seen as a way of capturing expert and design knowledge associated with a system architecture to support design reuse, as well as software reuse. In addition as interest in patterns has grown their use, and representational expressiveness has grown.

So what are design patterns? We will look at this question in more detail later in this chapter. For the moment they are essentially useful recurring solutions to problems within designs. For example, "I want to loosely couple a set of objects, how can I do this?", might be a question facing a designer. The Mediator design pattern is one solution to this. If you are familiar with design patterns you can use them to solve problems that occur. Typically early in the design process, the problems are more architectural/structural in nature, while later in the design process they may be more behavioural. Design patterns actually provide different types of patterns some of which are at the architectural/structural level and some of which are more behavioural. They can thus help every stage of the design process.

In this chapter we will discuss the motivation behind software design patterns, what design patterns are, how they are generally documented and when to use

J. Hunt, *Scala Design Patterns: Patterns for Practical Reuse and Design*,
DOI 10.1007/978-3-319-02192-8_2, © Springer International Publishing Switzerland 2013

design patterns. We will then explore the categories of pattern discussed in this book and the relationship between Scala and Design Patterns.

2.2 Motivation Behind Patterns

Design patterns have been adopted by many organisations, architects and developers as the basis of the systems they build! Why? What is the motivation behind this? There are in fact numerous motivations behind design patterns. These include:

1. The difficulty of designing reusable software. Finding appropriate objects and abstractions is not trivial. Having identified such objects, building flexible, modular, reliable code for general reuse is not easy, particularly when dealing with more than one class. In general, such reusable "frameworks" emerge over time rather than being designed from scratch.
2. Software components support reuse of code but not the reuse of knowledge.
3. Frameworks support reuse of design and code but not knowledge of how to use that framework. That is, design trade-offs and expert knowledge are lost.
4. Experienced programmers do not start from first principles every time; thus, successful reusable conceptual designs must exist.
5. Communication of such "architectural" knowledge can be difficult as it is in the designers head and is poorly expressed as a program instance.
6. A particular program instance fails to convey constraints, trade-offs and other non-functional forces applied to the "architecture".
7. Since frameworks are reusable designs, not just code, they are more abstract than most software, which makes documenting them more difficult. Documentation for a framework has three purposes and patterns can help to fulfill each of them. Documentation must provide:
   - the purpose of the framework,
   - how to use the framework,
   - the detailed design of the framework.
8. The problem with cookbooks is that they describe a single way in which the framework will be used. A good framework will be used in ways that its designers never conceived. Thus, a cookbook is insufficient on its own to describe every use of the framework. Of course, a developer's first use of a framework usually fits the stereotypes in the cookbook. However, once they go beyond the examples in the cookbook, they need to understand the details of the framework. However, cookbooks tend not to describe the framework itself. But in order to understand a framework, you need to have knowledge of both its design and its use.
9. In order to achieve high level reuse (i.e. above the level of reusing the class set) it is necessary to design with reuse in mind. This requires knowledge of the reusable components available.

The design patterns movement wished to address some (or all) of the above in order to facilitate successful architectural reuse. The intention was thus to address many of the problems which reduce the reusability of software components and frameworks.

2.3 Design Patterns

2.3.1 What Are Design Patterns?

A design pattern captures expertise describing an architectural design to a recurring design problem in a particular situation. It also contains information on the applicability of a pattern, the tradeoffs that must be made, and any consequences of the solution. Books are now appearing which present such design patterns for a range of applications. For example, the Gang of Four book (Gamma et al. 1995) is a widely cited book that presents a catalogue of 23 design patterns.

Design patterns are extremely useful for both novice and experienced object oriented designers. This is because they encapsulate extensive design knowledge and proven design solutions with guidance on how to use them. Reusing common patterns opens up an additional level of design reuse, where the implementations vary, but the micro-architectures represented by the patterns still apply.

Thus, patterns allow designers and programmers to share knowledge about the design of a software architecture. They thus capture the static and dynamic structures and collaborations of previous successful solutions to problems that arise when building applications in a particular domain (but not a particular language).

Most systems are full of patterns that designers and developers have identified through past experience and documented good practice. The patterns movement have essentially made these patterns explicit. Thus the programmatic idioms that have previously been used are now documented as behavioural patterns. In turn there are design patterns that express some commonly used design structure and architectural patterns which express structural patterns.

2.3.2 What They Are Not?

Patterns are not concrete designs for particular systems. This is because a pattern must be instantiated in a particular application to be used. This involves evaluating various trade-offs or constraints as well as detailed consideration of the consequences. It also does not mean that creativity or human judgment have been removed as it is still necessary to make the design and implementation decisions required. Having done that the developer must then implement the pattern and combine the implementation with other code (which may or may not have been derived from a pattern).

Patterns are also not frameworks (although they do seem to be exceptionally well suited for documenting frameworks). This is because frameworks present an instance of a design for solving a family of problems in a specific domain (and often for a particular language). In terms of languages such as Smalltalk, Java and Scala; a framework is a set of abstract, co-operating, types. To apply such a framework to a particular problem it is often necessary to customize it by providing user defined sub-types and to compose objects in the appropriate manner (e.g. the MVC framework). That is, a framework is a semi-complete application. As a result any given framework may contain one or more instances of multiple patterns and in turn a pattern can be used in many different frameworks.

2.3.3 Architectural Patterns

Architectural patterns are patterns that describe the structure of a system (or part of a system). For example the Model-View-Controller (or MVC) pattern (Krasner and Pope 1988), (Hunt 2002) describes how a user interface, the associated application and any event handlers should be structured. They can be used to help you to structure your architecture as well as to explore different possible architectures. There are a range of architectural patterns which have been documented, including:

- Distributed, in which various parts of the system reside in different processes, potentially on different processors.
- Layered, in which a system is decomposed along application specific versus application generic lines.
- Model-View-Controller, in which the display, the application and the control of user input are separated.
- Blackboard, in which a central "blackboard" acts as a communications medium for a number of co-operating agents.
- Sub-sumption, in which high level components can subsume the role of those lower down in the architecture.
- Repository-centric, in which a central repository is used.

For more information on Architectural design patterns see (Buschmann et al. 1996).

2.3.4 Documenting Patterns

The actual form used to document individual patterns varies, but in general the documentation covers the following:

1. The motivation or context that the pattern applies to.
2. Pre-requisites that should be satisfied before deciding to use a pattern.

Table 2.1 The design pattern template

Heading	Usage
Name	The name of the pattern
Intent/Context	This is a short statement indicating the purpose of the pattern. It includes information on its rationale, intent, problem it addresses etc.
Also known as	Any other names by which the pattern is known.
Motivation/Problem	Illustrates how the pattern can be used to solve a particular problem.
Applicability/Forces	This describes the situation in which the pattern is applicable. It may also say when the pattern is not applicable.
Structure	This is a (typically graphical) description of the classes in the pattern.
Participants	The classes and objects involved in the design and their responsibilities.
Collaborations/Responsibilities	This describes how the classes and objects work together.
Consequences	How does the pattern achieve its objective? What are the trade offs and results of using the pattern? What aspect of the system structure does it let you vary independently?
Implementation/Strategies (for implementation)	What issues are there in implementing the design pattern?
Sample code	Code illustrating how a pattern might be implemented.
Known uses	How the pattern has been used in the past. Each pattern has at least two such examples.
Related patterns	Closely related design patterns are listed here.

3. A description of the program structure that the pattern will define.
4. A list of the participants needed to complete a pattern.
5. Consequences of using the pattern, both positive and negative.
6. Examples of the patterns usage.

The pattern templates used in (Gamma et al. 1995), (Alur et al. 2001) and (Grand 2002) (which are very similar) provide a standard structure for the information that comprises a design pattern. This makes it easier to comprehend a design pattern as well as providing a concrete structure for those defining new patterns. Gamma's book (Gamma et al. 1995) provides a detailed description of the template; only a summary of it is presented in Table 2.1. The books mentioned above differ slightly in their terminology (for example Gamma et al. use the title Intent where as Alur et al. use the title Context).

A pattern language is a structured collection of patterns that build on each other to transform needs and constraints into architecture. That is a set of related patterns dealing with for example, 2D drawing tools, would represent a pattern language for 2D drawing tools. Some of these patterns would build on others and together they might be considered to describe how a framework for 2D drawing tools could be constructed.

2.3.5 When to Use Patterns

Patterns can be useful in situations where solutions to problems recur but in slightly different ways. Thus, the solution needs to be instantiated as appropriate for different problems. The solutions should not be so simple that a simple linear series of instructions will suffice. In such situations patterns are overkill. They are particularly relevant when several steps are involved in the pattern that may not be required for all problems. Finally, patterns are really intended for solutions where the developer is more interested in the existence of the solution rather than how it was derived (as patterns still leave out too much detail).

2.3.6 Strengths and Limitations of Design Patterns

Design patterns have a number of strengths including:

- providing a common vocabulary,
- explicitly capturing expert knowledge and trade-offs,
- helping to improve developer communication,
- promoting the ease of maintenance,
- providing a structure for change.

However, they are not without their limitations. These include:

- not leading to direct code reuse,
- being deceptively simple,
- easy to get pattern overload (i.e. finding the right pattern),
- they are validated by experience rather than testing,
- no methodological support.

In general, patterns provide opportunities for describing both the design and the use of the framework as well as including examples, all within a coherent whole. In some ways patterns act like a hyper-graph with links between parts of patterns (in a similar way that pages on the web and the links between them make a hyper-graph of information).

However, there are potentially very many design patterns available to a designer and number of these patterns may superficially appear to suit their requirements. Even if the design patterns are available on-line (via some hyper text style browser (Budinsky et al. 1996)) it is still necessary for the designer to search through them manually, attempting to identify the design which best matches their requirements.

In addition, once they have found the design that they feel best matches their needs, they must then consider how to apply it to their application. This is because a design pattern describes a solution to a particular design problem. This solution may include multiple tradeoffs which are contradictory and which the designer must choose between, although some aspects of the system structure can be varied independently.

2.4 Fundamental Patterns

These are patterns that represent fundamental approaches to the design and implementation of Scala applications. In this section of the book the following patterns are considered:

- Immutability
- Singleton
- Marker Trait
- Delegation
- Composition with Mixins

2.5 Code Reuse Patterns

The Code Reuse Patterns section of the book explores patterns focussed on the reusability and reuse of Scala types/functions. This section of the book looks at:

- Eager parameter evaluation pattern
- Functions and Code Reuse
- Traits and Code Reuse
- Currying and Code reuse
- Cake Pattern for DI
- Structural Injection
- Implicit Injection

2.6 GoF Design Patterns

This section considers the GoF patterns from the Design Patterns book (with a few additional patterns included that are commonly encountered). These patterns include:

- Factory (Object)
- Builder
- Adapter
- Decorator
- Chain of Responsibility
- Strategy
- Visitor

2.7 Functional Patterns

This final section of the book looks at Functional Design Patterns including:

- Functor
- Monoids
- Monads
- Foldable
- Zippers
- Lenses
- Views
- Arrows

2.8 Patterns and Scala

Design Patterns, whether Object Oriented or Function Oriented, are a valuable addition to the box of tools available to the Scala developer. Some readers may be surprised by this as it has been argued that design patterns exist in languages such as C++ and Java to overcome the inherit weakness in those languages. It is argued that in other languages with richer semantics that many of the original GoF patterns are either greatly simplified or eliminated (for example Peter Norvig demonstrates that 16 out of the 23 patterns in the Design Patterns book are simplified or eliminated via direct language support in Lisp or Dylan).

However, this is not an argument about whether the design patterns as a concept are appropriate or not, as it is still worth while understanding what approach you are adopting even if the particular pattern is made trivially easy to implement (see the Singleton pattern in Scala later in this book). In addition, developers who are moving to a new language will take significant experience form previous languages with them; it is therefore instructive to understand how to do those things you already know in one language in a new language (even if it is by using direct language support).

In my experience the issue with Scala is that it is a hybrid language in which both object oriented and functional concepts are married together. This results not only in a very powerful language but also one in which many of the design patterns already developed for lesser languages can be implemented in a much cleaner and simpler manner – which in no way undermines the value of the pattern; rather it enhances the clarity of the solution (as it should not be the case that more complex is better)!

This is as true for those design patterns that focus on the Object Oriented world, such as Adapter, Bridge, Strategy etc. and those that are focussed on the Functional world such as Functor, Monoid, Lens etc. In fact it is my contention that the marriage of the two paradigms present in Scala actually significantly adds to the power and flexibility of these design patterns. For example, functional elements can be exploited in the Strategy pattern and Object concepts aid in the creation of a Monoid etc.

2.9 Further Reading

A number of books and a great many papers have been written about patterns in recent years. The most influential of which is (Gamma et al. 1995) by the so called "Gang of four" who are Erich Gamma, Richard Helm, Ralph Johnson and John Vlissides. There are also a series of conferences on Patterns referred to as PLoP (for Pattern Languages of Program design). The 20th PLOP conference was held in 2013 and selected papers from this and previous conferences are available in the Pattern Languages of Program Design (PLoPD) series. For example see (Coplien and Schmidt 1995), (Vlissides et al. 1996), (Martin et al. 1997) and (Manolescu et al. 2006).

Two further patterns books are (Buschmann et al. 1996) (which represents the progression and evolution of the pattern approach into a system capable of describing and documenting large scale applications) and (Fowler 1997) which considers how patterns can be used for analysis to help build reusable object models.

There are many web sites dedicated to design patterns; here are some of my favourites:

Quick reference list of design patterns

- http://www.oodesign.com/

Introductory descriptions and examples of patterns

- http://sourcemaking.com/design_patterns

List of patterns based sites

- http://hillside.net/patterns/patterns-catalog

References

Alexander, C. (1979). *The timeless way of building*. New York: Oxford University Press.

Alexander, C., Ishikawa, S., Silverstein, M., with Jacobson, M., Fiksdahl-King, I., Angel, S. (1977). *A pattern language*. New York: Oxford University Press.

Alur, D., Crupi, J., & Malks, D. (2001). *Core J2EE patterns*. Upper Saddle River: Prentice Hall. ISBN 0130648841.

Birrer, A., & Eggenschwiler, T. (1993). Frameworks in the financial engineering domain: An experience report (pp. 21–35). *ECOOP'93*.

Budinsky, F. J., Finnie, M. A., Vlissides, J. M., & Yu, P. S. (1996). Automatic code generation from design patterns. *IBM Systems Journal, 35*(2).

Buschmann, F., Meunier, R., Rohnert, H., Sommerlad, P., & Stal, M. (1996). *Pattern-oriented software architecture – A system of patterns*. Chichester: Wiley. ISBN 0-471-95869-7.

Coplien, J. O., & Schmidt, D. C. (Eds.). (1995). *Pattern languages of program design*. Reading: Addison-Wesley. ISBN 0-201-60734-4.

Fowler, M. (1997). *Analysis patterns: Reusable object models*. Reading: Addison-Wesley. ISBN 0-201-89542-0.

Gamma, E., Helm, R., Johnson, R., & Vlissades, J. (1995). *Design patterns: Elements of reusable object-oriented software*. Reading: Addison-Wesley.

Grand, M. (Ed.). (2002). *Patterns in java: A catalog of reusable design patterns illustrated with UML* (2nd ed., Vol. 1). New York: Wiley. ISBN 0471227293.

Hunt, J. E. (Ed.). (2002). *Java and object orientation: An introduction* (2nd ed.). Berlin: Springer.

Johnson, R. E. (1992). Documenting frameworks with patterns. *Proceedings of OOPSLA'92, SIGPLAN Notices, 27*(10), 63–76.

Krasner, G. E., & Pope, S. T. (1988). A cookbook for using the model-view controller user interface paradigm in smalltalk-80. *JOOP, 1*(3), 26–49.

Manolescu, D., Voelter, M., & Noble, J. (2006). *Pattern languages of program design 5* (Software patterns). Reading: Addison-Wesley. ISBN 0321321944.

Martin, R. C., Riehle, D., & Buschmann, F. (1997). *Pattern languages of program design 3*. Reading: Addison-Wesley. ISBN 0201310112.

Vlissides, J. M., Coplien, J. O., & Kerth, N. L. (1996). *Pattern languages of program design 2*. Reading: Addison-Wesley. ISBN 0-201-89527-7.

Chapter 3
UML and Scala

3.1 Introduction

The Unified Modeling Language (UML) is part of a development to merge (unify) the concepts in the Booch, Objectory and OMT methods (Jacobson et al. (1998); Booch et al. 1996). The method is still under development (and has taken a low profile recently), however the notation underlying this method is nearing completion. This notation is now the focus of the current work of Booch, Rumbaugh and Jacobson and is receiving a great deal of interest. Microsoft Corporation, Hewlett Packard, Oracle, and Texas Instruments have all endorsed the UML.

UML is a third generation object oriented modeling language (Rational 1996) which adapts and extends the published notations used in the works of Booch, Rumbaugh and Jacobson (Booch 1994; Rumbaugh et al. 1991; Jacobson et al. 1992) and is influenced by many others such as Fusion (Coleman et al. 1994), Harel's statecharts (Harel et al. 1987; Harel 1988) and CORBA (Ben-Natan 1995), as illustrated in Fig. 3.1.

UML is intended to form a single, common, widely useable modelling language for a range of object oriented design methods (including Booch, Objectory and OMT). It is also intended that it should be applicable in a wide range of applications and domains. It should be equally applicable to client–server applications and to real-time control applications.

The justification for UML is that different organizations, applications and domains require (and use) different design methods. An organization may develop its own methods or modify other methods through experience. Different parts of the same organization may use different methods. The notation that they use acts as a language to communicate the ideas represented in part (or all) of the design.

For example, the production of shrink-wrapped, off-the-shelf software is different from the creation of one-off bespoke software. However, a software company may carry out both activities. Such an organization may well wish to exchange ideas, designs, or parts of a design amongst its departments or operational units.

J. Hunt, *Scala Design Patterns: Patterns for Practical Reuse and Design*, DOI 10.1007/978-3-319-02192-8_3,

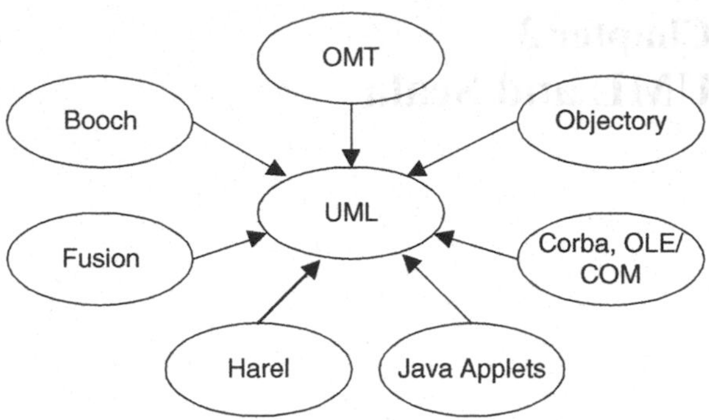

Fig. 3.1 The influences on the UML notation

This kind of exchange relies on the availability of a common language; UML provides such a language.

The Object Management Group (OMG) manages UML and provides for the standardisation process surrounding UML. This is an on going process with a number of versions of UML now ratified. For the latest information on the UML (and other developments on the unification front) see the Rational Software Corporation's Web site (http://www.rational.com).

This chapter provides a brief introduction to the UML and considers its applicability to Scala. It considers how the UML represents the classes, objects, relationships and attributes in an object-oriented system. It also considers sequence and collaboration diagrams, State diagrams and deployment diagrams.

3.2 The Models

The UML defines a number of models and their notations:

- *Use case diagrams* organize the use cases that encompass a system's behaviour (they are based on the use case diagrams of Objectory).
- *Class diagrams* express the static structure of the system (they derive from the Booch and OMT methods), for example the *part-of* and *is-a* relationships between classes and objects. The class diagrams also encompass the object diagrams. Therefore, in this book, we refer to them as the Object Model (as in OMT).
- *Sequence diagrams* (known as message-trace diagrams, in version 0.8 of the Unified Method draft) deal with the time ordered sequence of transactions between objects.
- *Collaboration diagrams* (previously known as Object-message diagrams) indicate the order of messages between specified objects. They complement sequence diagrams as they illustrate the same information. Sequence diagrams highlight the actual sequence, while collaboration diagrams highlight the structure required to support the message sequence.

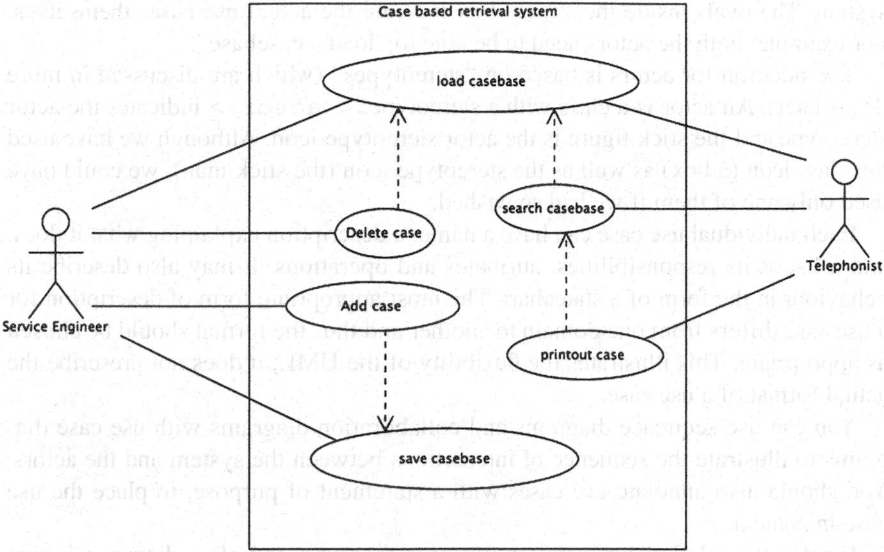

Fig. 3.2 Use case diagram

- *State machine diagrams* are based on statecharts, like those in OMT. They capture the dynamic behaviour of the system.
- *Component diagrams* (known as module diagrams, in version 0.8 of the Unified Method draft) represent the development view of the system. That is, how the system should be developed into software modules. You can also use them to represent concepts such as dynamic libraries.
- *Deployment diagrams* (previously known as platform diagrams) attempt to capture the topology of the system once it is deployed. They reflect the physical topology upon which the software system is to execute.

3.3 Use Case Diagrams

Use case diagrams explain how a system (or subsystem) is used. The elements that interact with the system can be humans, other computers or dumb devices which process or produce data. The diagrams thus present a collection of use cases that illustrate what the system is expected to do, in terms of its external services or interfaces. Such diagrams are very important for illustrating the overall system functionality (to both technical and non-technical personnel). They can act as the context within which the rest of the system is defined.

The large rectangle in Fig. 3.2 indicates the boundaries of the system (a telephone help desk adviser). The rectangles on either side of the system indicate external actors (in this case, a Service Engineer and a Telephonist) that interact with the system. The ovals inside the system box indicate the actual use cases themselves. For example, both the actors need to be able to "load a casebase".

The notation for actors is based on "stereotypes" (which are discussed in more detail later). An actor is a class with a stereotype: `<<actor>>` indicates the actor stereotype and the stick figure is the actor stereotype icon. Although we have used the class icon (a box) as well as the stereotype icon (the stick man), we could have used only one of them if we had so wished.

Each individual use case can have a name, a description explaining what it does, and a list of its responsibilities, attributes and operations. It may also describe its behaviour in the form of a statechart. The most appropriate form of description for a use case differs from one domain to another and thus the format should be chosen as appropriate. This illustrates the flexibility of the UML; it does not prescribe the actual format of a use case.

You can use sequence diagrams and collaboration diagrams with use case diagrams to illustrate the sequence of interactions between the system and the actors. You should also annotate use cases with a statement of purpose, to place the use case in context.

Finally, the relationship between use case diagrams and class diagrams is that use cases are peers of classes. Depending on the size of the system, they can be grouped with the object model in a package or remain totally independent.

3.4 The Object Model

The object model is the key element of the UML. The constituent diagrams illustrate the static structure of a system via the important classes and objects in the system and how they relate to each other. The UML documentation currently talks about class diagrams (and within this about object diagrams) stating that "class diagrams show generic descriptions of possible systems and object diagrams show particular instantiations of systems and their behaviour". It goes on to state that class diagrams contain classes, while object diagrams contain objects, but that it is possible to mix the two. However, it discusses both under the title *class diagrams*. To avoid confusion, we will adopt the term Object Model to cover both sets of diagrams (following the approach adopted in both the Booch and OMT methods).

3.4.1 Representing Classes

A class is drawn as a solid-outline rectangle with three components. The class name (in bold type) is in the top part, a list of attributes is in the middle part and a list of operations is in the bottom part. Figure 3.3 illustrates two classes: Car and File. The `Car` class possesses three attributes (name, age and fuel are string, integer and string types, respectively) and four operations (`start`, `lock` and `brake` take no

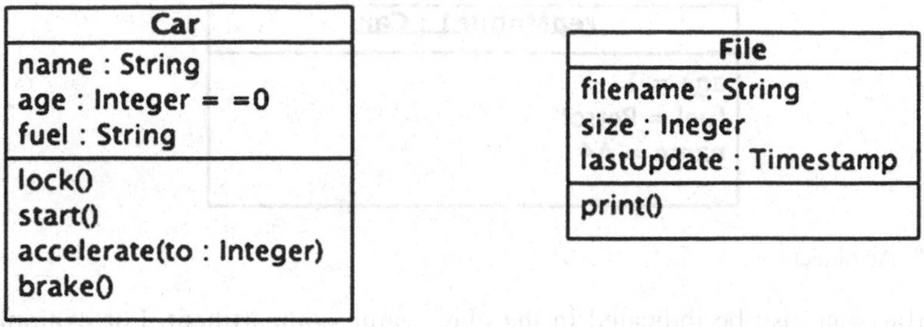

Car
name : String
age : Integer = =0
fuel : String
lock()
start()
accelerate(to : Integer)
brake()

File
filename : String
size : Ineger
lastUpdate : Timestamp
print()

Fig. 3.3 Classes with attributes and operations

Fig. 3.4 Class with additional annotations

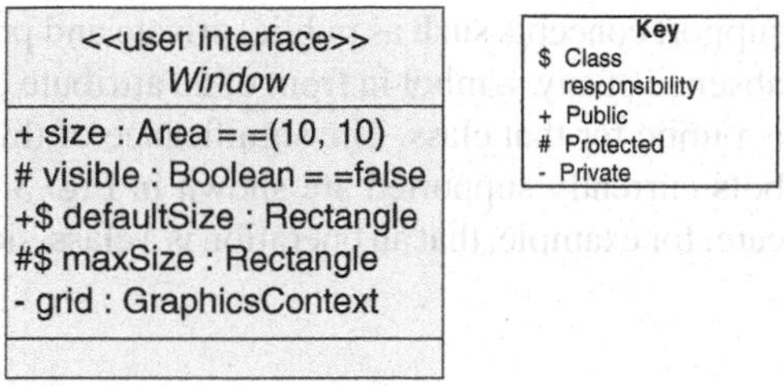

<<user interface>>
Window
+ size : Area = =(10, 10)
# visible : Boolean = =false
+$ defaultSize : Rectangle
#$ maxSize : Rectangle
- grid : GraphicsContext

Key
$ Class responsibility
+ Public
# Protected
- Private

parameters; `accelerate` takes a single parameter, `to`, which is an integer that represents the new speed).

An attribute has a name and a type specified in the following format:

```
name: type = initialValue
```

The name and type are strings that are ultimately language dependent. The initial value is a string representing an expression in the target language.

An operation has a name and may take one or more parameters and return a value. It is specified in the following format:

```
name (parameter : type = defaultValue, …): resultType
```

The constituent parts are language dependent strings.

You can hide the attribute and operation compartments from view to reduce the detail shown in a diagram. If you omit a compartment, it says nothing about that part of the class definition. However, if you leave the compartment blank, there are no definitions for that part of the class. Additional language dependent and user-defined information can also be included in each compartment in a textual format. The intention of such additions is to clarify any element of the design in a similar manner to a comment in source code.

A class *stereotype* tells the reader what "kind" of class it is (for example, exceptions, controllers, interfaces, etc.). You show the stereotype as a normal font text string between << >> centred above the class name (see Fig. 3.4).

However, UML makes no assumptions about the range of stereotypes that exist and designers are free to develop their own. Other (language specific) class

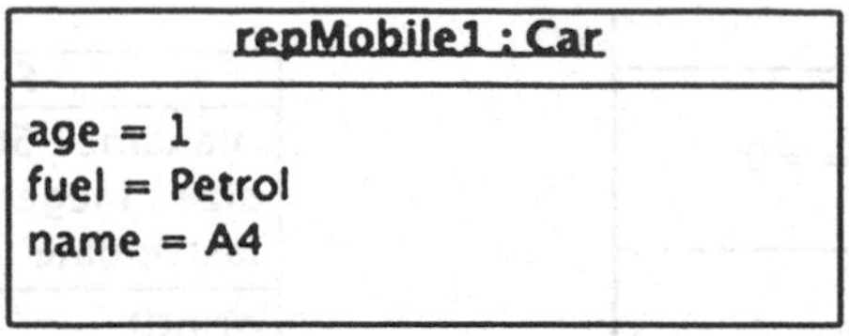

repMobile1 : Car
age = 1 fuel = Petrol name = A4

Fig. 3.5 An object

properties can also be indicated in the class name compartment. For example, in Fig. 3.4, the Window class is an abstract class.

You can also indicate the intended scope of attributes and operations in the class definition. This can be useful even for languages, such as Smalltalk, which do not support concepts such as public, private and protected attributes and operations. The absence of any symbol in front of an attribute or operation indicates that the element is public for that class. The significance of this depends on the language. The symbols currently supported are shown in Fig. 3.4. You can combine symbols to indicate, for example, that an operation is a class-side public method (such as `+$new()`).

3.4.2 Representing Objects

An object is drawn as a box with the type of the object underlined (see Fig. 3.5).

The object symbol is divided into two sections. The top section indicates the name of the object and its class in the format *objectName : className*. In Fig. 3.5, the object is `repMobile1` and the class is `Car` (see Fig. 3.3 for the definition of the `Car` class). The object name is optional, but the class name is compulsory. You can also indicate how many objects of a particular class are anticipated by entering the maximum value, range etc. in the top compartment. The lack of any number indicates that a single object is intended. The lower compartment contains a list of attributes and their values in the format *name type = value* (although the type is usually omitted). You can suppress the bottom compartment for clarity.

3.4.3 Representing Relationships

A relationship between classes or objects is represented by an association drawn as a solid line (see Fig. 3.6). An association between classes may have a name and an optional direction arrowhead that shows which way it is to be read. For example, in Fig. 3.6, the relationship called `hasEngine` is read from the `Car` class to the `Engine` class. In addition, each end of an association is a *role*. A role may have a name that illustrates how its class is viewed by the other class. In Fig. 3.6, the engine sees the car as a name and the car sees the engine as a specified type (e.g. Petrol, Diesel, Electric, etc.).

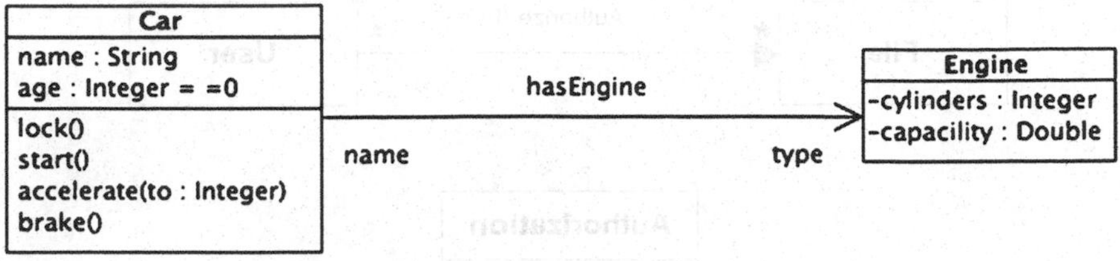

Fig. 3.6 Association between classes and links between objects

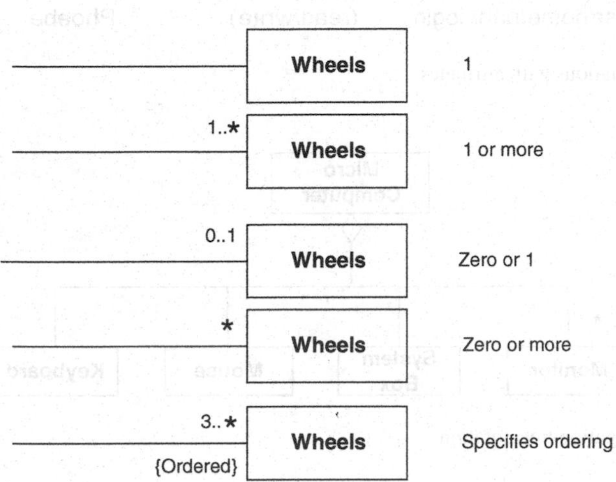

Fig. 3.7 Annotated associations

Each role (i.e. each end of the association) indicates the multiplicity of its class, that is how many instances of the class can be associated with one instance of the other class. This is indicated by a text expression on the role: * (indicating zero or more), a number, a range (e.g. 0..3). If there is no expression, there is exactly one association (see Fig. 3.7). You can specify that the multiple objects should be ordered using the text `{Ordered}`. You can also annotate the association with additional text (such as `{Sorted}`) but this is primarily for the reader's benefit and has no meaning in UML.

In some situations, an association needs attributes. This means that you need to treat the association as a class (see Fig. 3.8). These associations have a dashed line from the association line to the association class. This class is just like any other class and can have a name, attributes and operations. In Fig. 3.8, the associations show an access permissions attribute that indicates the type of access allowed for each user for each file.

Aggregation indicates that one or more objects are dependent on another object for their existence (*part-whole* relationships). For example, in Fig. 3.9, the Micro Computer is formed from the Monitor, the System box, the Mouse and the Keyboard.

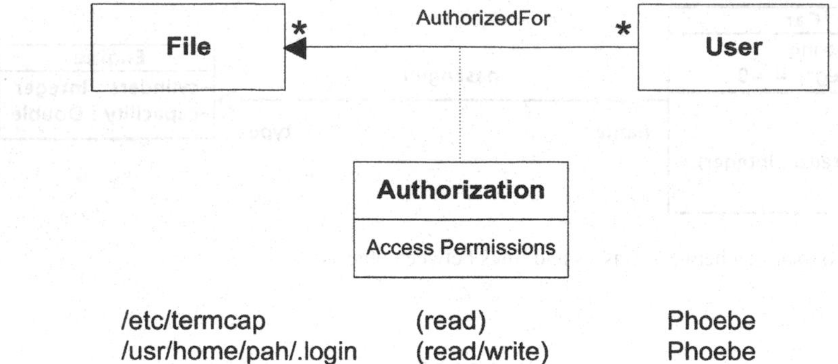

Fig. 3.8 Associations with attributes

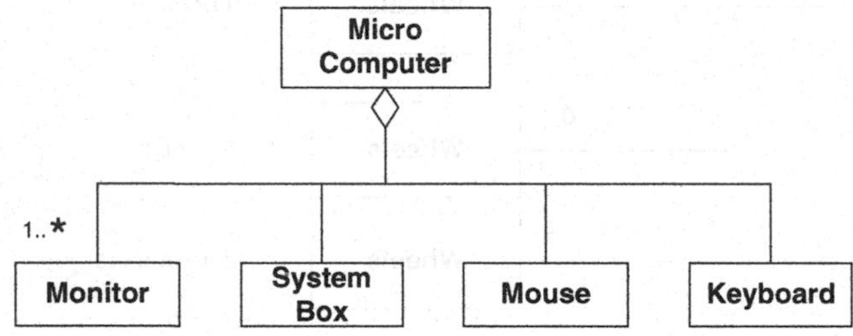

Fig. 3.9 Aggregation tree notation

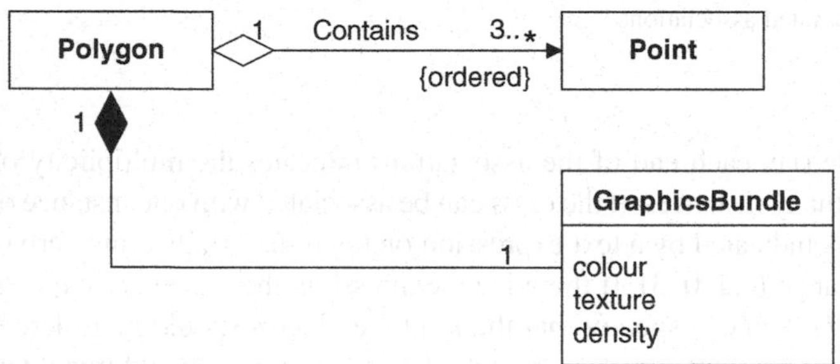

Fig. 3.10 Reference implementation

They are all needed for the fully functioning Micro Computer. Aggregation is shown by an empty diamond on the role attached to the whole object.

It is sometimes useful to differentiate between by-value and by-reference references (see Fig. 3.10). If the aggregation symbol is not filled, it indicates a by-reference implementation (i.e. a pointer or other reference); if the aggregation symbol is filled, it indicates a by-value implementation (i.e. a class that is embedded within another class).

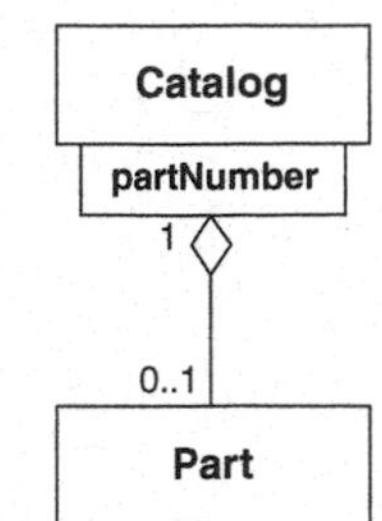

Fig. 3.11 Qualified associations

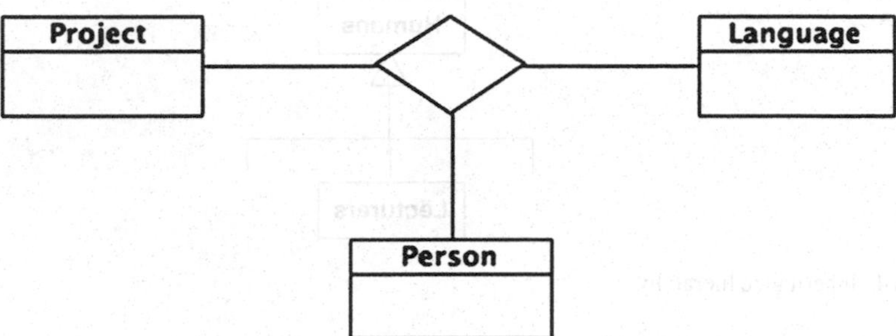

Fig. 3.12 Ternary associations

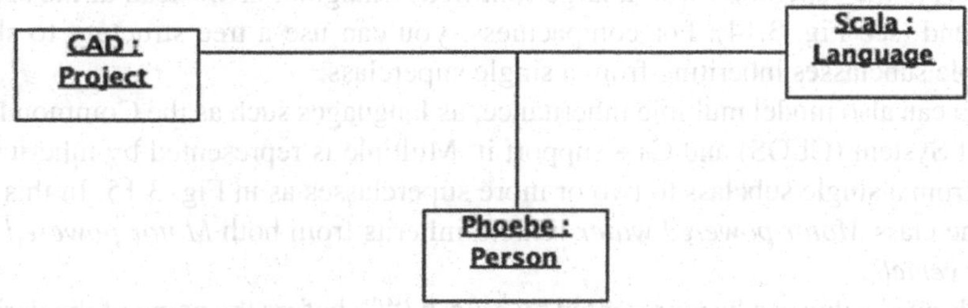

Fig. 3.13 Ternary links between objects

A qualified association is an association that requires both the object and the qualifier to identify uniquely the other object involved in the association. It is shown as a box between the association and the class. For example, in Fig. 3.11, you need the catalog and the part number to identify a unique part. Notice that the qualifier is part of the association, not the class.

A ternary (or higher order) association is drawn as a diamond with one line path to each of the participating classes (see Fig. 3.12). This is the traditional entity–relationship model symbol for an association (the diamond is omitted from the binary association to save space) (Fig. 3.13). Ternary associations are very

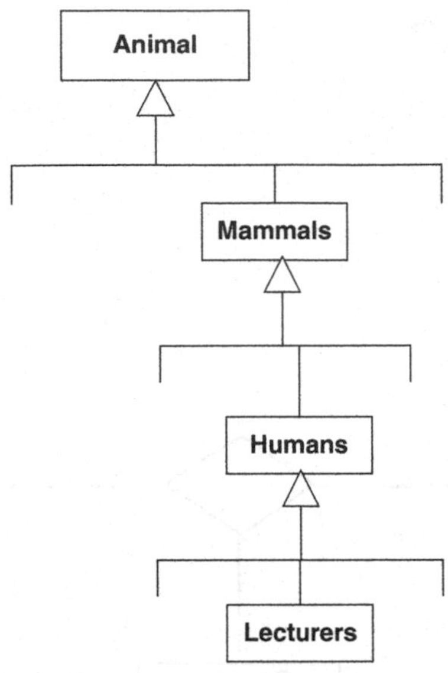

Fig. 3.14 Inheritance hierarchy

rare and higher order associations are almost non-existent. However, you can model them if necessary.

Inheritance of one class by a subclass is indicated by a solid line drawn from the subclass to the superclass with a large (unfilled) triangular arrowhead at the superclass end (see Fig. 3.14). For compactness, you can use a tree structure to show multiple subclasses inheriting from a single superclass.

You can also model multiple inheritance, as languages such as the Common Lisp Object System (CLOS) and C++ support it. Multiple is represented by inheritance lines from a single subclass to two or more superclasses as in Fig. 3.15. In this figure, the class *Motor powered water vehicle* inherits from both *Motor powered* and *Water vehicle*.

A derived value can be represented by a slash ("/") before the name of the derived attribute (see Fig. 3.16). Such an attribute requires an additional textual constraint defining how it is generated; you indicate this by a textual annotation below the class between curly brackets ({}).

A class may define a pattern of objects and links that exist whenever it is instantiated. Such a class is called a composite, and its class diagram contains an object diagram. You may think of it as an extended form of aggregation where the relationships among the parts are valid only within the composite. A composite is a kind of *pattern* or *template* that represents a conceptual clustering for a given purpose. Composition is shown by drawing a class box around the embedded components that are prototypical objects and links. That is, a composite defines a context in which references to classes and associations, defined elsewhere, can be used.

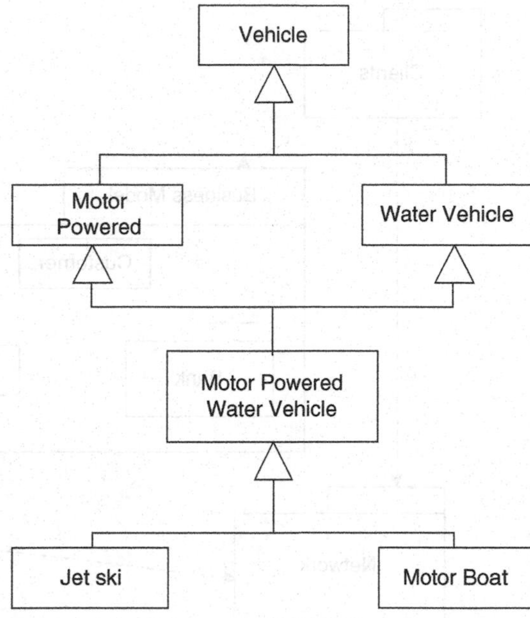

Fig. 3.15 Multiple inheritance

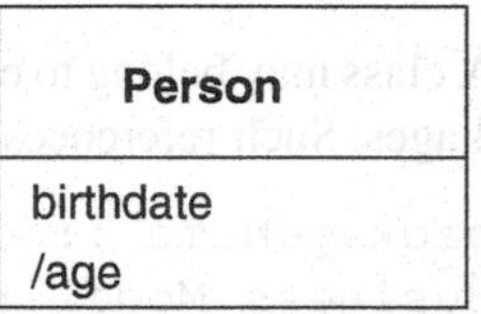

Fig. 3.16 Derived values

3.5 Packages

Packages group associated modelling elements such as classes in the object model (or subsystems in component diagrams). They are drawn as tabbed folders.

Figure 3.17 illustrates five packages called *Clients, Business Model, Persistent Store, Bank* and *Network*. In this diagram, the contents of *Clients, Persistent Store, Bank* and *Network* have been suppressed (by convention, the package names are in the body) and only *Business Model* is shown in detail (with its name in the top tab). *Business Model* possesses two classes, Customer and Account, and a nested package, *Bank*. The broken lines illustrate dependencies between the packages. For example, the package *Clients* directly depends on the packages *Business Model* and *Network* (i.e. at least one element in the *Clients* package relies on at least one element in the other two packages).

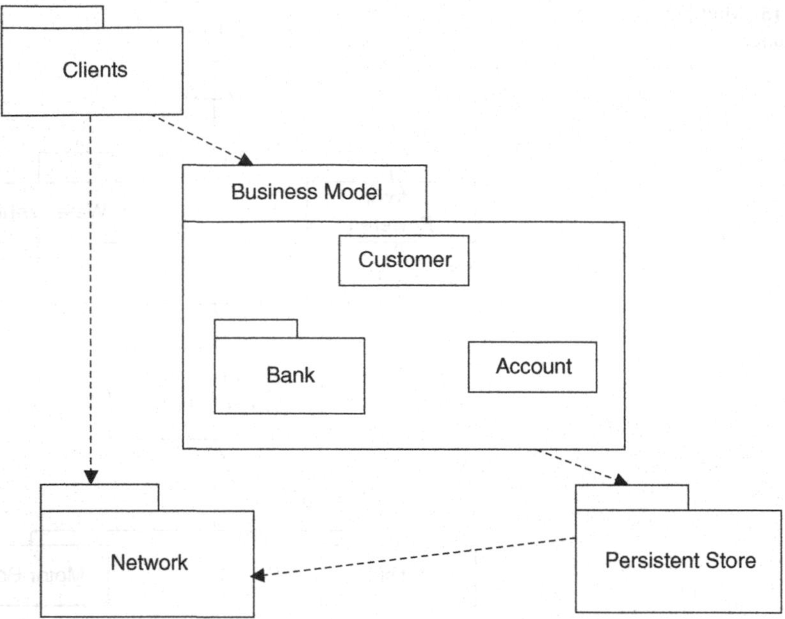

Fig. 3.17 Packages with dependencies

A class may belong to exactly one package but make reference to classes in other packages. Such references have the following format:

```
packageName :: className
Business Model :: Customer
```

Packages allow you to structure models hierarchically; they organize the model and control its overall complexity. Indeed you may use a package to enable top-down design of a system (rather than the bottom-up design typical of many object oriented design methods) by allowing designers to specify high level system functionality in terms of packages which are "filled out" as and when appropriate.

3.6 Sequence Diagrams

A *scenario* shows a particular series of interactions among objects in a single execution of a system. That is, it is a history of how the system behaves between one start state and a single termination state. This differs from an *envisionment*, which describes all system behaviours from all start states to all end states. Envisionments thus contain all possible histories (although they may also contain paths which the system is never intended to take).

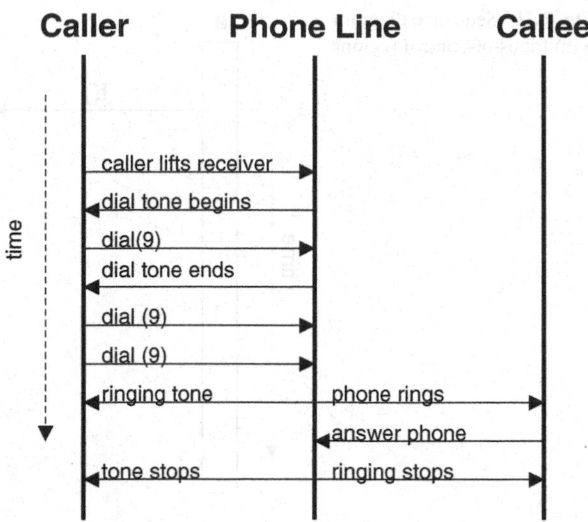

Fig. 3.18 A sequence diagram

Scenarios can be presented in two different ways: *Sequence Diagrams* and *Collaboration Diagrams*. Both these diagrams present the same information although they stress different aspects of this information. For example, sequence diagrams stress the timing aspects of the interactions between the objects, whereas collaboration diagrams stress the structure between these objects (which helps in understanding the requirements of the underlying software structure).

Figure 3.18 illustrates the basic structure of a sequence diagram. The objects involved in the exchange of messages are represented as vertical lines (which are labelled with the object's name). Caller, Phone Line and Callee are all objects involved in the scenario of dialling the Emergency services. The horizontal arrows indicate an event or message sent from one object to another. The arrow indicates the direction in which the event or message is sent. That is, the receiver is indicated by the head of the arrow. Normally return values are not shown on these diagrams. However, if they are significant, you can illustrate them by annotated return events.

Time proceeds vertically down the diagram, as indicated by the broken line arrow, and can be made more explicit by additional timing marks. These timing marks indicate how long the gap between messages should be or how long a message or event should take to get from the sender to the receiver.

A variation of the basic sequence diagram (called a focus-of-control diagram) illustrates which object has the thread of control at any one time. This is shown by a fatter line during the period when the object has control (see Fig. 3.19). Notice that the bar representing the object C only starts when it is created and terminates when it is destroyed.

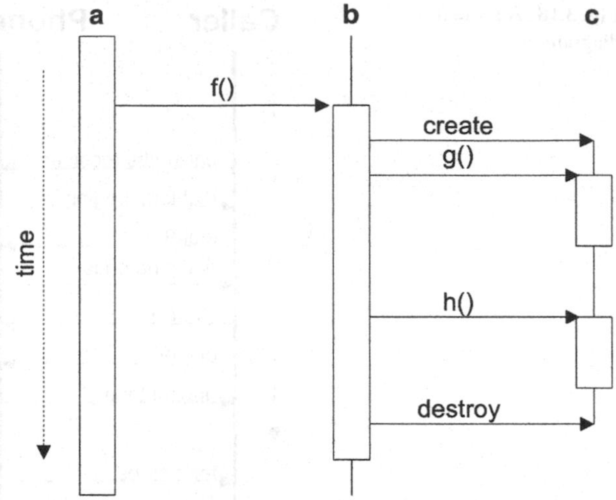

Fig. 3.19 Sequence diagram with focus-of-control regions

3.7 Collaboration Diagrams

As stated above, collaboration diagrams illustrate the sequence of messages between objects based around the object structure (rather than the temporal aspects of sequence diagrams). A collaboration diagram is formed from the objects involved in the collaboration, the links (permanent or temporary) between the objects and the messages (numbered in sequence) that are exchanged between the objects. An example collaboration diagram is presented in Fig. 3.20.

Objects which are created during the collaboration are indicated by the label *new* before the object name (e.g. the Line object in Fig. 3.20). Links between objects are annotated to indicate their type, permanent or temporary, existing for this particular collaboration. These annotations are placed in boxes on the ends of the links and can have the following values:

A Association (or permanent) link
F Object field (the target object is part of the source object)
G Global variable
L Local variable
P Procedure parameter
S Self reference

You can add role names to distinguish links (e.g. self, wire and window in Fig. 3.20). Role names in brackets indicate a temporary link, i.e. one that is not an association.

The messages which are sent along links are indicated by labels next to the links. One or more messages can be sent along a link in either or both directions. The format of the messages is defined by the following (some of which are optional):

1. *A comma-separated list of sequence numbers in brackets, e.g. [seqno, seqno]* which indicate messages from other threads of control that must occur before the current message. This element is only needed with concurrency.

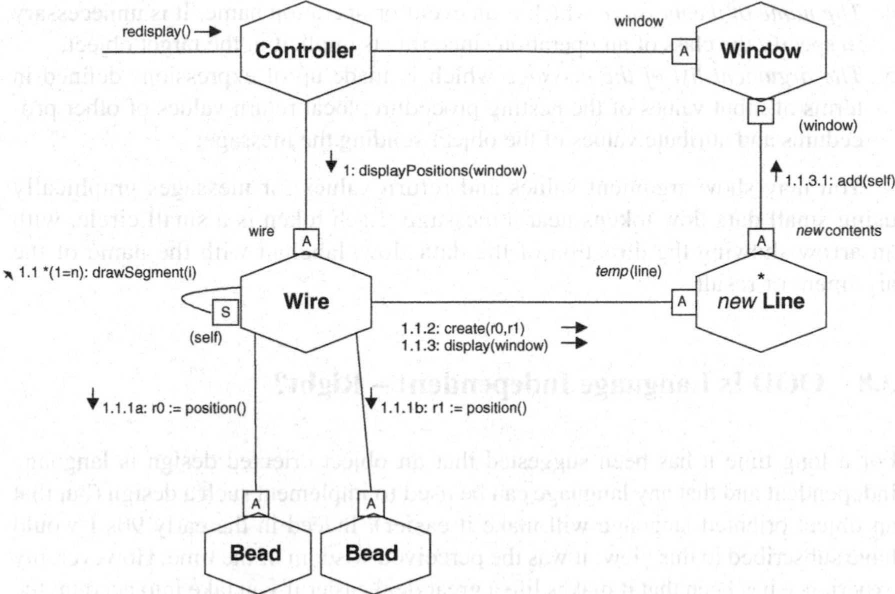

Fig. 3.20 An example collaboration diagram

2. *A list of sequence elements separated by full stops, "."* which represent the nested procedural calling sequence of the message in the overall transaction. Each element has the following parts:
   - A letter (or name) indicating a concurrent thread. All letters at the same level of nesting represent threads that execute concurrently i.e. 1.2a and 1.2b are concurrent. If there is no letter, it usually indicates the main sequence.
   - An integer showing the sequential position of the current message within its thread. For example, message 2.1.4 is part of the procedure invoked by message 2.1 and follows message 2.1.3 within that procedure.
   - An iteration indicator (*), optionally followed by an iteration expression in parentheses, which indicates that several messages of the same form are sent either sequentially (to a single target) or concurrently (to the elements of a set). If there is an iteration expression, it shows the values that the iterator assumes, such as "(i = 1..n)"; otherwise, the details of the iteration must be specified in text or simply deferred to the code.
   - A conditional indicator (?), optionally followed by a Boolean expression in parentheses. The iteration and conditional indicators are mutually exclusive.
3. *A return value name followed by an assignment sign* (":=") which indicates that the procedure returns a value designated by the given name. The use of the same name elsewhere in the diagram designates the same value. If no return value is specified, then the procedure operates by side-effects.

4. *The name of the message* which is an event or operation name. It is unnecessary to specify the class of an operation since this is implicit in the target object.
5. *The argument list of the message* which is made up of expressions defined in terms of input values of the nesting procedure, local return values of other procedures and attribute values of the object sending the message.

You may show argument values and return values for messages graphically using small data flow tokens near a message. Each token is a small circle, with an arrow showing the direction of the data flow, labelled with the name of the argument or result.

3.8 OOD Is Language Independent – Right?

For a long time it has been suggested that an object oriented design is language independent and that any language can be used to implement such a design (but that an object oriented language will make it easier). Indeed in the early 90s I would have subscribed to this view; it was the perceived wisdom of the time. However, my experience has been that it makes life a great deal easier if you take into account the target language (or languages) for which you are designing. Indeed this has been brought home to me on numerous occasions to such an extent that I know say that in practice you need to consider target "platform" issues and that if you don't you may well develop a design which is un-implementable (without a great deal of modification). That is, UML diagrams don't mean a thing unless you can implement them! For example, the concept of a parameterized class is supported in UML, however, to Java 1.2 such classes are meaningless! While it is not impossible to map such classes into Java 1.2 you would need to invent this mapping yourself. As such a mapping would at best be non-standard which could be confusing for others maintaining, updating or modifying your design / code.

In turn there are certain *idioms* that recur within object oriented programming languages, and each language has its own idioms. Java is certainly no exception to this and such idioms should be acknowledged and where appropriate exploited within a design. By idioms I mean essentially certain ways of doing things or using standard classes in combinations. Design patterns are an example of generic idioms, however Java has its own idioms which can be exploited. Some of these idioms have been made more formal than others and you can view the Enterprise JavaBeans as the ultimate example. They specify a very particular way of developing (and deploying) Java code that needs to be taken into account when designing a Java system (which employees Enterprise JavaBeans).

Finally, let us consider the various technologies that exist that may affect a design. These include (but are not limited to) various inter-process communications mechanisms such as RMI, JavaIDL, TCP/IP socket programming and IP Multicast sockets as well as Java streams, the Swing architecture (based on the model-view-controller pattern) and others (Scala related issues). All these may affect how you wish to structure your design.

3.9 Making UML Work for You

UML is a large notation designed to describe a wide variety of software systems. For example, MIS systems, Real time systems (at least to some extent), interactive system, batch oriented processing etc. However, in general you as a software engineer are not trying to produce all these systems in one go. Indeed many organizations (or at least departments within large organizations) specialize in particular types of systems. For example, interactive client side applications. Such a software system will not need (and is not best described) using every available aspect of the UML notation. It is much more appropriate (and actually much better for a project team) to identify an appropriate core notation set that will be used. This means that everyone can get familiar with this core set and can ignore the aspects of UML that they do not use.

It is also useful to accept that UML does not cover every eventuality that you might want to represent or describe. In such cases do not try to force UML to fit what you want. Either use a different notational format (for example by borrowing some notation from data modeling) or by inventing your own project notation (without of course trying to re-invent UML!). Also do not too hung up on "UML notational details", if what you have drawn is understood by those that need to understand it, then it is sufficient!

Also remember that a diagram can say a thousand words but that putting that diagram in context can make the thousand words comprehensible to the reader. Therefore use notes to explain what is being presented, any design decisions or tradeoffs. If these notes are simple enough you can place them as notes on the diagram. If they are more detailed and require it, link a word (or start office document) to your model.

Finally, remember that UML is not a method, the end goal or indeed the project documentation on its own. Rather it should be an aid to the main aim of this whole process – the production of working software systems!

3.10 Questions to Consider

UML allows many characteristics of a system to be modelled, but there are a number of questions you should consider when applying UML to any language and Scala in particular. These questions include:

1. Does the language support all of the features provided by the UML. Let us take one classic example; UML supports the concept of multiple inheritance. However languages such as Smalltalk and Java do not although C++ does. Scala is interesting in that it does not support multiple inheritance of classes but does allow multiple inheritance of behaviour through traits. This traits should be used for multiple inheritance but not classes..
2. What types does a language support? UML allows anything within reason to be used as a type. You should limit your types (particularly within the design phase)

to those types supported by the target language. For example, you should only use Scala types for compatible declarations. This may mean that you should leave specifying the type to be used until you know the implementation language. This is not necessarily a problem as early in the design phase (and the analysis phase you may wish to use abstract domain specific concepts rather than Scala types e.g. currency versus double).

3. Designs must be limited to the features of the language used. If the language being used inherently supports asynchronous concurrency (as Scala does) then your designs can make explicit use of this feature. If they don't then avoid this or consider how it might be provided in the target language.

3.11 The Scala Platform

At this point we will digress and consider what features a Scala specific design might focus on. That is what are the architectural elements in Scala, the implementation features and the technologies that might be of interest. These are listed below:

- **Packages**. Packages in Scala are collections of types (such as Class, Traits and functions) which exist within the same namespace and which have a shared (package) visibility. Note that compared with Java Scala has a more sophisticated package visibility / access control model and thus this can be exploited in your designs.
- **Traits and Classes**. Classes are only one of the two basic building blocks in Scala. Traits are the other. If you treat traits as essentially more flexible interfaces then you are missing the point. Traits are a very powerful construct in the Scala language which provide amongst other things strong typing. Contract based interactions, code reuse and extension. Exploiting these concepts in your design is likely to result in a better fit with the implementation features of Scala. Note that UML does not explicitly have a Trait concept but this can be indicated using a Trait stereotype.
- **Functions**. These are first class entities in the Scala world and can be treated as such with UML. This can be done by defining a Function Trait and defining the UML classifier in the form of a Function declaration. This is not the prettiest thing to view but is an effective way of representing Scala functions should you wish to do so.
- **Objects**. Scala has a keyword for creating objects (as well as the more familiar instantiation of an existing class). These objects are special in Scala in that they are singleton objects – their role can be indicated using a Object trait on a class.
- **Companion Objects**. Scala has a special meaning for an object with the same name as a class and defined in the same file as that class. It is a companion object which has privileged access to the contents of the class. This can be indicated using a Companion Object trait.
- **Fields**. In Scala we have field members for class and traits. These are all instance related fields – there is no such concept as a static field in Scala so you should not

use them in your models. Instead consider companion objects and fields held by those elements.

- **Methods**. Scala allows methods to be defined within types – however there is very little difference between Scala methods and functions; this is difficult to represent within UML and may be best left as an implementation consideration.
- **Constructors**. In Scala constructors are a very important concept however UML does not really have a concept of a constructor and thus does not distinguish them from other operations. Care must therefore be taken with the design and documentation of constructors. In addition as part of a constructor parameters can be marked as val or var which has significant meaning within Scala (making them into properties with getter and in the later case setters). UML has no such concept and so care needs to be taken within their use as well.
- Scala also provides a number of good software engineering features including reusable APIs which can be exploited to avoid re-implementing the wheel, asynchronous message based communication for multi-threaded applications and explicit exception handling. While a number of these should not impact on a high level design, they may impact on the lower levels of a design and should therefore be catered for.

3.12 Classes in UML

Mapping UML classes to Scala is straightforward, there can be a direct one to one relationship between UML classes and Scala classes. One of the nice features of UML classes is that you can use optional compartments so that you can also document the events handled by, and responsibilities of, a class.

You may wish to hi-light constructors as UML does not have a specific constructor concept (see later) and you need to be careful of inheritance as Scala only supports single inheritance of classes.

3.13 Fields in UML

UML fields map directly to instance variables (or field members) of various types in Scala. These types include Classes, Traits and Objects.

To ensure that the resulting design maps to Scala appropriately it is also important to following the guidelines:

- *Use Scala access control types* (such as public (the default), private, protected and explicitly package visibility) and no others. Also note that there are two concepts for private – private to the class and private to the object (private[this]) use these two concepts appropriately.
- *Use valid Scala names (and styles)*. Do not start variable names (or class, trait and object names) with a numeric – they must be a Unicode character. Also in Scala classes, objects and traits always start with a capital letter and methods,

functions and variables with a lower case letter. Subsequent words in both cases are hi-lighted using capital letters rather than underbars or other separators. It helps everyone involved if the designers adopt this standard as well as the implementers. You may note that this is essentially the same standards as are adopted by other languages such as Java (and to a lesser extent C#) and this should help people moving from other languages. Note if your organization adopts a different standard then that should be adopted by both designers and implementers.

- *Use valid Scala or user defined types*. Only use valid Scala types (particularly as the design nears the implementation stages) including user defined types. However, if you start adopting this style early on you will not have to change the types at a later stage. Of course early on you may wish to defer the decision regarding the exact type until a later stage and that is quite normal.
- *Specify valid Scala initial values*. Assume the standard default values for Scala member variables (such as false for boolean, 0 for Int, 0.0 for Double etc.). This will make your designs less cluttered. When you need to specify a non-standard default value then make sure you use a valid Scala value. Also consider when you wish to use the concept of Option.

3.14 Operations in UML

Operations are implemented as Scala methods or functions. The mapping from UML to Scala is the same as for fields with the same set of guidelines plus a few additional considerations. These are:

- *Parameter list as valid Scala parameters*. Parameters for an operation should follow the Scala conventions and should specify valid Scala types (these may include user defined types). This is particularly true as the design nears the implementation stage. However, if you start adopting this style early on you will not have to change the types at a later stage. Of course early on you may wish to defer the decision regarding the exact type until a later stage and that is quite normal.
- *Return type as valid Scala type*. The same is true for the operations return type. In Scala all methods and Functions have a return type (although this may be Unit indicating that no actual value is returned).

3.15 Constructors

Constructors have a special meaning in Scala. They act as initializers (so the name is a little unfortunate) allowing the newly created object to be initialised before being released for general use. There are some very specific rules governing constructors in Scala including:

- Constructors are not called via the dot notation and can only be *called* in a very limited way. This can either be done when the object is created using the new keyword or as the first line of another constructor.

- Constructors are not inherited by subclasses however, at least one constructor is always called for every parent class right back up the inheritance hierarchy.
- Additional, auxiliary constructors, can be defined in Scala but they are all called this and must invoke another constructor.
- Constructors must not have a return type, if they are given a return type.

UML does not distinguish between operations and constructors, but the distinction between them in Scala is very important. You therefore need to be very careful regarding the way in which you define and document what will become constructors in Scala. It is not a good idea just to ignore them in your design as they are fundamental to the operation of Scala and are very important in configuring objects before they are used.

3.16 Properties in Scala

Classes, objects and traits can all have properties associated with them. These properties can be marked as val or var. A val property is a read only property and a var is a readable and writable property. In effect when a property is marked with one of these keywords an internal representation is created for them along with the appropriate accessor (setter and getter) operations. UML does not have this concept in it, however this can be mimicked by defining the appropriate setter and getter. For example, in Scala the class Person might be written as:

```
class Person (val name: String="Denise", var age:Int=45)
```

Alternative, it could be written long hand as

```
class Person {
  private val _name = "Denise"
  private var _age = 0
  // Getters
  def age = _age
  def name = _name

  // Setters
  def age_=(value: Int): Unit = _age = value
  def name_=(value: String): Unit = _name = value
}
```

Both versions result in a class person with getters for both name and age but only a setter method for the age property.

It would this be possible to mimic the use of val and var within Scala by defining the appropriate setter and getter operations in UML. However, this may well be overkill for many situations and a Stereotype might present a better solution. In Fig. 3.21 I am using both a Property stereotype and a readonly stereotype to indicate that I expect this to be a Scala val member of the class Person (however readonly might be sufficient or event a Stereotype *val* might be appropriate):

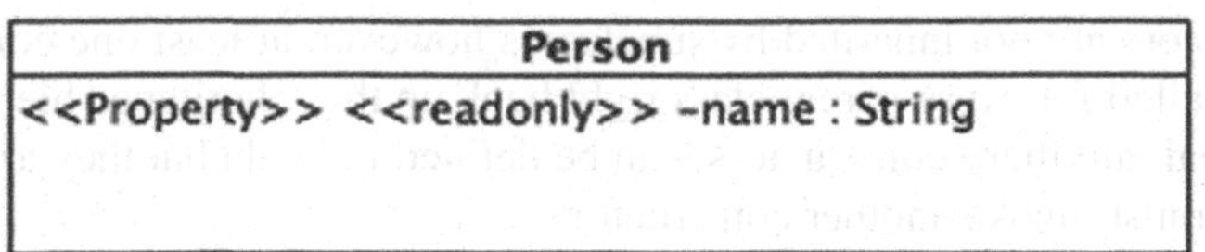

Fig. 3.21 Stereotypes on properties

3.17 Packages in UML

UML packages map directly to Scala packages, however this mapping is not as straight forward as it may at first seem. In Scala packages are encapsulated units which can possess classes, traits, functions and Objects. In addition there can be a package object defined. Packages are extremely useful:

- They allow you to associate related classes and interfaces.
- They resolve naming problems that would otherwise cause confusion.
- They allow some privacy for classes, methods and variables that should not be visible outside the package. You can provide a level of encapsulation such that only those elements that are intended to be public can be accessed from outside the package.

In UML packages have similarities to aggregation. If a package owns its content it is *composed aggregation* but if it refers to its contents (i.e. imports elements from other packages) it is *shared aggregation*. Don't be confused here with Scala imports, Scala imports are merely making types in other packages *visible* to the current package – there is no aggregation happening with Scala. This is the first major difference between Scala packages and UML packages.

The second major difference is associated with visibility. In UML packages, just like classes, can have visibility modified applied to them showing how other packages can access their contents. UML defines four different levels for package visibility. These four are:

- Private
- Protected
- Public
- Implementation

The first three may appear familiar to Scala, Java or C# developers (as these languages have private, protected and public visibility modifiers as well). Firstly the default visibility for the contents of a package is public (which is also the default in Scala but not in Java). Secondly packages in Scala themselves don't have a concept of visibility associated with them! This may not be a major difference, however, if we consider what each of them mean in UML we find very significant differences. The meanings of the different visibility modifiers are:

- **Public** means that other elements in other packages can see and use the contents of the package.

- **Private** means that only the package that owns an element or package that imports that element can use it. This is very different to Java, private means private to an object (top level classes cannot be private).
- **Protected** means that only the package that owns or imports the element can use it, however packages which inherit from this package will also be able to access the elements of the package (note inheritance of packages!).
- **Implementation** is similar to visibility with the additional idea that elements which have a dependency to a package cannot use the elements inside that package if it has implementation visibility.

In addition to a visibility modifier, UML packages can also have interfaces and can be *specialisation's* of other packages. In Scala there is no concept of an *interface* only classes, traits, functions and objects.

UML packages also support the concept of inheritance; however languages such as Scala and Java do not. You should therefore avoid using package inheritance as it has no direct mapping into Scala. Although it is quite an elegant way to describe how the models packages are related it will only complicate the process of translating the design into Scala. Secondly you should avoid using package visibility modifiers as again they really have no equivalent in Scala and indeed some aspects of package visibility can be quite confusing for the Scala developer (not least because the same names are used for different concepts).

Finally, Scala allows Package Objects to be defined that encapsulate package level data and functionality. These are a really useful feature of Scala which are not directly supported in UML. One approach is to use a Package Object trait to represent them.

3.18 UML Interfaces

UML interfaces do not map directly to any construct in Scala. One approach could be to use UML interfaces to model Scala traits – and conceptual this is a possibility. However, numerous UML tools default to certain assumptions about interfaces which cause problems when trying to model traits as UML Interfaces (such as presuming that all attributes will be implemented as class side / static fields). My preference would be to model traits using a Stereotype – see next section.

3.19 Scala Traits as Stereo Types

In many ways traits have a lot in common with an abstract class. That is, you cannot instantiate a trait, you can define whatever behaviour you need including variable and constant members, you can including methods, functions, types etc. However, traits cannot have constructors, and can be mixed into any other types as required into the type hierarchy or when a object is being instantiated.

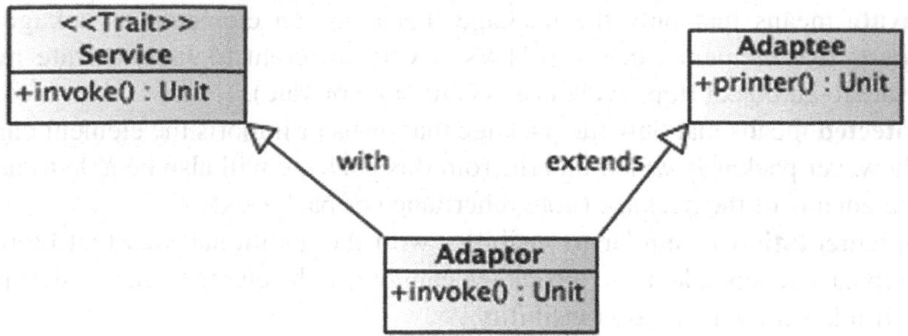

Fig. 3.22 Representing Traits in UML

They are therefore neither UML interface nor UML abstract classes. Personally I prefer to represent them using a Trait stereotype on a UML class. This can then be associated with other types as appropriate (with the inheritance associated annotated with a 'with' stereotype to show the relationship). This is illustrated in Fig. 3.22.

3.20 Templates

UML supports the concept of parameterised classes as templates. Such concepts are directly supported by languages such as C++, Java and Scala. They can therefore be used within your designs.

3.21 Associations

There are many possible ways of mapping the different types of associations in UML into Scala. The simplest and most obvious approach is to use a variable in one object to reference another object. However this has a number of limitations and is often too simplistic. The primarily problem with this approach is that it is impossible to directly use the instant variable approach for anything other than a single uni-directional link. In most cases you either require a bi-directional link, or multiple objects referenced by the link (possibly with some ordering or sorting) you may even require a key to determine which link to follow. Associations may also have attributes of their own. Each of these scenarios requires greater flexibility (and behaviour) than a single instance variable reference can provide.

Another option is to use a specific association class (or classes). These class represent the association. They sit between the two objects being associated (see Fig. 3.23). In this figure the link class represents an association between a Developer class and a Project class. The link may be uni-directional or bi-directional depending upon the application. Of course the references between the developer object, the link object and the project object are held in instance variables. However, the

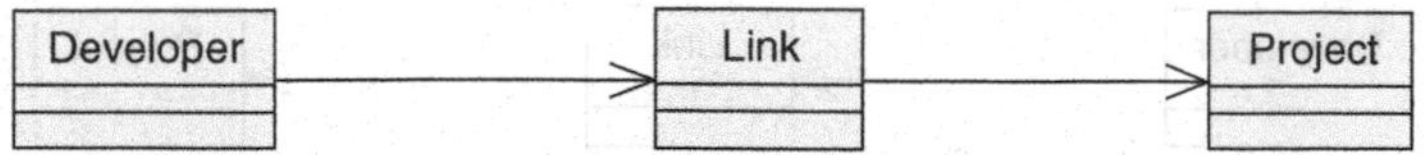

Fig. 3.23 A link class representing an association

association itself is not represented by a reference but by the link object. Thus the link object can have attributes and operations just link any other object. This is therefore a much more powerful alternative than merely using a reference.

To illustrate this idea, simple source code is provided for the three classes in Fig. 3.23 below. Note that we are only hi-lighting how the association may be implemented and are not focusing on the attributes or operations that may be supported by each class.

```
case class Developer(val link: Link)

case class Project(val name: String)

case class Link(val project: Project)

object test extends App {
  val proj = Project("CAD")
  val link = Link(proj)
  val dev = Developer(link)
  println(dev)
}
```

Which when run generates:

```
Developer(Link(Project(CAD)))
```

In some cases it is necessary to have a link object, for example when we are dealing with ternary associations (as illustrated in Fig. 3.24).

In some cases there will only ever be a single instance of a class within the system. Such objects are often referred to as singleton objects (and indeed the singleton pattern has become well documented) and is directly supported within the Scala language.

A singleton object may be referenced by many different objects throughout the system and therefore there needs to be an easy way to implement such associations. In Scala a type defined using the keyword Object is a singleton object and can be accessed by any code anywhere simply by importing that object (or the objects operations). For example:

```
object Single {
  val count = 0
}
```

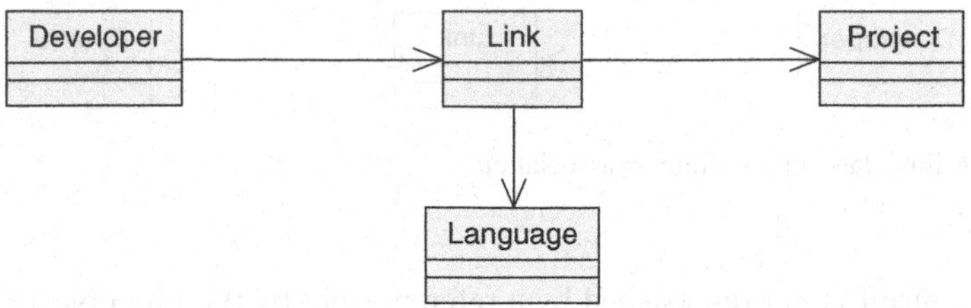

Fig. 3.24 Representing a ternary association

3.22 Multiplicity in UML

In UML it is possible to specify a range of different attributes of an association. These can indicate the number of associations (e.g. 1, or 2), they can also be used to indicate ranges of number (e.g. 1–3) as well as any ordering and sorting of the associations. However, such information has no direct mapping into Scala. Unless you implement code to support ranges, for example, Scala will not impose any such constraints.

There are types available provide support for ordering and sorting collections of objects (see the scala.collection sub package as there are both mutable and immutable collection types). However, these types are not explicitly intended for use with associations. Instead a developer needs to decide how to use such classes to implement the constraints on an association.

The end result is that an association may need to be implemented in Scala as a member variable or constant maintaining a reference, as a link object (as described above) or as a collection of references (or link objects).

Such decisions will impact not only on the potential performance of the system, but also the comprehensibility of the design versus the implementation. You should therefore produce guidelines that are adopted throughout a project and adhere to them. Where the guidelines are broken explicit reasons should be given to ensure that those enhancing or maintaining the design and implementation understand what they are being presented with.

3.23 Aggregation and Composition

As well as standard associations, UML supports the concepts of aggregation and composition. An aggregation is a specialised form of association in which a whole is related to its part(s). It is a *part of* relationship (where as an association is a *works with* or *uses* relationship). In turn composition is a variation on an aggregation that indicates that the sub part cannot exist on its own. For example, a human heart is something that is a aggregate of a human body which does not function outside of the body (thus it is a compositional relationship). In turn a car engine might or might not be a compositional part of a car. For example, in a warehouse of parts, an engine may well be an object in its own right that can exist outside the scope of the car.

Aggregation is a concept that is only supported by UML, there is nothing special in Scala which supports the general concept of aggregation. However, Scala does have a concept referred to as an inner class. An inner class is a class that defines an object which can only exist with reference to the outer class. That is, you cannot make an instance of an inner class without referring to an instance of the outer class. This can be very useful and might at first appear to support compositional aggregation.

Inner classes, however, may limit the reusability of a design. An inner class cannot be created as a stand-alone object, thus if we created a class Gearbox as an inner class of a Car, then we could only ever use the class Gearbox with reference to instance of the class Car. This would mean that we could not use the class Gearbox with a Lorry, a Tractor, a Motorcycle or similar. However, from the point of view of our design, each possesses an object called a *gearbox* that is an aggregate part of the main object. We have therefore imposed unnecessary restrictions on the design due to an implementation design we have made.

Care must be taken with using inner classes to represent aggregation (and particularly composition) as this may be an over simplification.

3.24 Singleton Objects

Singleton objects are a fundamental type in the Scala language. Each time a type is defined using the object keyword, that creates a singleton object. This can then be accessed directly within the need for any further instantiation.

Although this is a concept in the Scala language it is not a feature of the UML world. The semantics of an object could be represented by a Singleton stereotype. However, that would not encompass the full meaning of the Scala object; which is a singleton *as well as* being an object in its own right.

In UML I prefer to indicate that something is expected to be a Scala object by using an Object stereotype. For example see Fig. 3.25.

Which might be coded in Scala simply as

```
object Session {
  val id = 1
}
```

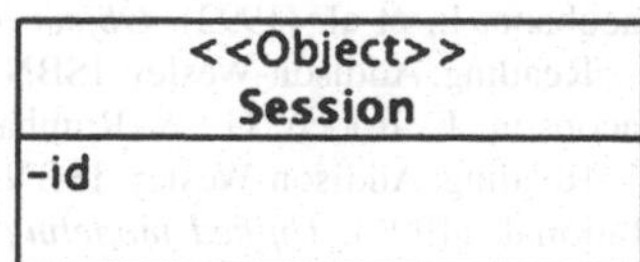

Fig. 3.25 A Scala Object

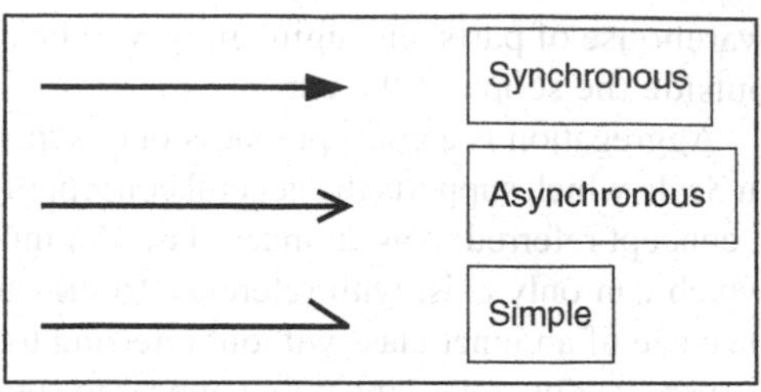

Fig. 3.26 UML message types

3.25 Synchronous and Asynchronous Messages

UML supports a number of different message types including simple, synchronous and asynchronous types (see Fig. 3.26). Simple messages indicate the direction of the flow of control, but not details about that flow of control.

A synchronous message is one in which the message being sent does not return until the operation initiated by the message is completed. An Asynchronous message is one that returns as soon as it is sent and the receiver process the message in a separate thread. This is the approach adopted by Actor messages in Scala. When a message is sent to an object, that message is added to a queue of messages to be processed by the receiving Actor. The sending process is able to immediately continue processing.

UML is agnostic as to which communication style is adopted. However, if the design does not make it clear the approach that is being used then it may be confusing. It is usual therefore to clearly indicate either using UML message types (or using stereotypes) the form of interaction expected.

References

Ben-Natan, R. (1995). *CORBA: A guide to common object request broker architecture*. New York: McGraw-Hill. ISBN 0-07-005427.

Booch, G. (1994). *Object-oriented analysis and design with applications* (2nd ed.). Redwood City: Benjamin Cummings.

Booch, G., Jacobson, I., & Rumbaugh, J. (1996). *The unified modeling language for object oriented development*. Documentation Set, Version 0.91 Addendum, UML Update. Rational Software Corporation. Available at http://www.rational.com/ot/uml.html

Coleman, D., et al. (1994). *Object oriented development: The fusion method*. Englewood Cliffs: Prentice Hall. ISBN 0-13-101040-9.

Harel, D. (1988). On visual formalisms. *Communications of the ACM, 31*(5), 514–530.

Harel, D., et al. (1987). On the formal semantics of Statecharts. In *Proceedings of the 2nd IEEE symposium on logic in Computer Science*, Ithaca, pp. 54–64.

Jacobson, I., et al. (1992). *Object-oriented software engineering: A use case driven approach*. Reading: Addison-Wesley. ISBN 0-201-54435-0.

Jacobson, I., Booch, G., & Rumbaugh, J. (1998). *The unified software development process*. Reading: Addison-Wesley. ISBN 0201571692.

Rational. (1996). *Unified modeling language for real-time systems design*. Rational Software Corporation. Available at http://www.rational.com/ot/uml.html

Rumbaugh, J., et al. (1991). *Object-oriented modeling and design*. Englewood Cliffs: Prentice Hall.

Part II
Fundamental Patterns

Chapter 4
Immutability

4.1 Introduction

Immutability indicates that once created, an objects' data cannot be changed (this is in contrast to mutable objects where the state of the object can be changed).

In Java strings are examples of immutable objects. Once a string has been created you cannot modify that string. When you concatenate that string with another string a new string is created, but the original string is unmodified. Unless you alter any references you have to the new string the effect of the catenation will not be observed.

Many in the Scala community will not consider Immutability a pattern that requires explicit description as such, since it is one of the underlying themes of the Scala language. This is illustrated by the presumption that collection classes are immutable (unless you explicitly state that you wish to use a mutable version). This is achieved by the use of the Scala PreDef object automatically placing the immutable collection classes into your default environment. However, this is certainly not the case for those of you who are moving to Scala from Java, C# or many other programming languages where collection classes are by default mutable. In Scala this goes much wider with Immutability being an overriding design pattern that permeates many classes and libraries.

This chapter considers Immutability and presents it as a Fundamental pattern which is adopted within the Scala class libraries and which can be adopted within your own applications. It also presents the reasons for and against immutability so that you can decide when it is appropriate to adopt.

4.2 Pattern Classification

Fundamental

J. Hunt, *Scala Design Patterns: Patterns for Practical Reuse and Design*,
DOI 10.1007/978-3-319-02192-8_4, © Springer International Publishing Switzerland 2013

4.3 Intent

To simplify design and implementation of applications by restricting side effects and limiting unintended modifications.

4.4 Context

In object-oriented and functional programming, immutable objects are objects whose state cannot be changed once they are created.

Immutable objects are useful because they simplify implementations and reduce the complexity inherent in multi-threaded environments (immutable objects are inherently thread safe – as they do not allow any thread to alter their state).

The tread safe aspect of immutable objects is significant. One of the most difficult areas of a multi threaded application to get right is that associated with protecting multi threaded access to shared mutable objects. In Java this issue is notorious for resulting in problems associated with:

- Deadlock due to thread1 waiting for data to be supplied by thread2 for a shared object, but thread2 is waiting for thread2 to do the same on another shared data object.

It is also far too easy to get data corruption (due to little synchronization of threads) or general performance degradation whatever happens. This situation is exacerbated by the fact that it is really hard to write effective multi-threaded tests that capture all the possible scenarios that might occur.

Immutability solves many of these problems merely by only allowing read access to that data, it is therefore never necessary to use any form of locking at all.

Note that in some cases an object may be considered immutable, even if an internal only attribute may change, if the external state does not appear to alter. An example of such a situation might occur when an internal attribute is used to cache the results of an expensive computation, but may clear that cache if it has not been accessed for a period of time. The same result will be returned whether it is generated or returned from the cache – thus making the object appear immutable.

4.5 Forces/Motivation

In many situations objects (such as collections) are created in one part of a system and passed to other parts of a system via method or function invocation. If those invocation may make unexpected or undesirable changes to the objects this may adversely effect an apparently unrelated body of code. In these situations tracking down the cause of the problem and rectifying that issue may be time consuming, costly and resulting in difficult to maintain code.

Much of the benefit that comes with the Immutable pattern is because immutable objects avoid unwanted side effects. That is, it is impossible for client code to inadvertently modify an immutable object. This therefore results in simpler designs as it is not necessary to manage numerous copies of objects, check for unexpected situations, handle production errors due to code side effects etc.

The main benefits associated with immutability are

- Immutable implementations are easier to understand.
- Resulting in simpler solutions that are easier to maintain.
- Allowing easier to extension to new scenarios or extended functionality.
- All of which can result in improved reliability.

4.6 Constituent Parts

The primary component of the Immutable pattern is an immutable implementation of a class or object (or indeed a trait). The immutable element is implemented such that it either does not incorporate any modification-oriented behaviour or that behaviour results in a new instance of the object that represents the changed state.

For example, creating variable to hold a string "John" and adding another string "Hunt" to that string results in a third string "JohnHunt"; it has no effect on the original string. For example:

```
var name = "John"
name: String = John
```

```
name + "Hunt"
res0: String = JohnHunt
```

```
println(name)
John
```

In many cases it is also common to have a mutable version of the same concept. These mutable versions are often in their own mutable package but may merely be denoted via a naming convention.

A refinement of the basic concept is to use two Marker traits one for Immutable and one for Mutable. Scala already provides Immutable and Mutable traits see scala.Immutable and scala.Mutable (both of which were introduced in Scala 2.8).

4.7 Implementation Issues

It is necessary to decide what is meant by immutable (and mutable) with respect to a particular type. For example, should an immutable object even contain operations that allow apparent data changes (but which result in a new copy of the object with the updated data being created).

Additionally, the key to an immutable object is that the external view of the object does not change state. However, in practice internal some attributes may change. The boundaries for such changes must be identified and a decision made regarding at what point the object actually becomes mutable rather than immutable.

4.8 Concrete Example

As an example of applying the Immutable pattern to a very simple application we will use the example of an Invoice. An invoice is a data oriented entity that holds information on a list of products and incorporates a number of properties related to the invoice, for example

- An invoice number or ID
- An invoice version number (which allows corrections to previously published invoices) allowing tracking of different versions of an invoice.
- A customer name and address.
- A total for all the products in the invoice.

There are numerous ways in which we could implement this invoice class and the most obvious might result in a *mutable* data entity. That is, an implementation that allows application code to directly modify the contents of the invoice after that invoice is created.

However, we have chosen to apply the Immutable pattern to our implementation of the invoice. The intention is to simplify the implementation thus avoiding the need to consider issues of concurrent update, dynamic behaviour and simplifying external management of the invoice.

Our Invoice class will thus only support the following functionality:

- The creation of an invoice
- The ability to copy an invoice
- Calculation of the total of an invoice.

It will adopt the approach of many Immutable types by generating a new instance of an Invoice if any products are added or removed from the Invoice.

Figure 4.1 illustrates the elements that make up this solution.

Note that we have continued with the Immutable theme by also making the Products that are contained within the Invoice immutable. This is indicated by the use of the Immutable trait. For example, the Product trait defines a single *val*

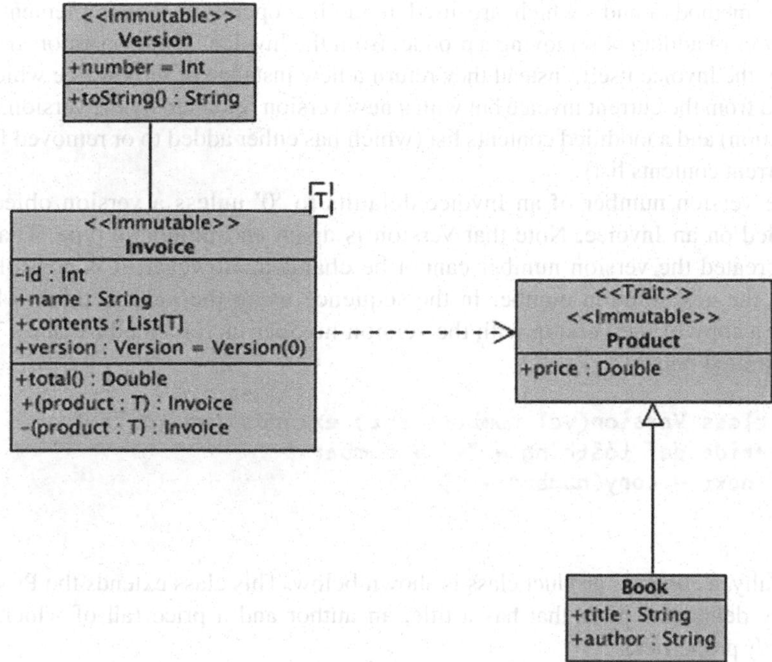

Fig. 4.1 Use of the immutable trait

property price; which means that it provides a read only property price ensuring that no client code unintentionally changes the price.

```
trait Product extends Immutable {
  val price: Double
}
```

The Invoice class uses type parameterization to indicate that it can contain products that mixin the trait Product (as shown below):

```
case class Invoice[T <: Product](val id: Int,
                                 val name: String,
                                 val contents: List[T],
                                 val version: Version = Version(0)) extends Immutable {
  def total = contents.map(_.price).sum
  def +(p: T) = Invoice(id, name, p :: contents, version.next)
  def -(p: T) = Invoice(id, name, contents diff List(p), version.next)
}
```

As can be seen in the definition of the Invoice, the id, name and version are all vals, and thus are *readonly* properties of the Invoice. The parameter contents passed into the Invoice's constructor is used to define the method *total* which merely sums the total of the contents of the Invoice.

The methods + and – which are used to define operators that implement the semantics of adding or removing a product from the Invoice. These operators do not modify the Invoice itself, instead they return a new instance of the Invoice which is derived from the current invoice but with a new version (indicted by the version.next invocation) and a modified contents list (which has either added to or removed from the current contents list).

The version number of an Invoice defaults to '0' unless a version object is provided on an Invoice. Note that Version is again an immutable type. That is, once created the version number cannot be changed. However, it is possible to obtain the next version number in the sequence using the *next* method (which makes a copy of the Version with the version number incremented by one). This is illustrated below:

```
case class Version(val number: Int) extends Immutable {
  override def toString = "v" + number
  def next = copy(number + 1)
}
```

Finally, a concrete product class is shown below. This class extends the Product trait by defining a book that has a title, an author and a price (all of which are *readonly* properties).

```
case class Book(val title: String,
                val author: String,
                val price: Double) extends Product
```

The following test application illustrates how these types are used. Note that the reference to the Invoice initially created is replaced by the reference to the new invoice that results from adding a second Book.

```
object Test extends App {
  val books = List(Book("Java", "John", 12.99))
  var i = Invoice(1, "Denise", books)
  println(i)
  i = i + Book("Scala", "Adam", 10.99)
  println(i)
}
```

This is illustrated below where we can see that the version number of the invoice has been increased from Zero to One:

```
Invoice(1,Denise,List(Book(Java,John,12.99)),v0)
Invoice(1,Denise,List(Book(Scala,Adam,10.99), Book(Java,John,12.99)),v1)
```

4.9 Pros and Cons

The benefits of using the Immutable pattern include:

- Immutable objects are often easier to use.
- Immutable objects reduce the number of possible interactions (aliasing) between different parts of the program
- Immutable objects can be safely shared between multiple threads.
- Implementing an immutable objects is often easier, as there is less that can go wrong and the design space is "smaller"
- It's easy to work with immutable objects in a functional language

The drawbacks of using the Immutable pattern include:

- Immutable objects often result in more objects being created
- It may not be obvious how to add, remove or modify elements in an immutable object.
- It may not be obvious that the *add*, *delete*, *concatenate* etc. methods actually return a new instance which must be referenced in order to pick up the changed data.
- Immutable objects may actually add to the complexity of a piece of code (due to the above) rather than simplify it.

4.10 Related Patterns

Marker Trait A marker trait could be used to indicate the semantics of immutable or mutable objects.

Chapter 5
Singleton

5.1 Introduction

The Singleton pattern describes a type that can only have one object constructed for it. That is, unlike other objects it should not be possible to obtain more than one instance within the same virtual machine. Thus the Singleton pattern ensures that only one instance of a class is created. All objects that use an instance of that type use the same instance.

5.2 Pattern Classification

Creational Pattern

5.3 Intent

To limit the number of instances of a given type to one within a specific context (such as the current virtual machine).

5.4 Context

The motivation behind this pattern is that some classes, typically those classes that involve the central management of a resource, should have exactly one instance. For example, an object that managements the reuse of database connections (i.e. a connection pool) could be a singleton.

J. Hunt, *Scala Design Patterns: Patterns for Practical Reuse and Design*,
DOI 10.1007/978-3-319-02192-8_5, © Springer International Publishing Switzerland 2013

5.5 Forces/Motivation

The Singleton pattern can be used where:

- There must be exactly one instance of a type and it must be accessible to clients from a well-known access point.

In some cases additional consideration need to be taken into account. For example:

- Whether the sole instance should be extensible by sub-typing and clients should be able to use an extended instance without modifying their code (in which case the constructor should be protected).
- When should the singleton be created?
- Should the singleton ever be killed?
- Does the singleton have a lifecycle which needs to be represented such as operations that are performed just after the singleton is created and/or just before the singleton is killed etc.
- There is a presumption of a singleton per virtual machine – what if the singleton concept needs to be shared across virtual machines, for example within a server farm?

5.6 Constituent Parts

The primary participant is the Singleton type itself. Its collaborators are the clients who access the singleton instance.

5.7 Implementation Issues

The question thus arises

> "How do you implement/ensure a single instance of an object?".

From one perspective this question is trivially easy in Scala as the language provides a singleton concept in terms of the Scala *object* keyword. This keyword can be used to create a single instance of an object that can be accessed by any code anywhere that the object is visible.

It therefore may appear that Scala removes any considerations associated with implementing a singleton away from the developer. This is true for the simplest case, a singleton per virtual machine that is initialised the first time it is accessed and remains available unless garbage collected.

However, there are other questions that may need to be considered associated with the singleton pattern that may result in a different implementation strategy being adopted. These questions include the lifecycle of a singleton, the ability to subclass a singleton and possibly the need for a slightly more flexible approach (such as the so called *duoton* which limits the number of instances to two etc.).

5.8 Concrete Examples

In this section we will look at a simple Singleton implementation in Scala and then compare this to a more sophisticated solution.

5.8.1 Basic Scala Singleton Implementation

This example relies on the use of the object type in Scala. A new object called Session is defined that guarantees a single instance of Session is available in the virtual machine. The Session object defines an id and overrides the toString method.

```
object Session {
  val id = "session"
  override def toString = "session singleton"
}
```

This object can be easily access within any client code with directly using the Session or by importing the Session and accessing its members. For example:

```
object Test extends App {
  val id = Session.id
  println(id)
  println(Session)
}
```

5.8.2 Extended Singleton Scenario

The previous section illustrates how simple it is to create a basic Singleton implementation in Scala. Due to this, it has been argued that Scala takes away any considerations of how to implement a singleton. However, this still leaves the question of when you should use a singleton and in answering that question other issues associated with the singleton may arise.

Take for example the question of "how to handle the Singletons lifecycle?". This illustrates that the simplicity of the singleton pattern can be misleading. Some questions to consider include:

- When should a singleton be created?
- When should a singleton be deleted? This is important if the presence of the Singleton results in significant usage of resources (such as memory) and where, if the singleton has not been accessed for some time, it may be beneficial to release those resources.
- How can a singleton be destroyed?
- Who should destroy the singleton?
- What behaviour should be invoked just after a singleton is created?
- What behaviour should be invoked just before the singleton is destroyed?

There are various solutions to these issues but all rely on expanding the singleton solution so that it does not just rely on the use of the Scala object construct (and typically also involves other patterns such as the factory pattern or the delegate pattern). These solutions may involve:

- Accessing the Singleton via a factory object method that actually returns a lightweight delegate to the singleton. Each client obtains its own delegate but all delegates reference the same Singleton.
- When the singleton is first requested any lifecycle methods/functions can be invoked.
- The factory object can be notified that the system is shutting down or that a particular singleton is no longer required. In this case, the factory object can invoke any pre destruction behaviour and then release the singleton.
- If a client does try to access the singleton behaviour after this point, then the singleton can be resurrected via the delegate that will obtain a new reference to the singleton from the factory.

This approach also allows the singleton type to be sub typed and the sub type used instead of the parent type if required. This may be configured externally or programmatically and can be controlled via the factory object.

Such an example is presented in the next section.

5.8.3 Extended Singleton Example

Figure 5.1 illustrates the types involved in this implementation.

The core concept in this implementation is the Session trait, which in this particular example only has an id associated with a session.

```
trait Session {
  val id: String
}
```

The Session trait can then be extended by sub traits mixed into classes as required.

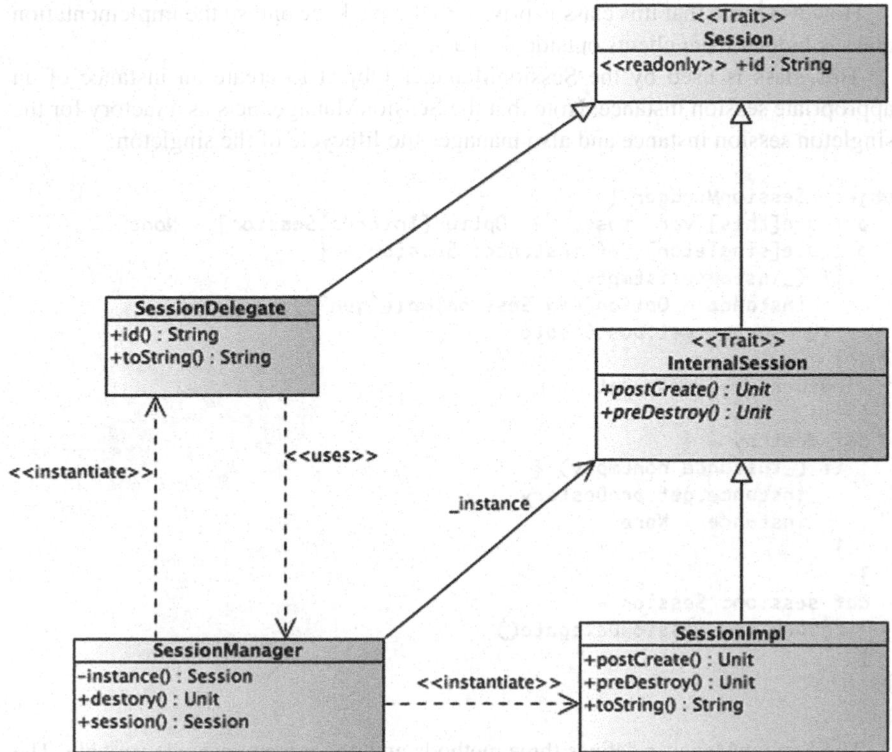

Fig. 5.1 Participant types in Session Singleton example

In this example, a sub trait is defined that extends the basic (external view) of the Session for the internal (to the package) view of a Session. This trait adds the abstract postCreate and preDestroy methods:

```
private trait InternalSession extends Session {
  def postCreate: Unit
  def preDestory: Unit
}
```

We now have two traits one for external consumption (the Session trait) and one for internal (private to the package) use (the InternalSession trait).

The private to the package SessionImpl class extends the InternalSession trait, implementing the postCreate and preDestory methods and overrides the toString method:

```
private class SessionImpl(val id: String) extends InternalSession {
  def postCreate = println("SessionImpl postCreate")
  def preDestory = println("SessionImpl preDestory")
  override def toString = "session " + id + " singleton"
}
```

However, note that this class is private to the package and so the implementation class is hidden from clients outside the package.

This class is used by the SessionManager Object to create an instance of an appropriate session instance. Note that the SessionManager acts as a factory for the singleton session instance and also manages the lifecycle of the singleton:

```
object SessionManager {
  private[this] var _instance: Option[InternalSession] = None
  private[singleton] def instance: Session = {
    if (_instance isEmpty) {
      _instance = Option(new SessionImpl("jeh"))
      _instance.get.postCreate
    }
    return _instance.get
  }
  def destroy = {
    if (_instance nonEmpty) {
      _instance.get.preDestory
      _instance = None
    }
  }
  def session: Session = {
    return new SessionDelegate()
  }
}
```

The SessionManager defines three methods and one private instance variable. The private (to the object) instance variable *_instance* holds a reference to an Option which wraps the InternalSession object (or the value None if no reference is currently held).

The three methods defined are instance, destroy and session:

- *instance*. This private to the package method returns an instance of type InternalSession if one is present (by getting the value held by the option). If the option is currently empty, that is no reference to an InternalSession is currently held, then a new singleton object is created and the post create method is invoked.
- *destroy*. This method checks to see if the _instance variable is empty or not. If it is not empty then it calls preDestory on the singleton instance and sets the _ instance variable to *None*.
- *session*. This method returns a new instance of the Session trait. In this case the concrete type used with the Session trait is actually a SessionDelegate. This delegate wraps a reference to the singleton object.

The SessionDelegate is presented below:

```
private class SessionDelegate extends Session {
  override val id: String = {
    SessionManager.instance.id
  }
  override def toString = SessionManager.instance.toString
}
```

Note that the implementation of the Session Delegate merely references the Session Manager and invokes the id from there. It can do this, as it is part of the same package as the SessionManager. This means that the SessionManager buffers the SessionDelegate from direct access to the Session singleton. Thus if the Singleton is currently not available, it is the SessionManager that will handle it. It also means that client applications cannot access the Session implementation directly; unless they are part of the same package.

The following test application illustrates the use of the SessionManager and the Session types:

```
object Test extends App {
  val s1 = SessionManager.session
  println(s1)
  println("-----------------")
  val s2 = SessionManager.session
  println(s2)
  println("-----------------")
  SessionManager.destroy
  println("-----------------")
  println(s2)
  println("-----------------")
  val s3 = SessionManager.session
  println(s3)
}
```

This test application first accesses the SessionManager session and stores a reference to it in s1. It then prints out s1. It then accesses the SessionManager session for a second time and stores it in s2 and prints it out. The result of doing this is shown below:

```
SessionImpl postCreate
session jeh singleton
-----------------
session jeh singleton
-----------------
```

As you can see from this the Singleton instance is created and the postCreate method called only once. Both s1 and s2 reference the same session instance (indicated by the id 'jeh').

Next the test application calls the destroy method on the SessionManager:

```
SessionManager.destroy
```

The result of invoking this method is that the preDestroy method is called and the _ instance method of the SessionManager is set to *None*.

```
------------------
SessionImpl preDestory
------------------
```

At this point we reuse the val s2 to print out the session id, however the singleton Session has been destroyed. However, the client is accessing the session singleton via the delegate, therefore, there is no null pointer error or problems with accessing a None value. The SessionManager seamlessly re-creates the singleton (with the same state as the original singleton) and makes this available to the Session Delegate. From the client's perspective they are working with the same Session object as before. However, the output from the application makes it clear that the singleton has been re created as the postCreate method is called again:

```
------------------
SessionImpl postCreate
session jeh singleton
------------------
```

Finally, the test application uses the SessionManager to obtain a third reference to the Session which is held in s3. This re references the Session singleton (via a new SessionDelegate object). This results in the final output:

```
session jeh singleton
```

5.9 Pros and Cons

Depending upon the implementation chosen there may be a number of advantages and drawbacks. For the basic Scala singleton implementation the advantages are:

- Simple implementation approach inherent within the Scala language
- Access to the sole instance based on visibility
- Reduced name space with little likely confusion between classes, traits and the object instance (as no class or traits is actually required).

However there are also several drawbacks

- Little control over the lifecycle of the singleton including the behaviour that should be invoked after construction or before the singleton is destroyed.
- No ability to sub-type the singleton.
- Little actual control on access to the singleton object and thus little ability to change the singleton transparently to the clients.

Approaches that extend the singleton pattern (such as that presented earlier in this section) also have advantages and drawbacks, which in general are the opposite of the basic Scala solution. The primary advantages are:

- More control over the lifecycle of the singleton and the behaviour that is invoked as part of that lifecycle.
- May allow the ability to sub-type the singleton and use that sub-type in place of the original type.
- More control over access to the singleton object.

The primary disadvantages are:

- Increased complexity, as the inherent facilities associated with the Scala object keyword are not directly being used.
- Increased namespace pollution and potential lack of clarity of who to use the singleton types.
- Greater confusion as the implementation does not align with developer's expectations.

5.10 Related Patterns

Factory This pattern can be used to manage the creation of the Singleton object in the extended singleton example.

Delegate This pattern can be used to hide the reference to the actual singleton from the client, thereby allowing the singleton to be created and destroyed independently of the client. When a client attempts to access a destroyed singleton it can be recreated with its state restored so that the client appears to still have access to the original singleton.

Chapter 6
Marker Trait

6.1 Introduction

The Marker Trait pattern uses traits that declare no methods, functions, types or properties to indicate additional semantics of a type (class, object or further traits). An alternative could be to use annotations, however annotations are not part of the type system of Scala, and thus can only provide additional semantic meaning where as a Marker trait also adds the ability to be treated as part of Scala the type system.

Marker traits are used within the Scala class libraries. For example see the scala. Mutable and scala.Immutable traits; these are marker traits indicating the semantics of mutability and immutability.

6.2 Pattern Classification

Fundamental Patterns

6.3 Intent

To semantically indicate the role of some type/entity within the domain.

6.4 Context

A trait that declares no functions, methods, properties or types is said to be a marker trait if it is used to indicate the semantic meaning of some concept in the problem domain. For example, a Marker trait was used to represent the concept of a domain

J. Hunt, *Scala Design Patterns: Patterns for Practical Reuse and Design*,
DOI 10.1007/978-3-319-02192-8_6, © Springer International Publishing Switzerland 2013

in the last chapter. Other examples of marker traits might be those used to indicate that something represents a form of agreement or trade etc. This is particularly useful in situations where the concrete implementations of an agreement are all very different with very different properties and operations, but where from a domain view point we wish to indicate their role, i.e. that of an agreement.

The Marker Trait pattern is particularly useful with libraries or utility classes but can be used in a wide range of situations.

6.5 Forces/Motivation

The Marker Trait pattern may be used where:

- it is useful to semantically indicate a role or concept that other entities may play with the application. However, these entities may be of varying types (from classes, to objects to further traits) and may inherit behaviour from various different places in the type hierarchy.
- semantically there is a common concept, but there is little or no common behaviour or data representation between the concrete implementations of the generic domain concept.
- client classes may need to know something about the type of an object without actually needing to know the specific type (at least at the interface level).

Using a trait, as the basis of a marker, is particularly convenient in Scala as a type may mix in any number of traits.

6.6 Constituent Parts

The constituent parts of the Marker Pattern are the marker trait and any client classes that mix in the marker trait. The generic concept is illustrated below:

```
trait Marker
```

This is an example of a Marker trait – it merely defines the trait without providing any additional definitions. This can then be mixed into a variety of other types. In the following example, the Marker trait is mixed into two case class Basic and Named.

```
case class Basic extends Marker

case class Named(val id: String) extends Marker {
}
```

The marker interface can be used with a Utility class to pass in anything that is a type of Marker. In this case this is sufficient to allow anything that is a Marker type to be printed using println (however pattern matching could be used to determine what action to take based on the actual type of the object passed to the utility printer method):

```
object Test extends App {
  Utility.printer(Basic())
  Utility.printer(Named("ABC123"))
}
```

The result of running this application is shown below:

```
Basic()
Named(ABC123)
```

6.7 Implementation Issues

The concept of a Marker trait is one that defines no abstract or concrete types, methods, functions or properties. However, as Scala traits are not the same as Java interfaces and can contain any behaviour, data or definitions required, it may be useful to define some self contained behaviour that could be of use to a type mixing in the trait, but still consider the trait as a Marker trait.

6.8 Concrete Example

The example shown here illustrates the concept of a Contract in some financial domain. This concept is represented by a Contract marker trait. However, the two classes that implement this trait are Loan Contract and Trade Contract that do not share any operations or properties in common (other than they are both classes). Therefore the marker trait acts as the unifying domain concept.

The Contract marker trait and the two concrete classes that mix in that trait are shown in Fig. 6.1.

The Contract trait is a Marker trait and is illustrated below:

```
trait Contract
```

It is mixed into the TradeContract and LoanContract classes. The TradeContract class has the concept of a buyer and a seller of the trade, with a notional amount, a fixed rate and a floating index (such as the Libor index), the

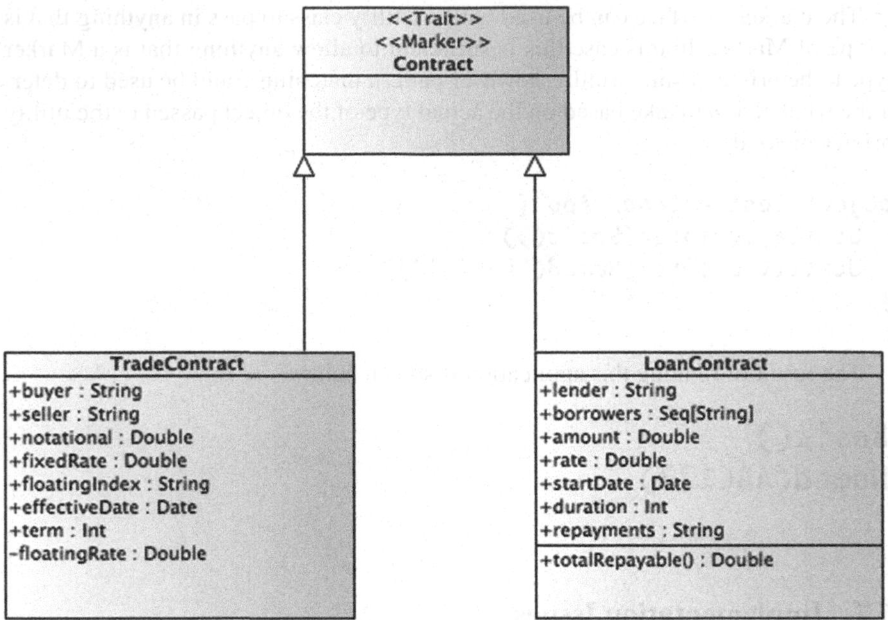

Fig. 6.1 Using the Marker trait in a financial model

effective date from which the trade commences, the term of the trade and when available it allows the floating rate to be provided. The implementation of this case class is shown below:

```
case class TradeContract(val buyer: String,
                         val seller: String,
                         val notational: Double,
                         val fixedRate: Double,
                         val floatingIndex: String,
                         val effectiveDate: Date,
                         val term: Int) extends Contract {
    var floatingRate: Double = 0.0
}
```

The LoanContract class in contrast is between a lender and one or more borrowers (to whom the loan is made). The loan also has an amount provided, an single interest rate to apply to the loan, a start date from when the amount of the loan will be made available, a duration (in terms of years) and an indicator of how often repayments are made (e.g. monthly or quarterly). It also has a method totalRepayable that calculates the compound interest on the loan amount. The code for this class is presented below:

```
case class LoanContract(val lender: String,
                        val borrowers: Seq[String],
                        val amount: Double,
                        val rate: Double,
                        val startDate: Date,
                        val duration: Int,
                        val repayments: String) extends Contract {
  def totalRepayable = {
    amount * Math.pow((1 + rate), duration)
  }
}
```

The following simple application illustrates how these two classes might be used:

```
object test extends App {
  val c1 = LoanContract("BankCo", Seq("John"), 1000, 0.05, new Date(), 3, "monthly")
  println(c1)
  println(c1.totalRepayable)
  println("----------------")
  val c2 = TradeContract("JayCo", "DeeCo", 100000, 1.4, "Libor", new Date(), 10)
  println(c2)
  c2.floatingRate = 0.7
}
```

The two concrete case classes both mix in the Contract marker trait. However this is the only thing they have in common (other than they extend the AnyRef class by default). Thus the marker trait provides the semantic indicator that helps identify both as a type of Contract.

6.9 Pros and Cons

The advantages of the Marker Trait pattern are:

- Client code can handle objects of various different types and from different parts of the type hierarchy without needing to depend on those specific types.
- The domain semantics of the concept represented by the marker interface are easy to identify within the application code.

The drawbacks of the Marker Trait pattern are:

- The marker trait is just that, a marker. It does not allow for access to any functionality or data and therefore may be of limited value beyond indicating the domain role of some object / type.

Chapter 7
Delegation

7.1 Introduction

The Delegation pattern is a response to all those examples in books that show inheritance between types as the fundamental approach to reuse in object oriented languages. There are of course many situations where inheritance is useful but equally there are times when delegating responsibility for implementing some behaviour to another type is better.

Inheritance on object-oriented languages is supposed to allow increased levels of reuse providing improved quality and speed of development. However, many project managers will state that they have achieved very low levels of reuse through inheritance. Why is this? In turn many non-object oriented languages (such as Ada83 and Modular2) place a great deal of emphasis on compositional reuse.

The lack of reference to compositional reuse is possibly indicative of the emphasis placed on inheritance within tutorials and books on object orientation rather than the potential contribution of the two approaches. One exception to this is (Szyperski 1998) whose book focuses on component based reuse but who devotes a whole chapter to the issue of inheritance and how to provide a disciplined approach to inheritance.

It is interesting to note that (Cox 1986) has also stated that "Inheritance is not a necessary feature of an object-oriented language, but it is certainly an extremely desirable one". This is an interesting statement as inheritance is often taken as the defining characteristic of object oriented systems. If we consider the four elements often presented as comprising object oriented languages (namely Encapsulation, polymorphism, abstraction and inheritance) various procedural programming languages can be seen to provide them all except inheritance. It is the unique element of object-oriented systems. It could be argued that without inheritance a programming language is at best object based (e.g. Ada83) and not object oriented.

J. Hunt, *Scala Design Patterns: Patterns for Practical Reuse and Design*,
DOI 10.1007/978-3-319-02192-8_7, © Springer International Publishing Switzerland 2013

7.2 Pattern Classification

Fundamental Pattern

7.3 Intent

Provides a way to extend and reuse functionality of a type, without using inheritance, by combining multiple objects together in such a way as the target object *delegates* the implementation for some of its behaviour to a sub-ordinate object.

7.4 Context

Inheritance is not without its own set of drawbacks. If inheritance is applied without due consideration problems can arise. In some situations it can:

- Reduce the comprehensibility of code.
- Make maintenance harder.
- Make further development harder.
- Reduce reliability of code.
- Reduce overall reuse!

For example, inheritance can pose a problem for a programmer trying to follow the execution of a system by tracing methods and method execution. This problem is known as the *Yo-Yo* problem (see Fig. 7.1) because, every time the system encounters a message that is sent to "this" (the current object), it must start searching from the current class. This may result in a developer jumping up and down the class hierarchy while trying to trace the system's execution path.

Inheritance can potentially increase the dependencies between the code in the parent class and the code in all subclasses. For example, consider the `Undo` framework in Swing. This comprises of a central `UndoManager`, and a number of `UndoableEdits` that represent each edit that can be undone (or redone). The idea is that you subclass `AbstractUndoableEdit` to create suitable edits for your application.

From the point of view of inheritance, the problem is that the `UndoManager` has two methods, `canUndo( )` and `canRedo( )` which determine whether there are edits available to undo or redo respectively. The `canUndo( )` method works correctly on its own. The `canRedo( )` method however, when used on its own, only allows a single redo, after which it declares that there are no more "redos" available on the stack (even when there are). However, if an application ignored `canRedo( )` and tried to redo regardless, then it is successful.

The problem here is that there is a (subtle dependency) between the methods called by a subclasses of `AbstractUndoableEdit` and the `canUndo()` and `canRedo()` methods in the parent class. Such subclasses are required to call the superclasses `undo( )` and `redo( )` method. This is not obvious. The one-line javadoc description of `undo()` and `redo()` does not mention this (only the full

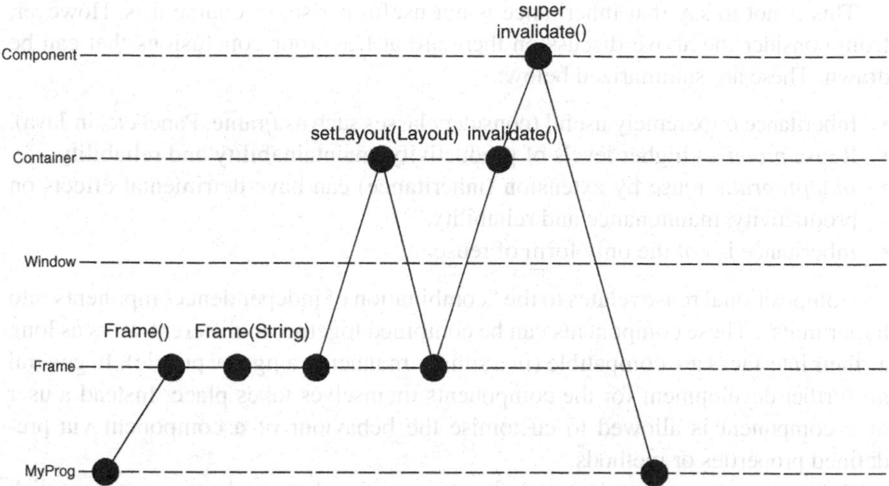

Fig. 7.1 The Yo-Yo problem

text does). This problem is compounded as a developer would expect `undo()` and `redo()` to do nothing in an abstract class.

This means that in order to evaluate a potential change to some class *X* it is necessary to consider the impact of this change on multiple subclasses. If care is not taken then it can be a simple matter to damage the operation of apparently unrelated parts of the system, while fixing an apparently simple "bug" in another part of the system.

This situation is exacerbated, as it may also be necessary to understand the implementation of the superclass when implementing a subclass. This can be because the implementation of the superclass

- assumes a particular behavior from one method or combination of methods,
- assumes that subclasses will provide a specific behavior in one or more methods,
- relies on the state of one or more variables which become critical to the operation of the class,
- contains an overly complex structure in order to allow for inheritance.

The emergence of an overly complex structure can arise when a developer has tried to force the potential for reuse amongst a set of classes. This commonly occurs when a developer has implemented a number of classes, has then noticed that they have some common features and has tried to create a suitable parent class to represent the commonalties. In these situations the developer is familiar with the structure of the subclasses and can design around them. They can therefore develop a parent class that is flexible enough to allow each subclass to provide the specialization required. However, for any other developer examining this parent class at a later date, it may be far from obvious what the purpose of the class is or why the class is structured in the way that it is.

The result is that in order to extend the parent class the developer must gain a detailed understanding of the structure of any subclass (this may be because instance variables are referenced, internal methods executed or internal states relied upon).

This is not to say that inheritance is not useful per se, of course it is. However, from consider the above discussion there are at least four conclusions that can be drawn. These are summarized below:

- Inheritance *is* extremely useful (consider classes such as Frame, Panel etc. in Java).
- Reuse *promises* higher levels of productivity, maintainability and reliability.
- *Inappropriate* reuse by extension (inheritance) can have detrimental effects on productivity, maintenance and reliability.
- Inheritance is *not* the only form of reuse.

Compositional reuse relates to the "combination of independent components into larger units". These components can be combined together in different ways as long as their interfaces are compatible (in a similar manner to a jigsaw puzzle). In general no further development for the components themselves takes place. Instead a user of a component is allowed to customise the behaviour of a component via pre-defined properties or methods.

Software components designed for compositional reuse have great potential. They can greatly improve a developer's productivity and the reliability of software. For example, in Java, `Buttons`, `TextAreas` and `Labels` are all Beans. They can therefore be used within a `Panel` or a `Frame` without further development. In addition a `Panel` or `Frame` is a component that works with a second object (a layout manager) to determine how components are displayed. Thus a graphical user interface can be developed without the need to subclass any existing classes. Instead all a developer must do it to write the code that will glue all these elements together.

The Delegation Pattern is a design pattern illustrating how composition reuse can be realized.

7.5 Forces/Motivation

The Delegation Pattern can be used when

- An object needs to be a different sub type of some given type at different times.
- If a type tries to hide inherited behaviour as it is not appropriate for that type.

7.6 Constituent Parts

There are two main roles within the Delegate patter, the Delegate and the Delegator. In addition there must be some mechanism for relating the two together.

Delegator This is the type that is using the Delegate to provide some or all of its implementation.

Delegate This is the type that is providing the implementation for the Delegator.

This is illustrated in Fig. 7.2.

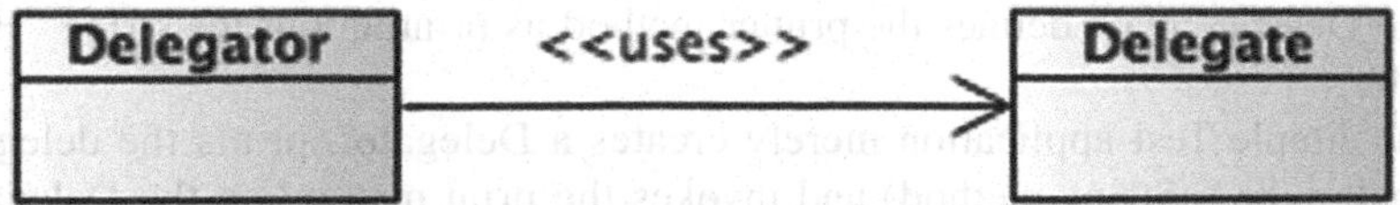

Fig. 7.2 Main roles in delegation pattern

7.7 Implementation Issues

The implementation issues are purely related to which Scala technology you will use to implement the delegate pattern. One option is the object-based approach; another is the trait-based approach.

7.8 Concrete Examples

7.8.1 Object Based Approach

The object-based approach relies on having two objects where the Delegator is a type of object and the Delegate is another type of object. In the Delegator a reference is maintained to the Delegate. Some of the Delegators methods merely invoke behaviour on the Delegate. For example:

```
case class Delegator {
  private val delegate = Delegate()
  def print = delegate.printer
  override def toString = "Delegator"
}

case class Delegate {
    def printer = println("Hello World")
}

object Test extends App {
  val d = Delegator()
  println(d)
  d.print
}
```

In this example the Delegator maintains a reference to the Delegate in the private val member delegate. The toString method prints out the name of the class and the print method *delegates* the responsibility for implementing its required behaviour onto the delegate's printer method.

The Delegate class defines the printer method as printing out the string "Hello World".

The simple Test application merely creates a Delegator, prints the delegator out (using the toString method) and invokes the print method on the Delegator. The produces:

```
Delegator
Hello World
```

7.8.2 Trait Based Approach

In Scala traits can also be used as a way of implementing the Delegate Pattern. However, the advantage of the trait-based approach is that only a single object is required at run-time. The trait providing the Delegate implementation can be mixed into the Delegator.

In this implementation the Delegate is a trait that provides the printer method. It is mixed into the Delegator, which can then directly reference the printer method in the Delegators print method:

```
trait Delegate {
   def printer = println("Hello World")
}

case class Delegator extends Delegate {
    def print = printer
}

object Test extends App {
  val d = Delegator();
  println(d)
  d.print
}
```

The test application is the same as that in the previous section. It creates a Delegator and invokes the print method on that.

7.9 Pros and Cons

The advantages of the Delegate Pattern are:

- Potentially simpler maintenance then may result from inheritance-based reuse.
- Can exploit the rich Scala language features such as Traits, Functions and Objects.

The drawbacks of the Delegate Pattern include:

- Delegates can be integrated into multiple Delegators and may be used in ways that were not intended by the Delegate developer.
- If an object composition model is adopted then additional objects are being created, relative to the inheritance approach.

7.10 Related Patterns

Adapter An adapter *delegates* some of its behaviour to an *adaptee* object, however the semantics of the adapter pattern differ from the delegate pattern.
Flyweight The Flyweight pattern can be used as the basis for the sharing of state objects by delegating state-based behaviour to the flyweight.
Decorator The decorator pattern adds additional behaviour to an existing object rather than *delegating* behaviour to that object.

References

Cox, B. J. (1986). *Object oriented programming: An evolutionary approach*. Reading: Addison-Wesley.
Szyperski, C. (1998). *Component software: Beyond object-oriented programming*. Reading/New York: Addison-Wesley/ACM Press. ISBN 0-201-17888-5.

Part III
Code Reuse Patterns

Chapter 8
Lazy Parameters

8.1 Introduction

In some situations a parameter to a method or function may be costly to process or evaluate, but might only need to be processed or evaluated in certain situations. It is therefore useful to allow for lazy evaluation of such parameters. This results in an *on demand* evaluation model that may have significant performance or processing benefits.

8.2 Pattern Classification

Code Reuse Pattern

8.3 Intent

To enable lazy evaluation of method and function parameters.

8.4 Context

Scala already possesses the ability to mark a val as lazy, for example the following standard definition of val is evaluated immediately:

```
val x = 15
```

J. Hunt, *Scala Design Patterns: Patterns for Practical Reuse and Design*,
DOI 10.1007/978-3-319-02192-8_8, © Springer International Publishing Switzerland 2013

However, you can use the prefix *lazy* to indicate that the val should only be evaluated the first time it is accessed:

```
lazy val x = 15
```

However, it is not possible to mark a parameter as lazy. In Scala parameters are by-value parameters, meaning that their value is determined before the method or function is invoked.

The solution in Scala is to use pass-by-name parameter passing mechanism. This allows a code block to be passed into a function or method, but be treated from a coding point of view, just like a normal parameter. However, the code block is only evaluated when accessed (although it is evaluated every time the parameter is accessed).

The advantage is that we now have lazy parameter evaluation semantics – with the value of the parameter only being determined if required rather than at method or function invocation time.

8.5 Forces/Motivation

The two motivating scenarios for this pattern are:

- If a process will take significant time, memory or processing cycles to evaluate.
- If the value of the parameter must be regenerated each time it is accessed.

8.6 Constituent Parts

The constituent parts of this pattern are:

- A function or method that takes one or more by name parameters.
- A function that will be evaluated when the parameter is accessed.

Note that internally to the function or method, the parameter looks just like any other parameter

8.7 Implementation Issues

The concept of the pass-by-name parameters relate to when expressions are evaluated.

The type of a value parameter may be prefixed by =>, e.g. x: => T. The type of such a parameter is then the parameterless method type => T. This indicates that the corresponding argument is not evaluated at the point of function application, but instead is evaluated at each use within the function. That is, the argument is evaluated using call-by-name semantics.

A very simple example of a pass-by-name parameter is shown below:

```
def myFunc(p: => Int) = p
```

This method takes a pass-by-name parameter p and returns an Int. It may be invoked as follows:

```
val count= 10
val total = myFunc(count + 1)
```

In this case count + 1 will not be evaluated when myFunc is called but when it is accessed inside the method.

To compare the difference with a *standard* method or function consider the following two methods. eagerEval is a normal method using by-value parameter passing while lazyEval uses by-name parameter passing:

```
object Evaluation {
  def eagerEval(x: Int) = { println("eager"); x; }
  def lazyEval(x: => Int) = { println("lazy"); x; }
}
```

The following test harness is used with these two methods. The test harness defines a third method, answer, that prints the string answer and returns the value 40. Both methods are invoked by calling answer and adds 2 to the result returned from answer.

```
object Test extends App {
  import Evaluation._
  def answer = { println("answer"); 40 }
  eagerEval(answer + 2)
  println("----------------")
  lazyEval(answer + 2)
}
```

The result of running this test application is:

```
answer
eager
-----------------
lazy
answer
```

As can be seen from this the string *answer* is printed out before the string *eager* in the first case but after the string *lazy* in the second case. Illustrating that the expression "answer + 2" is evaluated eagerly in the first case and lazily in the second.

8.8 Concrete Example

As a concrete example of where you might use this pattern consider a simple custom *assert* object. This object can be used to perform various tests and validate that the result is true. However, for performance reasons we wish to be able to disable the assertion logic. We therefore provide a Boolean member which can be set to true or false to determine whether the assertion test is performed or not. We might write such an object in Scala as:

```
object MyAssert {

  var assertionEnabled = true

  def basicAssert(predicate: Boolean) =
    if (assertionEnabled && !predicate) throw new AssertionError

}
```

The logic in the *basicAssert* method is that if the assertion is enabled then we check that the predicate passed in is true, if not we throw a new *AssertionError*. This can be invoked as follows:

```
object Test extends App {
  import MyAssert._
  basicAssert(5 < 3)
}
```

Therefore the test to determine if 5<3 return true or false will only occur if the *assertionEnabled* property is true. However, the expression 5<3 will always be evaluated whether the *assertionEnabled* property is true or false.

An alternative would be to write the assertion method using pass by-name syntax, for example:

```
object MyAssert {

  var assertionEnabled = true

  def byNameAssert(predicate: => Boolean) =
    if (assertionEnabled && !predicate) throw new AssertionError

}
```

This version of the assertion method takes a by-name parameter that will only be evaluated if the predicate variable is accessed within the body of the method. This will only occur if the *assertionEnabled* property is true.

This version of the assertion method is invoked in exactly the same way as the original version, for example:

```
object Test extends App {
  import MyAssert._
  byNameAssert(5 < 3)
}
```

However 5<3 will only now be evaluated if the *assertionEnabled* property is true.

This second version is now semantically is closer to the intention of the original plan for MyAssert; it only evaluate the assertions if the *assertionEnabled* property is set to true.

8.9 Pros and Cons

The main benefit of this pattern is that

- expensive or time consuming expression are only evaluated if required.

The main drawback of this pattern is that

- the *by-name* parameter is represented by a code block. This code block will be re-evaluated every time it is accessed. Thus for expensive operations this may be inefficient and it may be better to copy the value returned to a local variable and access that once the code block has been accessed for the first time.

Chapter 9
Partially Applied Functions

9.1 Introduction

Functions in Scala are very powerful and very flexible. This chapter looks at a particular facility in Scala known as partial applied functions.

Consider an operation (which could be a function or method) to find the hypotenuse of a right-angled triangle:

```
def hyp(a: Double, b: Double) = sqrt(a * a + b * b)
```

this method can be invoked as follows:

```
val h = hyp(5.0, 12.0)
```

One way of thinking about the parameter passing that happens when you invoke an operation is that the compiler substitutes a value for each parameter. These values are then used within the function body.

If we wanted to always have *a* bound to 5.0 we could of course right:

```
sqrt(5.0 * 5.0 + b + b)
```

In this case we have fixed the value of *a* to 5.0 – we could view this as partially applying the parameters to the hyp function. That is we have applied the value 5 to the parameter, but have not applied anything to the parameter b.

In fact Scala provides specific language structures to support these ideas. An operation (that is a method or a function with multiple parameters) can be partially applied in that it is possible to bind one or more of the parameters to create a new operation with fewer parameters. The remaining parameters must then be provided when the new operation is invoked.

J. Hunt, *Scala Design Patterns: Patterns for Practical Reuse and Design*, DOI 10.1007/978-3-319-02192-8_9, © Springer International Publishing Switzerland 2013

9.2 Pattern Classification

Code Reuse Pattern

9.3 Intent

To create new operations (either functions or methods) from existing operations by binding 1 or more parameters to specific values.

9.4 Context

You may have behaviour, defined in operations (either functions or methods) that take multiple parameters but that may be confusing to use due to the number of nature of the parameters. Using partial functions new, more specific, operations can be created that take fewer parameters and can be simpler for client code to invoke.

9.5 Forces/Motivation

The Partially Applied Functions Pattern can be used when

- Clients find it difficult to determine how to use operations due to the number, nature of complexity of the parameters.
- Semantically more meaningful operations can be created from more generic operations.
- Higher order functions are available that can be used to create partially applied functions where the functionality to be applied can be identified.

9.6 Constituent Parts

There are two main roles when using partially applied functions:

Operation This may be a function or a method that takes multiple parameters. One or more of those parameters can be a function itself.

Partially Applied Operation A function or method derived from a multiple parameter operation that binds 1 or more of the parameters of the original operations. Allowing remaining parameters to be supplied when the operation is invoked.

9.7 Implementation Issues

When implementing Partially Applied Functions there are two questions to consider:

- What functions are there available that we can build upon?
- What function definitions can be provided so that they can be built upon?

This may involve identifying new higher order functions to provide the flexibility required to apply different behaviour to some data.

9.8 Concrete Example

The following examples illustrate the way in which partially applied functions work and can be used.

Given a simple function sum that takes three *int* values and adds them together, we can either invoke that function directly (sum(1, 2, 3)) or we can partially apply it. This is done by providing 1 or more parameters and indicating those parameters that are being omitted. This is indicated by replacing the parameter with a '_'. Note that for any parameter that is omitted its type must be specified (this deals with any overloading of operations that make exist). The result returned from a partial application is a new function that takes fewer parameters than the original function. For example:

```
object PartiallyAppliedFunctions {

  def main(args: Array[String]): Unit = {
    var sum = (a: Int, b: Int, c: Int) => a + b + c
    println(sum(1, 2, 3))

    val partialSum = sum(1, _: Int, 3)
    println(partialSum(2))
  }

}
```

In this example, the partialSum function takes one parameter (an Int). Thus it is invoked with:

```
partialSum(2)
```

The values 1 and 3 are also provided for the parameters a and c. Thus when the body of the function is evaluated a = 3, b=2 and c=3. We have thus been able to reuse the implementation of the function sum to produce a new function partialSum that takes 1 parameter.

This can be taken further when we consider that functions can take other functions as parameters. These functions are referred to as higher order functions. These types of functions are found in all of the collection classes in Scala (and will be used throughout this book).

However, by allowing one function to take another function and combining this with partial functions we can create a very powerful form of reuse. For example, if we write a function that takes two parameters, where the first parameter is a function and the second parameter is some data that the function is applied to, then using partial functions we can create numerous concrete implementations that perform different operations on that data.

To illustrate this idea consider the apply function in the following Scala Object Processor:

```
object Processor {
  val apply = (func: Int => Int, x: Int) => func(x)
}
```

The apply function takes a functions whose signature is that it takes an Int and returns an Int. The apply function also takes a single Int value x. The body of the apply function invokes the function passed in and passes the value held in x to it. This is an example of a higher order function.

This function can be invoked directly as shown below:

```
val f = (x: Int) => x * 2
println(apply(f, 2))
```

Here we have a function ‘f’ that takes an Int and multiplies it by 2. This is used as a parameter to the apply function along with the value two. The result is that when the apply function executes it invoked the function ‘f’ on the value 2 producing the value 4.

We could also create a new function double that takes an integer and doubles it. We could do this by partially applying the *apply* function using the ‘f’ function, for example:

```
val double = apply(f, _: Int)
```

We have now partially applied the apply function by binding the first parameter to the function f. The resulting function stored in double is a function that takes a single Int as a parameter. Note the fact that the first parameter is a function does not matter, we have bound it in just the same way as if it were an Int, a Double, a String or any object.

We can now invoke the double function using a single parameter:

```
println(double(2))
```

The result of invoking double is that the number passed in is used with the function ‘f’ to multiple it by 2. In this case the result is again 2.

9.9 Pros and Cons

The advantages of Partially Applied Functions are:

- Very powerful framework for the reuse of behaviour (whether implemented as a function or a method).
- Can layer functionality on top of existing higher order functions.

The drawbacks of the Partially Applied Functions Pattern include:

- It may not be obvious that functions such as double in the previous section are partially applied functions and this may lead to confusion when the software needs to be maintained.

9.10 Related Patterns

Strategy Pattern When used with higher order functions the dynamic binding of the function could be viewed as providing a strategy to implement.

Template Operation The dynamic provision of a function to be used by the higher order function could be viewed as an example of the template operation in which part of the algorithm to be used will be provided when the function is invoked.

Chapter 10
Trait Based Template Operation

10.1 Introduction

When developing software systems a rich *interface* for a client may have many methods providing a semantically rich set of operations that can be invoked. In general this is thought of as providing the client with an easier to use and more expressive *interface*. However, a thinner interface, with fewer operations is easier to implement and to maintain and may be considered the preferable solution for a development team.

In many cases what is required is the best of both worlds, a semantically rich *interface* for the client code but low cost for the developers to create. This should aim to minimise the effort-required from both the developers of the component and the users of that component as well maximising the utility for the clients.

10.2 Pattern Classification

Code Reuse Pattern

10.3 Intent

To enable rich interfaces without the need for *fat* implementations.

J. Hunt, *Scala Design Patterns: Patterns for Practical Reuse and Design*,
DOI 10.1007/978-3-319-02192-8_10,

10.4 Context

In some situations it is useful to define a skeleton of an algorithm in a method or function but to defer some of the steps of that implementation to sub types. The Template Operation pattern is the derived from the Template Method behavioural pattern from the Gang of Four Design Patterns book (Gamma et al. 1995). However, it is modified here to utilize traits and the way that traits can be mixed into and extended by classes and objects.

10.5 Forces/Motivation

Traits can be used for the production of rich *interfaces* when

- The invariant parts of an algorithm can be implemented separately from the variant parts that are provided by types using the trait.
- The behaviour to add to a type can be defined separately and reused amongst types.
- The behaviour can be built on a core function or method that can be provided by a concrete type.
- Where the behaviour of a type needs to be extended by composition rather than by inheritance.

10.6 Constituent Parts

There are two main roles within the Trait reuse pattern.

Trait This is the trait defining the behaviour to add plus an abstraction operation that must be provided by the Target type. The behaviour defined within the Trait builds on the abstract operation.

Target This is the type that will mix in the trait and provide the concrete implementation for the abstraction operation defined by the trait.

The Trait will provide additional behaviour for the target. And the target will fill in the missing details of the template operation.

10.7 Implementation Issues

When implementing code reuse through the use of traits there are a number of issues to consider:

- How is the functionality/data to be organised such that it can be mixed into other types.
- What functionality/data must the host type provide to allow the trait to operate.
- How will the trait be used with the host types?

10.8 Concrete Example

An example of the use of a trait that implements the Template operation is the Ordered trait. The Ordered trait is defined in the *scala.math* package and is a trait that is used with totally ordered data. The Ordered trait defines 1 abstract method *compare*. It also defines several *logical* comparison methods that are based on the compare method.

It is therefore only necessary to mix in the Ordered trait and define the method compare to provide a rich interface of comparison methods (but with a light implementation) for a given type.

As an example, consider the Rational class. This is used to represent a Rational number and defines two read-only properties number and denom (for the denominator). In addition it defines a method compare that takes another Rational number and compares it with the current rational number.

```
class Rational (val number : Int, val denom : Int) extends Ordered[Rational] {
  def compare (that: Rational): Int = (this.number * that.denom) - (that.number * this.denom)
}
```

However instance of the class Rational support a range of operations including <, <=, => and >. These all build on the compare method. This means that we can write:

```
object TraitTest2 {
  def main(args: Array[String]): Unit = {
    val x = new Rational(2, 3)
    var y = new Rational(6, 9)
    println( x < y)
  }
}
```

10.9 Pros and Cons

The advantages of the Trait Based Template operation pattern are:

- Data, functionality, types etc. can be reused in a wide range of types by mixing the traits with appropriate types.
- The *features* defined by the trait and by those left abstract represent the interface between the trait and the host type.

The drawbacks of Template operation pattern include:

- It may not be clear from the host type that a particular method is used by a trait to build additional behaviours.

10.10 Related Patterns

Strategy The template operation pattern uses Scala's type system to vary the implementation provided for part of an algorithm. The strategy pattern uses Scala's language facilities to alter the whole implementation used for an algorithm.

Reference

Gamma, E., Helm, R., Johnson, R., & Vlissades, J. (1995). *Design patterns: Elements of reusable object-oriented software*. Reading: Addison-Wesley.

Chapter 11
Stackable Traits

11.1 Introduction

Traits in general allow types to be constructed based on existing implementations that are mixed together to provide the resultant interface and implementation. Stacking such traits extends this concept further allowing traits to extend behaviour as well as define it.

11.2 Pattern Classification

Code Reuse Pattern

11.3 Intent

To enable the behaviour of an operation to be extended rather than replaced.

11.4 Context

Let us say that you have a class that provides an implementation for some behaviour, however you wish to modify that behaviour depending upon the scenario by pre or post processing data or by being able to decide whether to pass the request onto the underlying implementation or not.

Stackable traits provide a flexible mechanism that allows this to be done in a type safe manner that is directly supported by the Scala language itself.

J. Hunt, *Scala Design Patterns: Patterns for Practical Reuse and Design*,
DOI 10.1007/978-3-319-02192-8_11, © Springer International Publishing Switzerland 2013

For example, if the actual operation is expensive to perform and it might be useful to cache the values generated, rather than generate them each time, a caching trait could be defined that is stacked with the original implementation. This trait would then first look to see if the value required is in the cache. If it is then that value could be used directly. If it isn't then the request could be passed onto the actual calculator method. When a result is returned this result could be cache for future use.

Using stackable traits, no change needs to be made to the original class. Instead either a subclass that mixes the original class with the trait can be created or a new instance is created based on the original class and mixing in a trait at the point of instantiation.

11.5 Forces/Motivation

Stackable traits can be used where it is useful to *wrap* modifications to the behaviour of a type.

11.6 Constituent Parts

There are two main roles within the Trait reuse pattern.

Trait This is the trait defining the behaviour to add.
Target This is the type that will mix in the trait.

The Trait will extend existing behaviour by wrapping that behaviour.

11.7 Implementation Issues

When implementing code reuse through the use of traits there are a number of issues to consider:

- What functionality might the trait need to extend?
- Will the trait merely pre and/or post process the parameters/results or will it determine whether further process of the data is required/appropriate?

11.8 Concrete Example

An example of the use of a trait which provides an additional wrapping behaviour is shown below.

For example, consider the abstract class IntQueue. This abstract class defines two operations put and get. The *get* method returns an Int and the *put* methods takes an Int:

```
abstract class IntQueue {
    def get(): Int
    def put(x: Int)
}
```

Based on this abstract class we can create a concrete class:

```
import scala.collection.mutable.ArrayBuffer

class BasicIntQueue extends IntQueue {
  private val buf = new ArrayBuffer[Int]
  def get() = buf.remove(0)
  def put(x: Int) { buf += x }
}
```

This class provides concrete implementations of the get and put methods that use an ArrayBuffer to store the Integer data. The put method adds the data to the buffer and the get method removes the data item from the front of the buffer.

Next we will define a *stackable* trait. This trait declares a superclass (that is an abstract class *not* a trait):

```
trait Doubling extends IntQueue {
  abstract override def put(x: Int) {
    super.put(2 * x)
  }
}
```

The trait also defines an abstract method that *overrides* one inherited from the IntQueue class. This abstract override method uses a reference to *super* to multiply the parameter x by two and then call super.put. However, super in this context will be bound dynamically to the type that this trait is mixed into rather than invoke the method defined in a *super* type. Also note that this trait can only be used with IntQueue types (that is with an IntQueue or a subclass of IntQueue).

We can now create a new class that extends the BasicIntQueue and mixes in the Doubling trait:

- **class** MyQueue **extends** BasicIntQueue **with** Doubling

Or indeed the trait can be mixed into an object when it is instantiated rather than being made a permanent feature of the class hierarchy:

```
object StackableTraitsTest {
  def main(args: Array[String]): Unit = {
    val queue = new BasicIntQueue with Doubling
    queue.put(10)
    println(queue.get())
  }
}
```

In either case when the method *put* is invoked on the object the Doubling trait will have been mixed into the definition of the object.

When the method put is now called on the queue above, it first calls the version of put in the Doubling trait (which doubles 10) and then invokes the version of put in the BasicIntQueue class (which ads 20 to the ArrayBuffer).

When the queue.get method is invoked it returns the value 20. We have therefore expanded the functionality originally defined in the put method to always double whatever number is passed into it.

```
trait Incrementing extends IntQueue {
  abstract override def put(x: Int) {
    super.put(x + 1)
  }
}

trait Filtering extends IntQueue {
  abstract override def put(x: Int) {
    if (x >= 0) super.put(x)
  }
}
```

We can define additional traits that all extend the IntQueue abstract class. For example, we have defined the Incrementing and Filtering traits above, The Incrementing trait merely adds 1 to the integer passed in. In contrast the Filtering trait checks to see that the parameter is greater than zero. If it is then it passes the value on it not then it merely returns. This illustrates that stackable traits can be used to decide whether to allow the wrapped behavior to be invoked or not.

Each of the above traits can now be stacked with the BasicIntQueue classes defined earlier. In actual fact we can define multiple stacked traits using the keyword with for any additional traits. The order of the *with* clause determines the order of the wrapping methods. For example:

```
object StackableTraitsTest2 {

  def main(args: Array[String]): Unit = {
    val queue = new BasicIntQueue with Incrementing with Doubling
    queue.put(10)
    println(queue.get())
  }

}
```

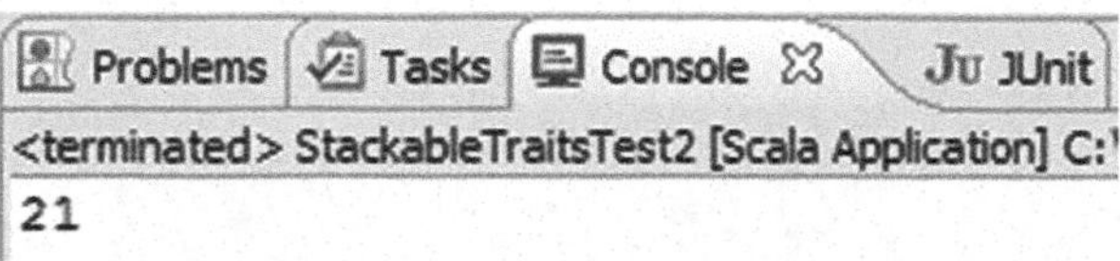

Fig. 11.1 Executing the example

In this case, when the method put is invoked on the queue object, the call is first passed to the version of put in the Doubling trait. This doubles the value to 20. It is then passed to the version of the put method defined by the Incrementing trait. This adds 1 to the value 20 passed to it. Finally the version of put defined in the BasicIntQueue class is invoked. This method stores the number 21 into the ArrayBuffer.

When the get method is invoked on the queue it goes straight to the version defined in the BasicIntQueue class (as there were no definitions of this method in the Doubling or Incrementing traits). This removes the value 21 from the ArrayBuffer that is then printed out in Fig. 11.1.

11.9 Pros and Cons

The advantages of Stackable traits for reuse are:

- That functions/methods can be wrapped one on top of another.
- Each behaviour is independent of the next behaviour.
- The behaviours can decide whether to continue processing the request or not.
- The wrapped methods also get access to the return result of the next in the wrapped chain of methods and so can post process the result as well as pre process the parameters.
- Stackable traits are a form of aspect-oriented programming (AOP) (Kiczales et al. 1997).

The drawbacks of Stackable traits include:

- It may not be clear in the host type that a trait is extending the behaviour of the type by wrapping existing behaviour.

11.10 Related Patterns

Adapter An adapter *delegates* some of its behaviour to an *adaptee* object, however the semantics of the adapter pattern differ from the delegate pattern.

Reference

Kiczales, G., Lamping, J., Mehdhekar, A., Maeda, C., Lopes, C. V., Loingtier, J., & Irwin, J. (1997, June). Aspect-oriented programming. In *Proceedings of the European Conference on Object-Oriented Programming (ECOOP)*, Springer LNCS, 1241.

Chapter 12
Currying and Code Reuse

12.1 Introduction

The code reuse approaches previously discussed for partially applied functions work well in Scala and are extremely useful in many situations. However, they do have some limitations:

- The syntax can seem somewhat convoluted.
- The resulting structures do not look as though they are part of the language. That is they still look like functions calls.

An alternative approach to partially applied functions is to use a technique/pattern known as Currying in the Scala/Functional world. The name Currying may seen obscure but the technique is named after Haskell Curry (for whom the Haskell programming language is named).

Currying allows new *language* structures to be created. The language features can resemble normal function invocations or can resemble language constructs. This allows the constructs developed to be presented to client code as if they are merely an extension to Scala (which in many ways they are). For example, structures such as:

```
transaction {
    ...
}
```

can be created where *transaction* is a function that has been curried such that it is linked to an appropriated database etc.

A curried function is a function that is applied to *multiple* argument lists (in contrast a Partially applied function have one argument list). Note that functions can have one or more parameter lists.

A standard single parameter function is illustrated below. This function takes two parameters (x and y) and multiplies them together. It is used with println in this example to print out eh result of multiplying 2 and 3:

DOI 10.1007/978-3-319-02192-8_12,

```
def basicSum(x: Int, y: Int) = x * y

println(basicSum(2, 3))
```

In Scala we can re-write this function as a multiple argument function, on which case each argument list takes a single argument. The arguments can still both be used in the body of the function (and thus we can still multiple x and y together):

```
def sum(x: Int)(y: Int) = x * y

println(sum(2)(3))
```

Both of these functions return the value 6 and both allow you to pass in two parameters to the function. However, in effect the second version results in two functions invocations back to back. It is a bit like chaining two functions together. The first function invocation takes a single Int parameter x and returns a function value for the second function. The second function takes the Int parameter Y and applies it to the first functions result.

Why is this useful? It is because we can provide a value to use for the *first* function before we wish to provide a value for the *second* function. As the result of providing the value for the first function is to return a function value to use with the second we can essentially *store* that functions and its subsequent invocation for later use. For example, given the following function definition in the class CurryTest:

```
class CurryTest {

  def sum(x: Int)(y: Int) = x + y

}
```

This function has multiple argument lists and could be called directly as follows:

```
val test = new CurryTest
println(test.sum(2)(4))
```

However we could curry the function such that we provide the first argument but not the second. Note that in comparison with Partially Applied Functions where any argument can be applied, when Currying it is only the left hand side arguments that can be applied. Thus in this case we could not supply the second argument rather than the first. Also note that because of this currying does not require that you specify the types of the omitted parameters.

The approach used with multiple argument lists is to provide the arguments from the left and to use '_' to indicate that the remainder of the function invocation has been left out:

```
val plusOne = test.sum(1)_
println(plusOne(10))
```

The plusOne function is now a curried function that takes the y argument and adds it to the value 1 which was provide for the x argument when the plusOne val was defined. Note that as far as the client code of plusOne is concerned this is just a normal single parameter function.

12.2 Pattern Classification

Code Reuse Pattern

12.3 Intent

To provide a code reuse and framework development design strategy.

12.4 Context

If you need to create a framework to be used by Scala programmers, but want to provide a flexible way to configure that framework and allow the developers to view the end results as merely part of the Scala environment then Currying has many advantages.

For example, the use of currying allows you to build new language structures based on multiple argument lists. For example you can then exploit the '{}' syntax for a single parameter. If this parameter is itself a function the end result is a construct that looks like a language feature:

```
write (file) {
  writer => writer.println(new Date)
}
```

The above is a function *write* that has two argument lists; one that takes a file and one that takes a function. The round bracket syntax could be used for both parameters. However, by using the '{}' syntax for the last parameter this looks more like a language structure!

12.5 Forces/Motivation

The Currying Pattern can be used when

- A framework is being developed which should be resemble a language structure to the client code.
- The framework may need to be parameterised for the context in which it is being used (for example to a specific database or file structure).

12.6 Constituent Parts

There are two main roles within the Curry pattern:

Multiple argument list function This is the raw definition of the function with all parameter lists specified.

Curried versions of the function with fewer argument lists These represent versions of the raw function with one or more of the argument list parameters specified.

12.7 Implementation Issues

When considering implementing functions that may be curried at a later date it is important to understand how the function will be used and which of the arguments will be partially applied. This allows an appropriate structure to be constructed.

12.8 Concrete Example

A simple printer Object and associated write function will be used to illustrate the use of Currying. The printer Object is a Scala singleton object with a single method write that needs to be supplied with a file to write to and the operation to invoke to determine what is written to the file. This object could be written using a single argument list as:

```
object Printer {

  def write(file: File, op: PrintWriter => Unit) {
    val writer = new PrintWriter(file)
    try {
      op(writer)
    } finally {
      writer.close()
    }
  }

}
```

This would be invoked as follows:

```
write(
  new File("date.txt"),
  writer => writer.println(new Date())
)
```

While this is perfectly acceptable, we could refactor the write method such that it uses multiple argument lists, for example:

```
def write(file: File)(op: PrintWriter => Unit) {
  val writer = new PrintWriter(file)
  try {
    op(writer)
  } finally {
    writer.close()
  }
}
```

This could then be used as follows:

```
val file = new File("date.txt")
write (file)(writer => writer.println(new Date))
```

With each parameter now having its own argument list. Of course we could also exploit the '{}' syntax which means that we could also write:

```
write (file) {
  writer => writer.println(new Date)
}
```

Which makes the write function appear more of a language construct than a straight function call.

However, we could take this further. If we are creating a logging system in which we always want client code to write to the same log file, we could use currying to create a fileWriter function that is guaranteed to write the file we wish to specify:

```
val fileWriter = write(file)_

fileWriter {
  writer => writer.println(new Date)
}
```

Client code can now invoke the fileWriter merely providing the function that will determine the actual value to write. If this is return to client code via a factory or explicitly imported, they will merely see this as a part of the language.

In fact this can be written more concisely yet using the implicit parameter syntax:

```
fileWriter {
  _ println new Date
}
```

Which is very clean and simple to present to client code.

12.9 Pros and Cons

The advantages of Currying are:

- Allows new *language* constructs to be created.
- Allows constructs to be bound at run time to specific objects etc. If this approach is combined with the Factory pattern then the details can be hidden from client code.

The drawbacks of Currying include:

- Partially applied functions are more flexible in terms of which parameters are applied and which are not yet applied.

12.10 Related Patterns

Partially Applied Functions The purpose of Partially Applied Functions is similar to the Currying pattern. However the resulting semantics of the new functions formed are typically different. Partially Applied functions are typically used for straight function reuse where as Currying can also be used to create language constructs.

Chapter 13
Cake Pattern

13.1 Introduction

The aim of the Cake pattern is to provide a Scala programmatic approach to the classic Dependency Injection strategy used when connecting dependent objects with the types they depend upon.

Dependency injection (or DI) involves at least three elements, these are:

- A dependent consumer
- A declaration of a component's dependencies
- Some way of injecting (or providing) the objects/types that a dependency consumer requires.

The dependent consumer is an object whose data or behaviour is dependent upon the data or behaviour of one or more separate objects or types (note that in Java we would only be using the term object here however in Scala the language itself offers a wider range of options than merely providing a reference to an object as a way of expressing and implementing dependency).

The elements that the dependent consumer relies on must be made available to that consumer in some way. Traditionally this would be done by the dependent consumer instantiation of actively access the required objects. The Inversion of Control approach (or more specifically the subset of this known as Dependency Injection) involves externally obtaining the objects required and making them available to, or injecting them into, the dependent consumer.

There are various technologies available to achieve such dependency injection. A widely used technology is the Spring framework which is ideally suited to use with Java. Although Spring can be used out of the box with Scala if care is taken, it is easier to integrate Spring and Scala using the Spring Scala bridge.

However, Scala is a rich language with many features not present in languages such as Java. In this chapter and the following two chapters, we will explore some language features that provide for static compile time dependency injection patterns.

J. Hunt, *Scala Design Patterns: Patterns for Practical Reuse and Design*,
DOI 10.1007/978-3-319-02192-8_13, © Springer International Publishing Switzerland 2013

This chapter explores the Cake Pattern (Oderskey and Zenger 2005), named after the layers in many sponge cakes that are combined placed one on top of another, to produce the final cake product.

13.2 Pattern Classification

Code Reuse Pattern

13.3 Intent

To provide a strategy to be used when needing to inject objects into a dependent consumer.

13.4 Context

Traditionally a given type knew all it needed to know about the types that it was dependent upon and typically created instances of those types within its constructor (for Java) or initialization functions as required. In this situation the dependent object is responsible for the creation of the objects on which it depends make the relationships easy to understand and simple to follow. However, these relationships are hard coded within the dependent object and become difficult to control, modify or update either dynamically at runtime or static at compile time.

It may be useful to be able to change the related objects based on different scenarios, requirements environments to aid with testing, maintenance or flexibility of the systems. Spring is probably the best-known Dependency Injection framework for Java. Whilst it is certainly possible to use Spring with Scala (possibly using the Spring to Scala bridge) Scala provides its own frameworks that allow for similar functionality to be achieved without the need for external frameworks.

This chapter, and the subsequent two chapters, provide Scala language features that provide for strongly typed dependency injection.

13.5 Forces/Motivation

The Cake pattern can be used when

- The decisions about the objects to provide to a dependent object can be generated at runtime but need to be type safe.
- Compile time configuration is acceptable.

13.6 Constituent Parts

The constituent parts of the Structural Injection pattern are:

A Configuration Trait This is an abstraction that defines the objects that will be available for injection into dependent objects.

One or more Concrete Configuration Traits These are the types that define how the objects to be made available will be created. For example, they could be loaded from a configuration file, from a database or maintained in memory.

A Context Trait This trait which identifies the appropriate concrete configuration to load.

A Dependent Component This is a component that depends on objects supplied by a Concrete Configuration.

The configuration traits wrap around the dependent component providers layers that provide the data and behaviour on which the root component depends.

13.7 Implementation Issues

Questions to consider with respect to the cake pattern include:

How are the configuration objects configured? Configuring these configuration objects externally to the application code makes it possible to change the objects made available at runtime. This configuration information may be provided in the form of XML files, from a database or via some property file.

The other implementation issue to consider is how the appropriate Concrete Configuration is identified. This may be done using a Factory object.

13.8 Concrete Example

The implementation defines a Context marker trait that is used to indicate an object that will be a context for the Cake Pattern and will make a configuration object available.

```
trait Context
```

The Config trait defines a loan method that returns Unit and a value text. This represents that the load method can be used to load a configuration and that the data to be loaded is the text. It also defines the method load as being executed when an object that mixes the trait is instantiated.

```
trait Config {
  load
  val text: String
  def load: Unit
}
```

A concrete configuration type is defined by the InMemoryConfig case class that mixes in the Config trait. This defines the load method as printing out a message (mimicking the action of loading this data from some persistent store) and declaring the text string has being Hello.

```
case class InMemoryConfig extends Config {
  lazy val text = "Hello"
  def load = println("load: " + text)
}
```

The MyContext trait, that will make available a configuration object, uses a *this* self type annotation/reference that indicates that a Config type will be mixed into (depends upon) the object or class that uses this trait. It can therefore refer to any data or methods defined in the Config trait as if it were its own trait. Note that any number of traits could be mixed in here so that the *this* reference may relate to multiple traits mixed together, for example:

this: ConfigContext with DAOContext with ConnectionManagerContext

The actual MyContext trait is shown below:

```
trait MyContext extends Context {
  this: Config =>
  def welcome = this.text
}
```

In this case the welcome method references the text property provided by the Config trait via the *this* self type annotation.

The MyContext trait is mixed with the InMemoryConfig trait for the Env Scala Object. Note we could have defined a class to mix these two traits together and then instantiated that class. However, the *environment* may well benefit from being a singleton shared where required and so we have selected a Scala object as the best way to represent the dependency injection environment:

```
object Env extends MyContext with InMemoryConfig
```

This environment object is used in the following simple Test application:

```
object Test extends App {
  println(Env.text)
}
```

The result of which is that the load method is executed and the string "Hello" is printed out:

```
load: Hello
Hello
```

13.9 Pros and Cons

The advantages of the Cake Pattern are:

- Provides for type safe injection of objects via the *this* self-type reference.
- Implementations can be changed at the point of use by altering which traits are mixed in.

The drawbacks of the Cake Pattern include:

- It may not be obvious how the dependent object obtains the data or behaviour it depends upon.
- Which traits will be mixed into the dependent object must be known at compiler time, runtime systems may offer greater flexibility.

13.10 Related Patterns

Factory Object May be used to supply the Concrete Configuration.

Structural Injection Provides an alternative approach to the injection of objects to a dependent consumer.

Implicit Injection Also aims to provide possible implementations that address the aims of dependency injection.

Reference

Oderskey, M., & Zenger, M. (2005). Scalable component abstractions. In *OOPSLA 2005, Proceedings of the 20th annual ACM SIGPLAN conference on object-oriented programming, systems, languages and applications* (pp. 41–57). New York: ACM. ISBN 1-59593-031-0.

Chapter 14
Structural Injection

14.1 Introduction

Injecting (or wiring) objects together is a common recurring theme within modern software systems. This chapter and the preceding and following chapters explore this concept within Scala.

As has previously been said, Dependency Injection (or DI) involves at least three elements, these are a dependent consumer, the objects that consumer depends upon and some technique for handling these dependencies.

This chapter explores the use of structural typing in Scala to provide an elegant, type safe approach to the injection of objects to a dependent consumer.

14.2 Pattern Classification

Code Reuse Patterns

14.3 Intent

To remove the hard coding of dependencies for an object and allow them to be changed in a type safe, verifiable manner.

14.4 Context

The Structural Injection pattern uses structural typing to provide one approach for DI in Scala.

J. Hunt, *Scala Design Patterns: Patterns for Practical Reuse and Design*,
DOI 10.1007/978-3-319-02192-8_14,

14.5 Forces/Motivation

The Structural Injection pattern can be used when

- The decisions about the objects to provide to a dependent object can be generated at runtime but need to be type safe.
- Compile time configuration is acceptable.

14.6 Constituent Parts

The constituent parts of the Structural Injection pattern are:

A Configuration Abstraction This is an abstraction that defines the objects that will be available for injection into dependent objects.

One or more Concrete Configuration types These are the types that define how the objects to be made available will be created. For example, they could be loaded from a configuration file, from a database or maintained in memory.

A Dependent Component This is a component that depends on objects supplied by a Concrete Configuration.

14.7 Implementation Issues

The first implementation issue to consider is how the Concrete Configuration objects generate the objects they make available. By configuring such a configuration object externally to the application code makes it possible to change the objects made available at runtime.

The other implementation issue to consider is how the appropriate Concrete Configuration is identified. This may be done using a Factory object.

14.8 Concrete Example

The simple application we will use to explore the Structural Injection pattern uses a Session type that is dependent on information provided by a Config object. The components in this application are shown in Fig. 14.1.

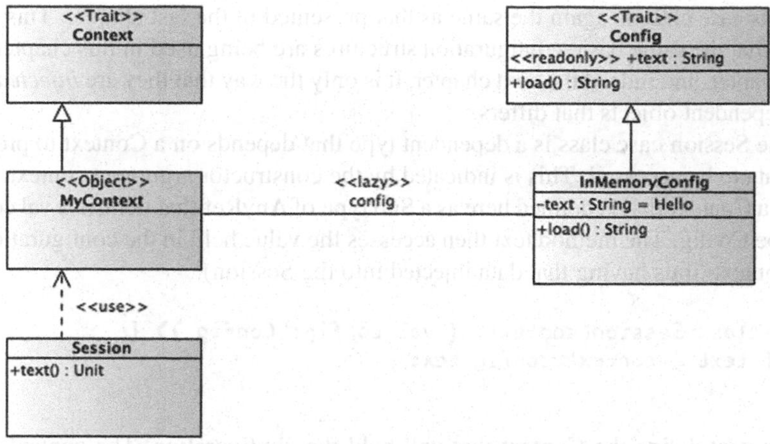

Fig. 14.1 Types in the Session Structural Injection example

The implementation defines a Context marker trait that is used to indicate an object that will be a context for the Structural Injection pattern and will make a configuration object available. This is exactly the same trait as was used in the previous chapter.

```
trait Context
```

The Config trait defines a loan method that returns Unit and a property text. This represents that the load method can be used to load a configuration and that the data to be loaded is the text. It also defines the method load as being executed when an object that mixes the trait is instantiated. Again this trait is exactly the same as that presented in the previous chapter.

```
trait Config {
  load
  val text: String
  def load: Unit
}
```

A concrete configuration type is defined by the InMemoryConfig case class which mixes in the Config trait. This defines the load method as printing out a message (mimicking the action of loading this data from some persistent store) and declaring the text string has being Hello.

```
case class InMemoryConfig extends Config {
  lazy val text = "Hello"
  def load = println("load: " + text)
}
```

This case class is again the same as that presented in the last chapter. This indicates that the same basic configuration structures are being used in this chapter, the last chapter, and indeed the next chapter. It is only the way that they are *injected* into the dependent objects that differs.

The Session case class is a dependent type that depends on a Context to provide the data to be accessed. This is indicated by the constructor argument context. This takes a Context that is defined here as a Sub type of AnyRef that defines a val config of type Config. The method text then accesses the value held in the configuration of the context (thus having that data injected into the Session).

```
case class Session(context: { val config: Config }) {
  def text = context.config.text
}
```

We next define the Context that will hold the configuration. The context is an object so that we can treat it as a singleton object and share the context with any objects that need the configuration held within the context. Also note we have made the config val member of the MyContext class a lazy value – and thus it is only evaluated if it is actually used. This is an implementation choice and is not required.

```
object MyContext extends Context {
  lazy val config = InMemoryConfig()
}
```

Finally the Test application used to illustrate the use of these types is presented below:

```
object Test extends App {
  val session = Session(MyContext)
  println(session.text)
}
```

This simple application creates an instance of the Session class passing in the MyContext object. We then print out the object returned from the text method (which is the value accessed from the config object). The result of running this application is:

```
load: Hello
Hello
```

14.9 Pros and Cons

The advantages of the Structural Injection Pattern are:

- Provides for Type safe injection of objects via a Concrete Configuration object.
- Highly flexible in terms of the way in which the context is provided.

The drawbacks of the Structural Injection Pattern include:

- It may not be obvious that the context provides the reference to the configuration object.
- It is less flexible than some purely runtime approaches.

14.10 Related Patterns

Factory Object May be used to supply the Concrete Configuration.
Cake Pattern Relies on stackable traits to achieve a similar goal.
Implicit Injection Also aims to provide possible implementations that address the aims of dependency injection.

Chapter 15
Implicit Injection Pattern

15.1 Introduction

Constructing objects from other objects is a fundamental recurring theme in Object Oriented Systems. Scala is just as much an object oriented language, as it is a functional language. Therefore there are many situations in which when one object is constructed it requires references to other objects.

One approach to such construction is to require the dependent object to create the objects it needs. Another approach, often referred to as Dependency Injection, is to provide the required objects to the dependent consumer through some framework (such as Spring) or via some language feature.

This chapter and the two preceding chapters explore this concept within Scala. Dependency injection (or DI) involves at least three elements, these are:

- A dependent consumer
- A declaration of a component's dependencies
- Some way of injecting (or providing) the objects that a dependency consumer requires.

This chapter explores the use of implicit declarations in Scala to provide a simple yet type safe approach to the injection of objects to a dependent consumer.

15.2 Pattern Classification

Code Reuse Patterns

15.3 Intent

Provides a simple and straightforward approach to providing objects that can be *injected* into a dependent consumer.

J. Hunt, *Scala Design Patterns: Patterns for Practical Reuse and Design*,
DOI 10.1007/978-3-319-02192-8_15,

15.4 Context

Being able to externally control the objects that are made available to a dependent consumer can be very useful not just for maintenance and reuse purposes but also for testing. By externalizing the construction of the objects required different implementations can be provided depending upon the context.

15.5 Forces/Motivation

The Implicit Injection pattern can be used when

- The decisions about the objects to provide to a dependent object can be generated at runtime but need to be type safe.
- Source level configuration is acceptable.

15.6 Constituent Parts

The constituent parts of the Implicit Injection pattern are:

The Configuration Abstraction Defines the generic way that the objects to be made available are configured and what data/objects is available.

One or more Concrete Configuration types These are the types that define how the objects to be made available will be created. For example, they could be loaded from a configuration file, from a database or maintained in memory. This object provides the context through which values will be made available to a dependent consumer. It will be implicitly extracted from the runtime environment of the consumer.

A Dependent Component This is a component that depends on objects supplied by a Concrete Configuration.

These roles are illustrated in Fig. 15.1:

15.7 Implementation Issues

It is important to decide how the configuration information will be provided. The actual concrete configuration may be a class, an object and in a package object etc. They can then be imported into the context where they are required.

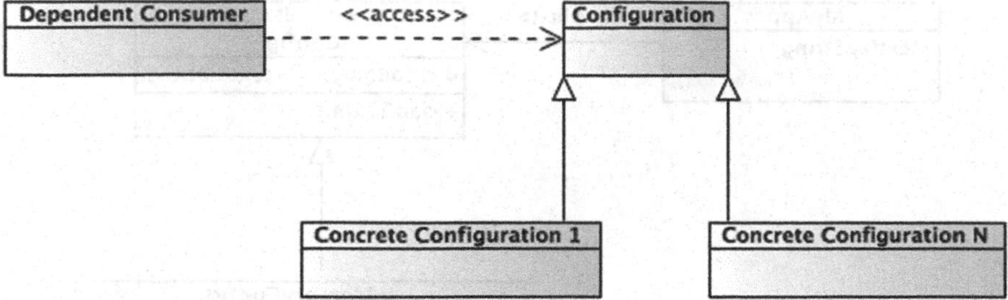

Fig. 15.1 Key roles within the Implicit Injection Pattern

The other implementation issue to consider is how the appropriate configuration object provider is identified. This may be done using a Factory object.

15.8 Concrete Example

The components in this application are shown in Fig. 15.2.

The Config trait defines a load method that returns Unit and a value text. Note that this is exactly the same trait as was defined in the last chapter. This trait indicates that the load method can be used to load a configuration and that the data to be loaded is the text String. It also defines the method load as being executed when an object that mixes the trait is instantiated.

```
trait Config {
  load
  val text: String
  def load: Unit
}
```

A concrete configuration type is defined by the InMemoryConfig case class that mixes in the Config trait. Again this is exactly the same class as was defined in the last chapter. This class defines the load method as printing out a message (mimicking the action of loading this data from some persistent store) and declaring the text string has being Hello.

```
case class InMemoryConfig extends Config {
  lazy val text = "Hello"
  def load = println("load: " + text)
}
```

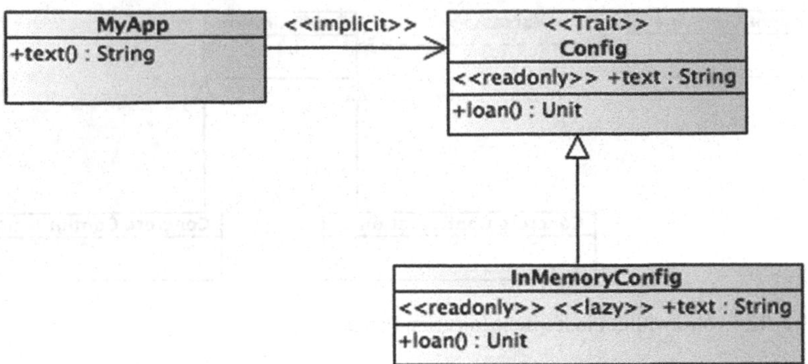

Fig. 15.2 Key components in sample application

The case class MyApp represents the dependent consumer of the configuration class. It has a constructor argument config that is marked as being implicit. This means that if a value is not provided by the client code, the system will look in the current environment to see if there is a object that can be used instead. This is indicated in the client code by an object marked with keyword implicit. The MyApp class is shown below:

```
case class MyApp(implicit config: Config) {
  def text = config.text
}
```

The MyApp class uses the data held in the config to provide an implementation for the text method. This method returns the value provided by the config object.

The InMemoryConfig class and the MyApp class are used in the following simple test application:

```
object Test extends App {
  implicit val config = InMemoryConfig()
  println("----------------")
  val myApp = MyApp()
  println(myApp text)
  println("----------------")
}
```

This application creates a val config that is marked as being capable of being used whenever an implicit parameter is required. A new instance of MyApp is created without a parameter being made available. This means that Scala looks in the invoking environment for an appropriate implicit value – and find the config object. This is passed into the MyApp as a form of dependency injection. This can be used within the MyApp class.

When this application is executed the following output is generated:

```
load: Hello
=================
Hello
=================
```

15.9 Pros and Cons

The advantages of the Structural Injection Pattern are:

- Simple and easy to use and the Scala language structure used is well understood and widely used.

The drawbacks of the Structural Injection Pattern include:

- The actual wiring, or definitions of the objects that provide the objects that the dependent consumer requires are scattered in application code.

15.10 Related Patterns

Factory Object May be used to supply the Concrete Configuration.
Cake Pattern Relies on stackable traits to achieve a similar goal.
Structural Injection Also aims to provide possible implementations that address the aims of dependency injection.

Part IV
Gang of Four Patterns

Chapter 16
Gang of Four Design Patterns

16.1 Introduction

The book which first raised awareness of the concept of design patterns and is still widely cited by any wiki, web site or book on design patterns is the Design Patterns book. The four authors, Erich Gamma, Richard Helm, Ralph Johnson and John Vlissides (collectively known as the "Gang of Four", or GoF for short) popularized the patterns concepts and ideals. The patterns in this book are often referred to as GoF Patterns and the book as the GoF Design Patterns book (to distinguish it from various other books with similar titles).

The GoF Design Patterns book is a weighty tome in its own right (over 370 pages). It is also focussed on C++ and Smalltalk as the implementation languages. This is not surprising as the book was originally published in 1995 Since then numerous works have considered how these design patterns relate to other languages such as the books written by Mark Grand (Patterns in Java Vol 1 and Patters in java Vol 2). The first of which is essentially the GoF patterns translated in Java.

I am performing a similar role in this section of this book for the Scala language.

16.2 GoF Patterns

There are 23 GoF patterns divided into three categories. The categories are "Creational Patterns", "Structural Patterns" and "Behavioural Patterns":

Creational Patterns These patterns provide guidance on the creation of objects. They help hide the details of the object instantiation form the code that uses those objects. That is they make a system independent of how its objects are created, composed and represented. This leads to high cohesion between the objects and their users, but low couple between the users and the way the objects are created. For example, if I have a Java interface that is implemented by three different classes, then using a Factory pattern I might instantiate one of the three classes

J. Hunt, *Scala Design Patterns: Patterns for Practical Reuse and Design*,
DOI 10.1007/978-3-319-02192-8_16, © Springer International Publishing Switzerland 2013

depending on the current situation. All the user of the object returned needs to know is what interface they all implement. The actual implementation may change each time the factory is used, but this detail is hidden.

Structural Patterns Such patterns describe the organization of objects. That is how classes and objects are composed to form larger structures. For example a large department store near where I live, appears form the outside to be a single entity with a very grand frontage. However, behind this frontage is a completely new shop containing various independent stores. This means that as a customer I see form the outside a single and quite grand whole. But form the inside there are multiple smaller shops/brands all working together. This is the essence of the Façade pattern.

Behavioural Patterns Behavioural patterns are concerned with organizing managing and assigning responsibilities to objects during execution. That is, the focus on the patterns of communication between the objects involved during some task. Typically, these patterns characterize complex control flows that are difficult to follow at runtime. They therefore help to shift the emphasis away from the low level flow of control to the higher level object interactions.

Chapter 17
GoF Patterns Catalog

17.1 Introduction

There are a growing number of patterns catalogs available including the Gang of Four patterns (from the original Patterns book), the J2EE patterns from Sun, various anti-patterns and Java based patterns (Grand 2002). In this chapter we will focus on the patterns that formed the seminal patterns book (Gamma et al. 1995). The patterns in this book are often referred to as GoF (for Gang of Four) patterns to distinguish them from other patterns.

17.2 Creational Patterns

There are 5 different patterns within the creational patterns category. They are Factory Method, Abstract Factory, Builder, Prototype and Singleton. These patterns are presented below.

17.2.1 Factory Method

This provides a pattern that describes the use of a factory class for constructing objects. The methods on the factory return objects that implement a given interface. The user of the factory only knows about the interface. Thus different objects can be created depending on the current situation (as long as they implement the interface).

J. Hunt, *Scala Design Patterns: Patterns for Practical Reuse and Design*, DOI 10.1007/978-3-319-02192-8_17, © Springer International Publishing Switzerland 2013

17.2.2 Abstract Factory

Describes a pattern for creating families of related or dependent objects.

17.2.3 Builder

This pattern separates out the construction of a complex object from its use. Thus the client can specify what type of object is required and what its content might be, but never need to know about how that object is constructed and initialised.

17.2.4 Prototype

This patterns allows a user object to create a customized object, based on a prototype of what is required. That is, the pattern describes how a new object can be created based on a customisation of an existing object.

17.2.5 Singleton

The Singleton pattern describes a class that can only have one object constructed for it. That is, unlike other objects it should not be possible to obtain more than one instance within the same virtual machine. Thus the Singleton pattern ensures that only one instance of a class is created. All objects that use an instance of that class use the same instance.

The motivation behind this pattern is that some classes, typically those classes that involve the central management of a resource, should have exactly one instance. For example, a object that managements the reuse of database connections (i.e. a connection pool) could be a singleton.

17.3 Structural Patterns

The structural category has seven patterns. These patterns are Adapter, Bridge, Composite, Decorator, Façade, Flyweight and Proxy. Each is discussed briefly below.

17.3.1 Adapter

The adapter pattern is used to convert the public interface of one class into the interface of another class. For example, let us assume that we have one piece of code that requires a method with the signature String getPersonName() and a class Person

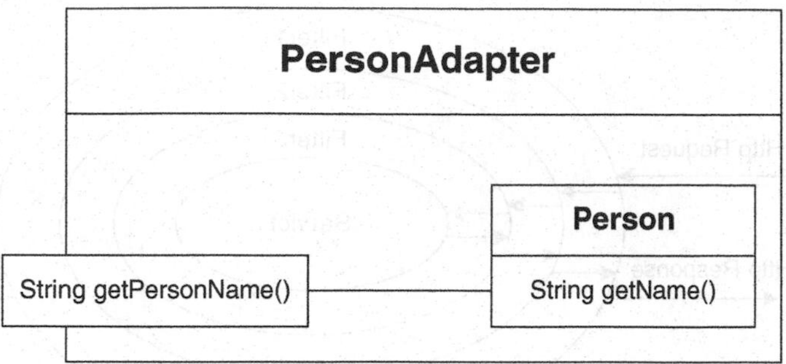

Fig. 17.1 An implementation of the adapter pattern

that has a method with the signature String getName(). We could wrap an adapter around the person object that maps the getPersonName() method to getPerson() (see Fig. 17.1).

17.3.2 *Bridge*

Provides an intermediary object between an abstraction and its implementation. This is particularly useful when there is a hierarchy of abstractions and another (corresponding) hierarchy of implementations. Rather than combine the two into many distinct classes, the Bridge pattern implements the abstractions and implementations as independent classes that can be combined dynamically.

17.3.3 *Composite*

The Composite pattern allows multiple objects to be treated as a single object or as an individual in the same way.

17.3.4 *Decorator*

This is used to wrap around an object to extend its functionality. The resulting wrapped object should be indistinguishable from the original to clients. For example, image an object that generates comma delimited tables. We could wrap different objects around this to post process the output into HTML, XML etc. If the interface presented to the client is the same as the original object then clients need not know that there is a decorator wrapped around the original. A good example of this pattern is the use of filters in the J2EE. A filter is an object that can be wrapped around a servlet and has the chance to pre and post process the requests and responses being sent to and from the servlet (or JSP) (Fig. 17.2).

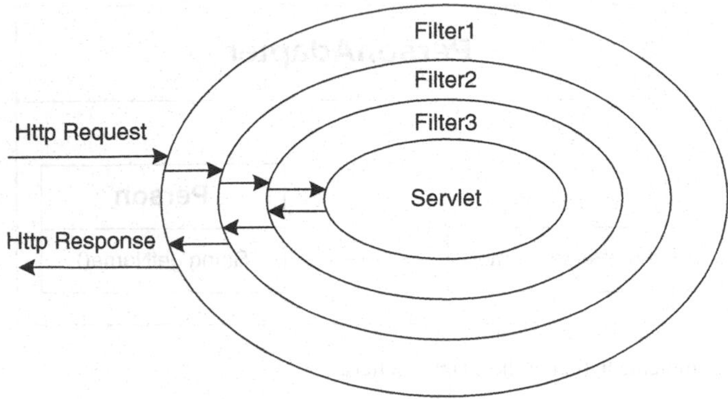

Fig. 17.2 A filter chain wrapped around a servlet

17.3.5 *Façade*

This pattern allows a (simplifying) object to unify a (potentially more complex) interface to a set of objects. The Façade can often be viewed as an interface to a subsystem. It has the effect of simplifying the interface between the clients and the subsystem objects. This is illustrated in Fig. 17.3 where a client only has to deal with a single Façade object. The Façade object then deals with the interactions with multiple subsystem objects.

17.3.6 *Flyweight*

This pattern allows a single instance (or a few instances) to represent many instances all of whole share the same data. This means that the application can avoid some of the expense of multiple instances that all contain the same information by sharing just one (or a few).

17.3.7 *Proxy*

The proxy pattern provides a buffer between a client and the object that will actually service method requests. Thus buffer is a surrogate or placeholder for the actual object. It can be used to control access to the actual object, to determine which object should actually receive the call, to handle network communication etc. A good example of the use of proxys is Remote Method Invocation (or RMI) in Java. In RMI local proxys are used to mimic remote objects and to handle all network communication see Fig. 17.4.

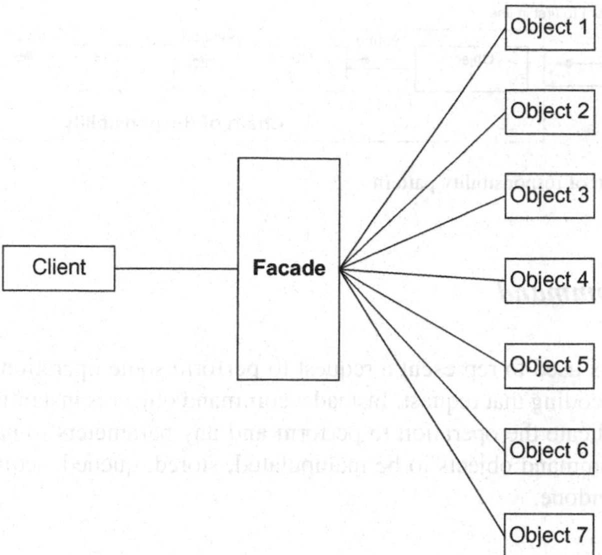

Fig. 17.3 The facade pattern

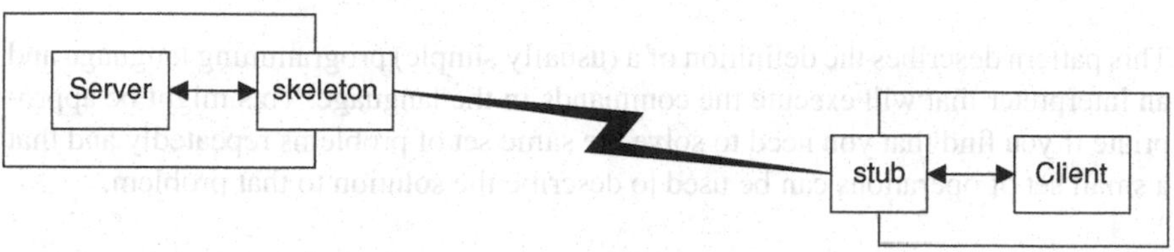

Fig. 17.4 Using the skeleton and stub proxy classes in RMI

17.4 Behavioural Patterns

There are 11 patterns in the behavioural patterns category of the GoF patterns. These are discussed briefly below.

17.4.1 Chain of Responsibility

This patterns allows a request for an action to be sent from a client object to a set of objects. Each object receives the rest sequentially and is given a chance to process that request and then to pass the request onto the next object in the sequence. This is illustrated in Fig. 17.5 where a client sends a method request to Object 1. This is then set onto Object2. Object 2 in turn sends the request onto Object3 and so on. Each object can itself process the request, if it so wishes, before it sends the request on.

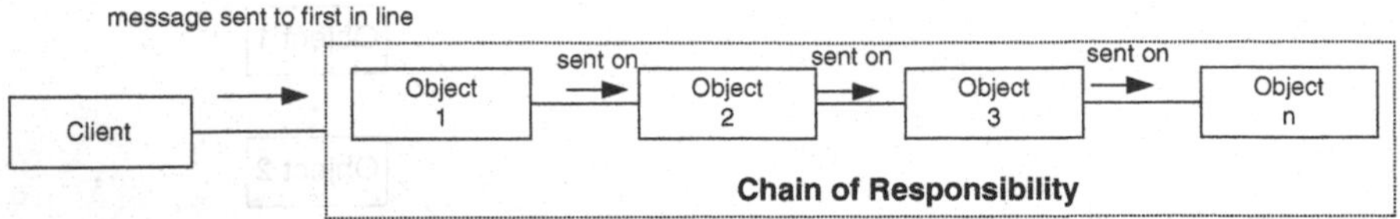

Fig. 17.5 Chain of responsibility pattern

17.4.2 Command

This pattern is used to represent a request to perform some operation on an object without hard coding that request. Instead a command object is instantiated and configured to indicate the operation to perform and any parameters to pass. This also allows the command objects to be manipulated, stored, queued, sequenced and in some cases undone.

17.4.3 Interpreter

This pattern describes the definition of a (usually simple) programming language and an interpreter that will execute the commands in the language. This might be appropriate if you find that you need to solve the same set of problems repeatedly and that a small set of operations can be used to describe the solution to that problem.

17.4.4 Mediator

The mediator pattern is one that promotes the loose coupling of a set of communicating objects. This pattern was discussed in the last chapter. The aim of the Mediator is to define an object that encapsulates how a set of objects interact. The Mediator pattern promotes loose coupling by keeping objects from referring to each other explicitly.

The motivation behind this is that object oriented design encourages the distribution of behavior among objects. However, this can lead to a multiplicity of links between objects. In the worst case every object needs to know about/link to every other object. This can be a problem for maintenance and for the reusability of the individual classes. This is illustrated in figure Fig. 17.6. In this example, there are five objects that all need to communicate with each other. This results in 10 bi-directional links (in Scala terms 20 references). If a sixth object wished to be added to this communications network we would end up with 15 bi-directional links (or 30 Scala references) and potential changes to five existing classes. This has major implications for maintainability as well as stability.

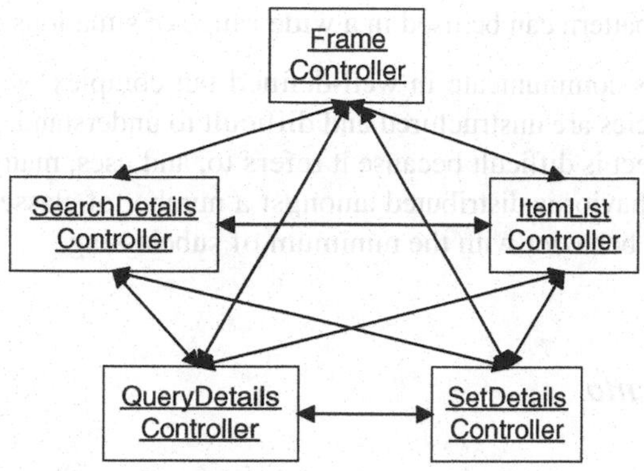

Fig. 17.6 Communicating objects

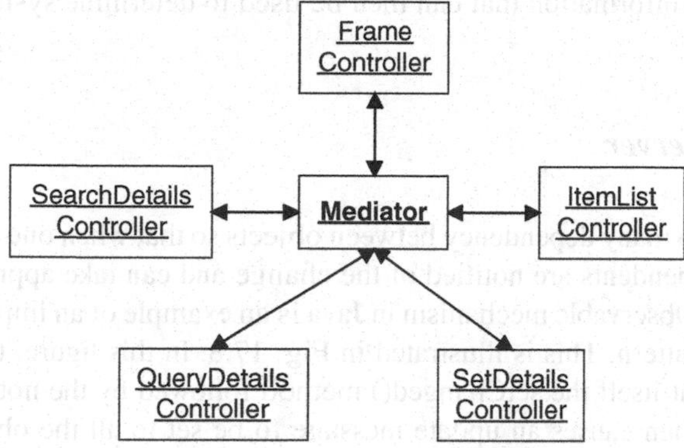

Fig. 17.7 Objects communicating via a mediator

These problems can be overcome by using a mediator object. In this scheme other objects are connected together via a central mediator object in a star like structure. The mediator is then responsible for controlling and coordinating the interactions of the group of objects.

The example illustrated in Fig. 17.6 could be reconfigured using the mediator pattern as illustrated in Fig. 17.7. In this case there are only 5 bi-directional links and if we add a sixth object there would be only 6 di-directional links.

The mediator handles communication between colleague objects. In turn each colleague knows its mediator object. It communicates with this mediator object in order to communicate with other colleagues. Thus the mediator object receives messages from its colleagues and relays them to other colleagues as appropriate. Exactly what form these messages take and how the mediator passes them onto its colleagues is not part of the design pattern – it is a responsibility of those applying the pattern to decide on these details. Examples of the form that messages can take include strings, objects, serializable objects, ints etc. In turn how the mediator sends this information onto the colleagues is implementation dependent – it could be implemented as a simple iteration through a list, via some form of IP broadcast mechanism or via some messaging system (for example via the JMS API).

The mediator pattern can be used in a wide range of situations including:

- a set of objects communicate in well-defined but complex ways. The resulting interdependencies are unstructured and difficult to understand.
- reusing an object is difficult because it refers to, and uses, many other objects.
- a particular behavior is distributed amongst a number of classes and we wish to customize that behavior with the minimum of subclassing.

17.4.5 Memento

This pattern is used to obtain a snap shot of the state of an object without violating its encapsulation. The memento object can be passed around from object to object capturing state information that can then be used to determine system activity.

17.4.6 Observer

Defines a one to many dependency between objects so that when one object changes state, all its dependents are notified of the change and can take appropriate action. The Observer/Observable mechanism in Java is an example of an implementation of the Observer pattern. This is illustrated in Fig. 17.8. In this figure, the Observable object must sent itself the setChanged() method followed by the notifyObservers() method. This then causes an update message to be set to all the objects currently registered with the Observable object. These Observer objects can then update themselves as required.

17.4.7 State

This pattern describes a state based set of operations. That is, when an objects state changes so does it behaviour.

17.4.8 Strategy

This pattern describes a set of structures that defines an abstract parent class method that can be implemented with different algorithms in different subclasses. Thus a different solution strategy can be adopted by selecting a different subclass. If the client works with variables of the superclass but actually has subclasses supplied (possibly by a factory method) then the client does not need to know about the changes in strategy.

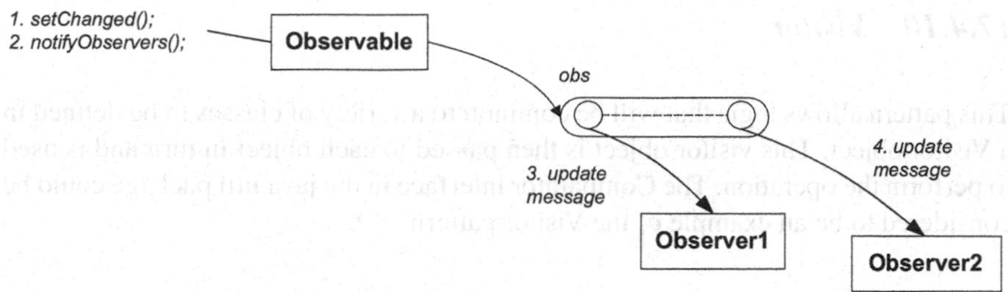

Fig. 17.8 The Observer/Observable pattern implemented in java

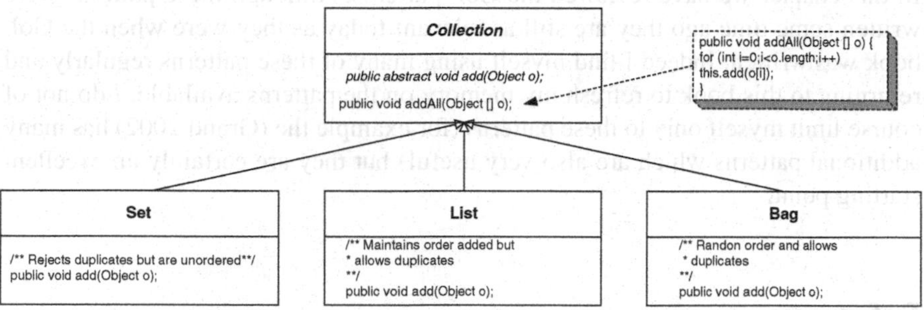

Fig. 17.9 The template method pattern

17.4.9 Template Method

This pattern is used to describe how a skeleton algorithm, that calls methods that are abstract in the current class, can be implemented in the subclass. This is illustrated in Fig. 17.9. In this figure an abstract super class Collection defines two methods. One, the addAll(Object [] o) method takes an array of objects and loops through the array calling the method add on each object. The method add however is abstract in the Collection class. This is not a problem because it is not possible to make an instance of an abstract class. Any concrete subclasses will have to implement the add method, thus any concrete subclasses will be able to execute the addAll method. Each subclass in this example, then implements the add method in a different way. For example, the Set class does not worry about maintaining the order in which objects were added, but does ensure that there are no duplicates. The List class in contrast allows duplicates but maintains the order the objects were added in. The bag class allows duplicates but does not maintain the order objects are added. Thus each of the subclasses will provide a different version of the template method defined in Collection.

17.4.10 Visitor

This pattern allows logic that will be common to a variety of classes to be defined in a Visitor object. This visitor object is then passed to each object in turn and is used to perform the operation. The Comparator interface in the java.util package could be considered to be an example of the Visitor pattern.

17.5 Summary

In this chapter we have reviewed the GoF patterns. Although these patterns were written some time ago they are still as relevant today as they were when the GoF book was written. Indeed I find myself using many of these patterns regularly and returning to this book to refresh my memory on the patterns available. I do not of course limit myself only to these patterns (for example the (Grand 2002) has many additional patterns which are also very useful) but they are certainly an excellent starting point.

References

Gamma, E., Helm, R., Johnson, R., & Vlissades, J. (1995). *Design patterns: Elements of reusable object-oriented software*. Reading: Addison-Wesley.

Grand, M. (2002). *Patterns in java: A catalog of reusable design patterns illustrated with UML* (2nd ed., Vol. 1). New York: Wiley. ISBN 0471227293.

Chapter 18
Factory Operation

18.1 Introduction

This chapter describes a Factory Operation pattern that can be used to construct objects of a given type. The methods on the Factory Operation return objects that implement a given trait or (typically abstract) super class. The client of the factory only knows about the trait or parent superclass. Thus different objects can be instantiated depending on the current situation/requirements (as long as they implement the trait or extend the superclass).

This pattern is the Scala equivalent of the Factory Method in the original Gang of Four Design patterns Book.

18.2 Pattern Classification

GoF Creational Pattern

18.3 Intent

To hide the instantiation of a specific type from a client thereby allowing flexibility in that instantiation.

18.4 Context

Let us say that we wish to create an application that allows the user to open documents of different types, using different implementations, but were a common facility is used. As far as the user is considered all they want to do is open a word document, a pdf document, an Open Office document or an image document. Which

J. Hunt, *Scala Design Patterns: Patterns for Practical Reuse and Design*,
DOI 10.1007/978-3-319-02192-8_18, © Springer International Publishing Switzerland 2013

actual implementation of the Document Viewer or Editor concept is used is not of interest to them, they merely wish to open a document.

One approach could be to have an application that is given the name of a document to open and uses an appropriate tool or library to achieve this. There are many different ways in which this application functionality could be implemented. One way would be to use a Factory Operation. This (singleton) object is passed the document name to open and determines the appropriate type to instantiate based on the file type (and potentially environmental and application specific information).

The various types available to the Factory Operation may be predefined or may be dynamically provided (for example from some central registry or via some configuration information such as an XML configuration file). These types may all implement a basic Document Viewer trait or super type.

18.5 Forces/Motivation

In situations where the object to instantiate may different depending on configuration information or environmental information it may be necessary to encapsulate this instantiation process within a factory. This factory object can then instantiate objects that inherit from a given type (trait or superclass).

If the actual set of types that can be instantiated may be dynamic, then hiding this behind a factory can be very useful. This allows the identification of the appropriate types to create to be encapsulated in one place and any complexity hidden from the client code.

18.6 Constituent Parts

The constituent parts of the Factory Operation Pattern are the root type of the objects to be created (for example a trait or an abstract class), the Factory Operation and the creation method(s) required. These methods may take parameters that may be used to identify the type of object to create and/or may be used as parameters to the constructors used with those types.

This is illustrated in Fig. 18.1:

The equivalent Scala code that illustrates the Factory Object pattern is presented below.

A type in the role of Product is the abstract super type of objects produced by the Factory Object pattern.

```
trait Product
```

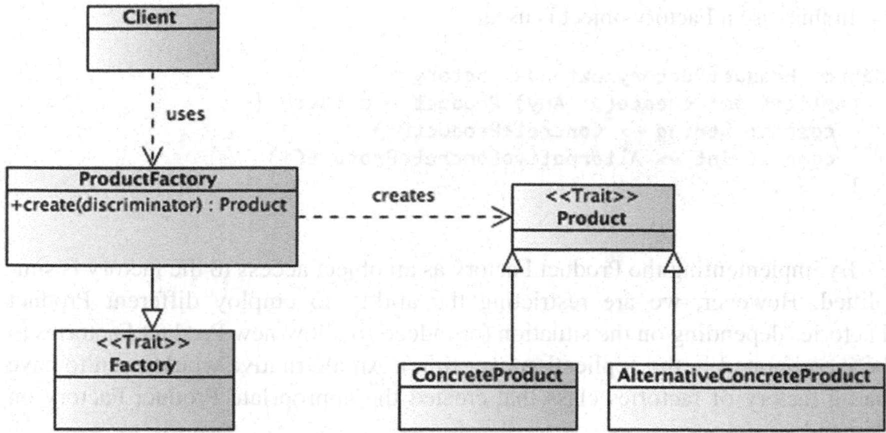

Fig. 18.1 Constituent parts of Factory Operation pattern

In this case the root concept being managed by the Factory Object is a trait (the Product trait).

The Concrete Product role (and the Alternative Concrete Product role) are the concrete classes that will be instantiated by the Factory object. That is they are the concrete types that participate in the Factory Object pattern. If these concrete classes share no logic then a trait may be used as the Product. If they share some logic then either a trait or an abstract super class may be the Product. If a large amount of logic is shared then an abstract super class may be the most appropriate parent for the concrete products.

```
case class ConcreteProduct(S: String) extends Product
case class AlternativeConcreteProduct(i: Int) extends Product
```

Two concrete case classes have been implemented to mix in the Product trait and the Factory object is used to handle the instantiation of these case classes.

The Factory trait is an application/client independent specification for the behaviour that the Factory Operation must provide. This trait may incorporate functionality or not as required. The Factory may also be implemented by a class or by a Scala Object. If the factory is to be treated as singleton then the Factory Object approach makes the most sense although it does limit the options for customization of the factory itself.

The Factory trait is shown below:

```
trait Factory {
  def create(a: Any):Product
}
```

In this case a Factory object is used,

```
object ProductFactory extends Factory {
  implicit def create(a: Any):Product = a match {
    case s: String => ConcreteProduct(s)
    case i: Int => AlternativeConcreteProduct(i)
  }
}
```

By implementing the Product Factory as an object access to the factory is simplified. However, we are restricting the ability to employ different Product Factories depending on the situation (or indeed to allow new Product Factories to be incorporated in the application over time). An alternative would been to have had a factory of factories class that created the appropriate Product Factory on demand.

Note that the create method has also been marked as implicit so that the factory operation can be applied implicitly if required. This is optional and many people believe that this is a dangerous approach to take, however it is one that is supported by the Scala language.

A simple example of using these classes is shown below:

```
object Test extends App {
  val a = ProductFactory.create("John")
  println(a)
  val b = ProductFactory.create(32)
  println(b)
  import ProductFactory._
  val c: Product = "Adam"
  println(c)
  val d: Product = "Denise"
  println(d)
}
```

The result of running this example is shown below:

```
ConcreteProduct(John)
AlternativeConcreteProduct(32)
ConcreteProduct(Adam)
ConcreteProduct(Denise)
```

18.7 Concrete Example

The example presented in this section defines a ProductFactory object that defines a single creation method that takes a string and returns a ProductViewer (or throws a Runtime exception indicating that the type specified in the string parameter was unknown).

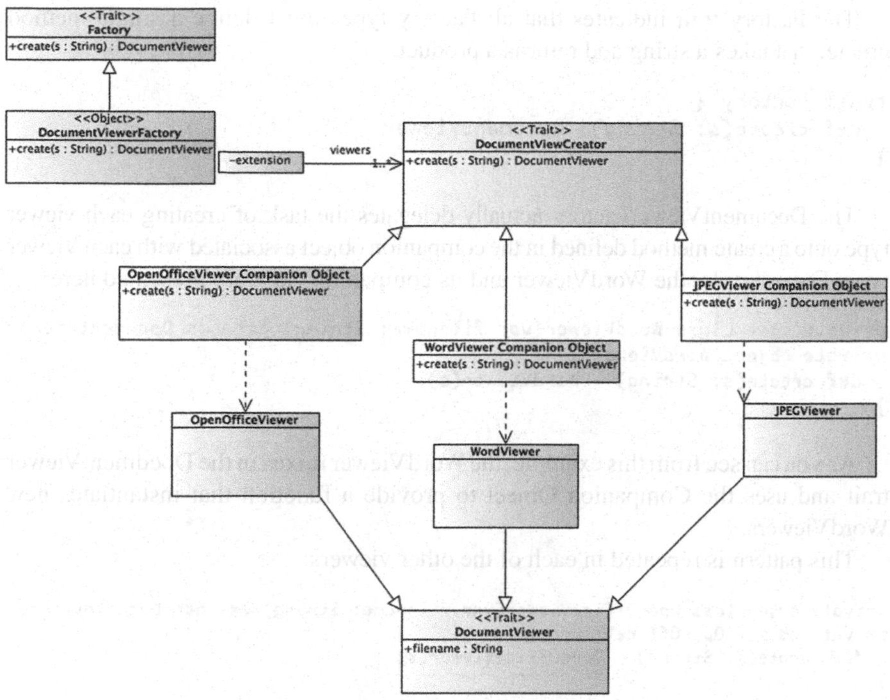

Fig. 18.2 Types used in simplified Document Viewer example

In this example we will have a Factory trait and a DocumentFactory object implementation. The create method will take a filename that will be tested for its extension type and one of a set of Document Viewers will be created. If an unknown extension type is passed in the Factory will throw an exception. Note that it could use a default Document Viewer type. The set of Document Viewers will be registered with the ProductFactory dynamically. In our example this will be done in a test application. However, in a real world application this information could come from a configuration file, a property file or a database etc.

Due to space considerations we will assume that the Document Viewer types available support .docx, .odt and .jpg (for Word, Open Office and JPEG documents).

The types used in this example are shown in Fig. 18.2.

The basic Document Viewer trait is shown below:

```
trait DocumentViewer {
  var filename: String
}
```

This indicates that all document viewers must define a filename readonly property.

The Factory trait indicates that all Factory types must define a single method create, that takes a string and returns a product:

```
trait Factory {
  def create(s: String): DocumentViewer
}
```

The DocumentViewerFactory actually delegates the task of creating each viewer type onto a create method defined in the companion object associated with each Viewer type. For example, the WordViewer and its companion class are presented here:

```
private case class WordViewer(var filename: String) extends DocumentViewer
private object WordViewer {
  def create(s: String) = WordViewer(s)
}
```

As you can see from this example, the WordViewer mixes in the DocumentViewer trait and uses the Companion Object to provide a function that instantiates new WordViewers.

This pattern is repeated in each of the other viewers:

```
private case class OpenOfficeViewer(var filename: String) extends DocumentViewer
private object OpenOfficeViewer {
  def create(s: String) = OpenOfficeViewer(s)
}

private case class JPEGViewer(var filename: String) extends DocumentViewer
private object JPEGViewer {
  def create(s: String) = JPEGViewer(s)
}
```

The create methods of the companion objects can then be registered with the DocumentViewerFactory using that object's *viewers* property:

```
DocumentViewerFactory.viewers.put(".docx", WordViewer.create)
DocumentViewerFactory.viewers.put(".odt", OpenOfficeViewer.create)
DocumentViewerFactory.viewers.put(".jpg", JPEGViewer.create)
```

Then when a new DocumentViewer is required the client code merely invokes the create method on the DocumentViewerFactory passing in the filename of the document to be viewed:

```
val p1 = DocumentViewerFactory.create("info.docx")
println(p1)
val p2 = DocumentViewerFactory.create("info.odt")
println(p2)
val p3 = DocumentViewerFactory.create("info.jpg")
println(p3)
```

The actual DocumentViewerFactory object is presented below:

```
object DocumentViewerFactory extends Factory {
  private[document] val viewers = HashMap[String, String => DocumentViewer]()

  def create(s: String): DocumentViewer = {
    var pos = s.lastIndexOf(".")
    if (pos < 0) { pos = 0 }
    val endsWith = s.substring(pos)
    val funcOption = viewers.get(endsWith)
    if (funcOption.nonEmpty) {
          val func = funcOption.get
          return func(s)
        } else {
      throw new RuntimeException("Unknown Document Type")
    }
  }
}
```

Note that the file extension is assumed to be the key in the HashMap used to hold the mapping from the extension to the DocumentViewer creation methods.

The result of running this example is:

```
WordViewer(info.docx)
OpenOfficeViewer(info.odt)
JPEGViewer(info.jpg)
```

18.8 Pros and Cons

The primary advantages of the Factory Operation pattern are that:

- The client and the creation process are separated and independent of each other.
- The actual type being instantiated is hidden from the client and can therefore change without the client code needing to be altered.
- The set of product types being instantiated may change dynamically and independently of the client.

The primary drawback of the pattern is

- The separation of the instantiation process from the client code. It may therefore not be clear until run time what the actual product type instantiated is, and this may lead to extra complexity and potential confusion.

18.9 Related Patterns

Singleton The Factory Object is a singleton object that implements the Factory method(s).

Marker Trait The common trait amongst all the types that the Factory instantiates may be a marker trait.

Delegate In our example the Document Factory actually delegated the takes of instantiating each of the viewer types to an appropriate companion object that provided the appropriate create methods.

Chapter 19
Abstract Factory Pattern

19.1 Introduction

The aim of the Abstract Factory pattern is to provide a way to obtain an appropriate *concrete* factory that can provide the specific type of product required by a client. The client need only be aware of the Abstract Factory type and obtains the concrete factory either by directly accessing it or by obtaining it from a Factory of Factories.

Each concrete Factory provides an implementation of a product and this by using an appropriate Factory the client can obtain different implementations as required.

19.2 Pattern Classification

Gang of Four Creational Pattern

19.3 Intent

To provide a way of creating families of different products without needing to know the actual implementing types.

19.4 Context

There are a number of common scenarios in which you will find the Abstract Factory pattern occurring. It could be used to abstract the windowing system being used away from the client. In such a situation a abstract WidgetFactory might be extended by a OSXWidgetFactory and a WindowsWidgetFactory. Each providing a range of different products (such as Window, a Dialog, a Menu, Menu bar etc. but

J. Hunt, *Scala Design Patterns: Patterns for Practical Reuse and Design*,
DOI 10.1007/978-3-319-02192-8_19, © Springer International Publishing Switzerland 2013

implemented based on OSX or MS Windows technologies). The client merely needs to access the appropriate factory to obtain the appropriate version of the products required.

19.5 Forces/Motivation

The Abstract Factory Pattern can be used when

- A client must be able to work with a set of products for which there are multiple different implementations and we wish to hide that detail from the client.
- It should be possible to configure the set of products made available to the client based on some configuration information.
- We wish to enforce consistency amongst the implementations of products created.
- The different types of product should only be used with products associated with the same family (for example, OSX Dialogs should only be used with OSX Windows and menus etc.).
- Clients (and other client code) should be unaware of the different implementations of Products.
- We wish to be able to extend the range of implementations of a set of Products without having to alter clients.

19.6 Constituent Parts

There are a number of roles in the Abstract Factory Pattern:

Abstract Factory Defines the *abstract* type that will be used to define the *interface* supplied by the factories to clients.

Concrete Factory This role is played by one or more implementing types that provide the concrete realization of the operations defined in the Abstract Factory. These operations instantiate different version of the products in the associated product hierarchies.

Factory of Factories (Factory Provider) This role is used to provide an object that can supply the appropriate type of Concrete Factory based on some criteria or configuration information.

Product An abstraction that represents a type of product object. There may be many different products associated with an Abstract Factory hierarchy.

Concrete Products One or more concrete implementations of the Product abstractions.

Client Uses the operations defined by the Abstract Factory on a Concrete Factory to obtain concrete implementations of the Products.

This roles and their relationships are illustrated in Fig. 19.1.

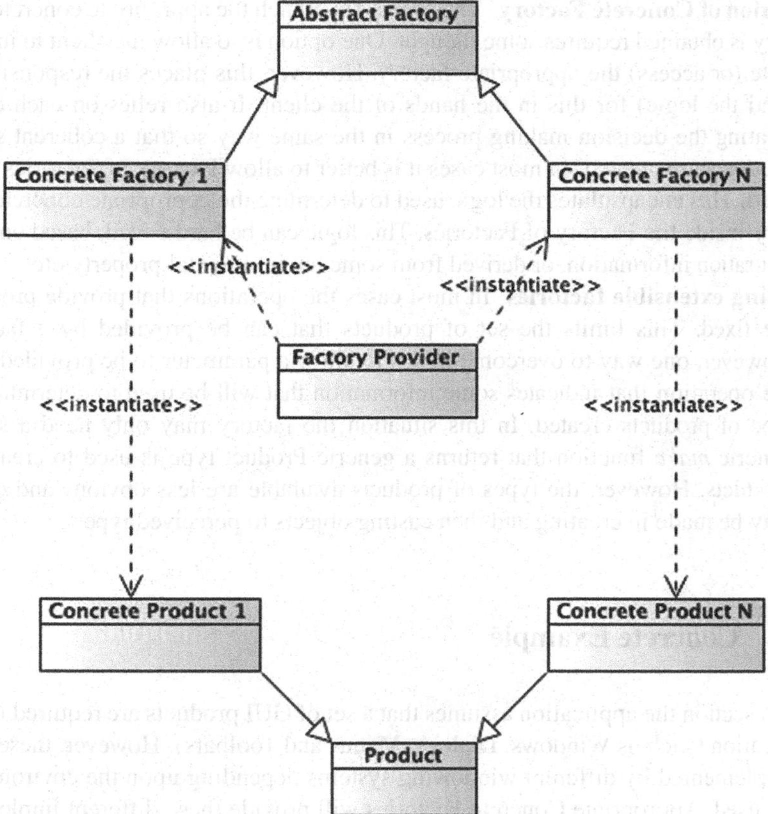

Fig. 19.1 Primary participants in the Abstract Factory pattern

19.7 Implementation Issues

There are a number of issues to consider when implementing the Abstract Factory pattern.

Scala Implementation features The traditional object oriented view of the Abstract Factory pattern has the Abstract Factory and the Concrete Factory as a hierarchy of classes. However, a Factory Object could be created by mixing in the appropriate Concrete Factory traits in Scala. Therefore ensuring the required implementation is available. Thus could be done using the type hierarchy or at the point of object creation. Both approaches ensure static type checking and compile time validation.

Factories as singletons An application typically only needs one instance of a Concrete Factory per product family. It is therefore practical to implement the factories as singleton objects.

Selection of Concrete Factory The process by which the appropriate concrete factory is obtained requires some thought. One option is to allow the client to instantiate (or access) the appropriate factory. However, this places the responsibility (and the logic) for this in the hands of the client. It also relies on each client treating the decision making process in the same way so that a coherent set of products are created. In most cases it is better to allow Factory of Factories to be used. This encapsulates the logic used to determine the appropriate concrete factory inside the Factory of Factories. This logic can be hard coded, based on configuration information, or derived from some environmental property etc.

Defining extensible factories In most cases the operations that provide products are fixed. This limits the set of products that can be provided by a factory. However, one way to overcome this is to allow a parameter to be provided with the operation that indicates some information that will be used to determine the type of products created. In this situation the factory may only need a single generic *make* function that returns a generic Product type is used to create all products. However, the types of products available are less obvious and errors may be made in creating and then casting objects to perceived types.

19.8 Concrete Example

In this section the application assumes that a set of GUI products are required for an application (such as Windows, Dialogs, Menus and Toolbars). However, these may be implemented by different windowing systems depending upon the environment being used. Appropriate Concrete Factories will provide these different implementations, for the different windowing systems. The concept will be illustrated using sample widgets rather than actual OSX, Windows, or other windowing system.

The types that comprise this application are illustrated in Fig. 19.2.

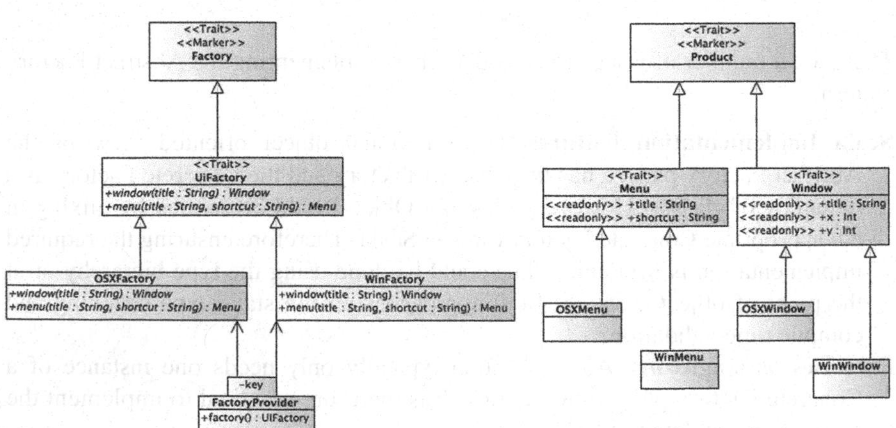

Fig. 19.2 Types used in the simplified GUI application

The first thing we do in this example is to define two Marker traits. These traits are used to indicate the roles of the Product and the Factory:

```
trait Factory

trait Product
```

These Marker traits are then used with the traits that define the behaviour / data associated with the actual factory type and the various product types that use the Abstract Factory pattern in this example.

Two product types are defined (to keep the example simple). One is used to represent Windows and the other Menus:

```
trait Window extends Product {
   val title: String
   var x: Int
   var y: Int
}

trait Menu extends Product {
  val title: String
  val shortcut: String
}
```

Any concrete implementation of a window will have a title and x and y coordinates. Any menu will have a title and a shortcut. These product traits can then be realized as appropriate using the different windowing technologies available.

The Factory trait is mixed into the UIFactory trait that represents the features required of a concrete factory associated with the UI products.

```
trait UIFactory extends Factory {
   def window(title: String): Window
   def menu(title: String, shortcut: String): Menu
}
```

As can be seen from this example, a factory must be able to supply an appropriate Window object and an appropriate Menu object.

The OSFactory is a concrete case class that mixes in the UIFatory trait. It therefore provides implementations for the two abstract methods defined in the Factory trait. These methods return OSX based objects (e.g. an OSXWindow and an OSXMenu).

```
case class OSXFactory extends UIFactory {

  class OSXMenu(val title: String, val shortcut: String) extends Menu {
    override def toString = "OSXMenu: " + title + " (" + shortcut + ")"
  }
  class OSXWindow(val title: String, var x: Int = 0, var y: Int = 0) extends Window {
    override def toString = "OSXWindow: " + title + "(" + x + ", " + y + ")"
  }

  def window(title:String) = new OSXWindow(title)
  def menu(title: String, shortcut: String) = new OSXMenu(title, shortcut)

}
```

The concrete classes used to instantiate the OSXWindow and the OSXMenu are defined as inner classes within the scope of the OSXFactory. This is not required (they could be top level types) but helps to reduce the pollution of the namespace within multiple, similarly named, types. In this simple example the only behaviour defined for each class is to override the toString method so that a more meaningful description is provided when objects of these classes are printed out.

The Windows version of the Factory is basically the same as the OSX version:

```
case class WinFactory extends UIFactory {

  class WinMenu(val title: String, val shortcut: String) extends Menu {
    override def toString = "WinMenu: " + title + " (" + shortcut + ")"
  }
  class WinWindow(val title: String, var x: Int = 0, var y: Int = 0) extends Window {
    override def toString = "WinWindow: " + title + "(" + x + ", " + y + ")"
  }

  def window(title:String) = new WinWindow(title)
  def menu(title: String, shortcut: String) = new WinMenu(title, shortcut)

}
```

The *factory of factories* object, here called the Factory Provider is a Scala Object (as the singleton nature of the Scala Object is beneficial in this situation). The Factory Provider sets up the available factories (note that this information could be loaded form a configuration file or the object could be programmatically configured if required). When a request is made for a factory it either uses a system property to determine the appropriate factory to return or returns the default factory (which in this case is the OSXFactory).

```
object FactoryProvider {
  private val default = OSXFactory()
  private val factories =
    HashMap[String, UIFactory]("WIN" -> WinFactory(), "OSX" -> default)
  def factory = factories.getOrElse(System.getProperty("factory"), default)
}
```

Note that this means that, with respect to the Factory Provider, each of the concrete factories is a singleton object.

Usage of the simple framework developed here is illustrated in the Test application:

```
object Test extends App {
  val f = FactoryProvider.factory
  println(f.window("Main"))
  println(f.menu("File", "CTRL-F"))
}
```

This Test application accesses the current factory and then uses that factory to obtain a window and a menu (both of which are printed out). The output from this example is presented below:

```
OSXWindow: Main(0, 0)
OSXMenu: File(CTRL-F)
```

19.9 Pros and Cons

The advantages of the Abstract Factory Pattern are:

- **Separation of hierarchies**. The client is separated from the creation of the concrete classes. This both allows you to change the classes created and to control the set of classes instantiated.
- **Consistent product set**. A consistent set of products is enforced by the use of a particular concrete class.

The drawbacks of the Abstract Factory Pattern include:

- **Constraints imposed by product types**. The concrete classes are arranged into Product hierarchies that make it easy to exchange one concrete product for another; these hierarchies may not naturally fit with all implementations.
- **Fixed set of product types**. Extending the abstract factories to produce new kinds of Products is not easy. This is because the Abstract Factory defines the set of Products to be created. Supporting new kinds of products requires the Abstract Factory to be extended and all sub types of the Abstract Factory may need to provide an appropriate product (or some default).

19.10 Related Patterns

Factory Object The Factory Object pattern may be used to implement each of the Concrete Factories.

Singleton The Concrete Factory classes can be singleton objects.

Marker Trait This pattern can be used to indicate the role of a Product or a Factory.

Chapter 20
Builder

20.1 Introduction

The aim of the Builder pattern is to separate the construction of a complex object from the client of that object so that the creation process can create different implementations as required without affecting the client. Thus the client does not have visibility of the object's construction process. Instead the client provides information on the type of object that is required and what its content might be. The Builder then determines how object is constructed and initialised.

20.2 Pattern Classification

Gang of Four Creational Pattern

20.3 Intent

To encapsulate the construction process used to create complex objects from clients of those objects.

20.4 Context

In some situations there may need to be flexibility about the way in which a complex object is constructed and in some cases flexibility about the exact object itself. For example, consider a RTF to other document format exchange application.

J. Hunt, *Scala Design Patterns: Patterns for Practical Reuse and Design*,
DOI 10.1007/978-3-319-02192-8_20,

This application reads RTF format documents and converts them into various other different formats. The object created is a complex document made up of different types of constituent parts depending upon whether an ASCII, Word, OpenOffice, PDF etc. document is being created. Each of the different types of document will be created in different ways, with different constituent parts and different construction processes. However, they will all produce a type of output document that can be written to a file. In addition, the list of document types is open ended and may be extended in the future to include new format types such as XML, HTML as required by the client systems.

What is required in this situation is a flexible way to create these complex document objects that can be easily extended. The Builder pattern provides one approach to this requirement.

20.5 Forces/Motivation

The Builder Pattern can be used when

- The steps required to create a complex object are independent of the elements that make up that object and how they are assembled.
- The construction process must allow different representations of the object to be constructed.

20.6 Constituent Parts

There are a number of different roles within the Builder pattern:

Product A Product represents the abstraction of the complex object under construction.

Concrete Product One or more implementations of the Product; made up of multiple components related as required to meet the overall requirements of the Product.

Builder This role indicates the abstract concept of the producers of the Product objects.

Concrete Builder The concrete implementation of the Builder abstraction used to construct the parts of the product.

Director The role of the director is to use the Builder to construct appropriate parts of the product and then combine them together as required.

Client The Client creates an appropriate Concrete Builder and uses it to configure the Director. The client then requests a configured product from the Director. It is required to supply appropriate information to the Director to allow the director to construct the appropriate representation of the Product.

This is illustrated in Fig. 20.1.

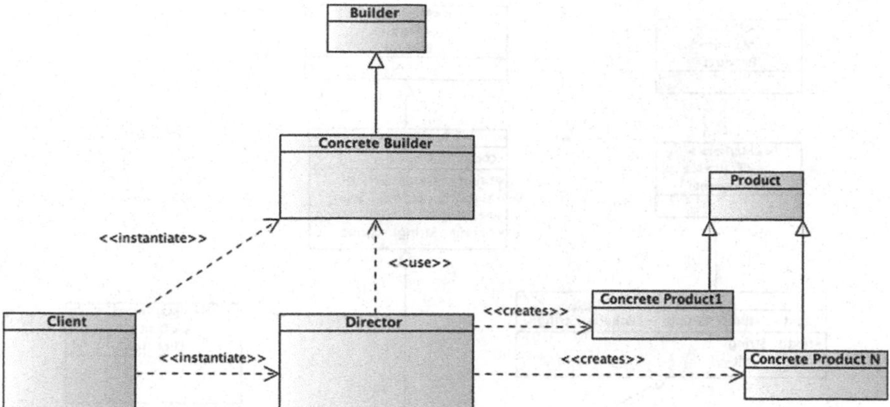

Fig. 20.1 The main participants in the Builder pattern

20.7 Implementation Issues

There are a number of implementation issues to consider with respect to the Builder pattern:

Implementation approach In any Scala implementation there are a variety of different types that could be employed. These range from a Scala Object to a trait, a class and a function. How these types are used within the Builder pattern may vary depending upon your requirements. For example, the Builder and Concrete Builder could be traits that are mixed into the Director as required or could be objects that are referenced by the director. Alternatively the functionality provided by the Builders could be represented as Function types that are passed to, and directly referenced by, the director.

Construction Model Another key implementation issue to consider is that model used for the construction and assembly of the complex object. A model where the results of the construction requests from the Director to the Builder objects may be sufficient or there may need to be a more complex assembly process.

Product Marker The Product abstraction may merely be a Marker trait as the results of the construction process may all differ and have no shared functionality or data.

Builder *interface* The interface made available by the builder to any Director needs to be flexible enough to allow the different elements required as part of the construction process to be created.

20.8 Concrete Example

The simple document creation application takes a series of plain text strings and provides a simple form of textual mark-up for them to create a Text Document version.

The types used in this example are presented in Fig. 20.2.

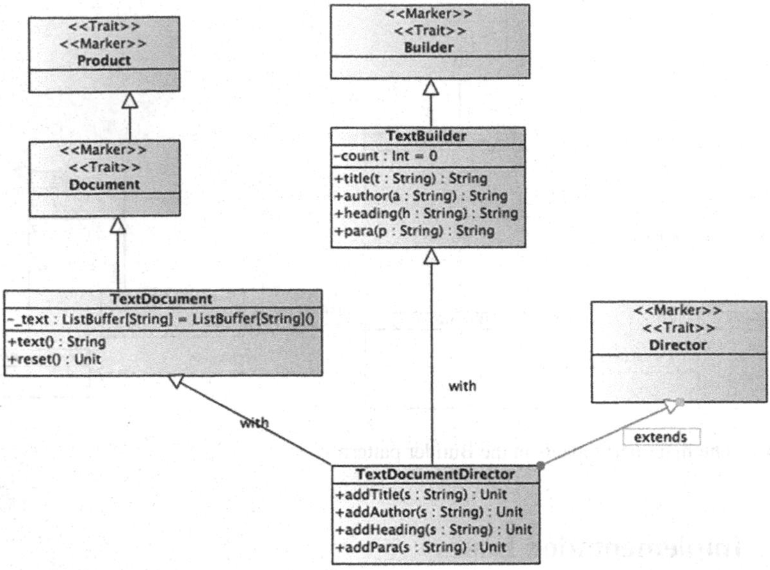

Fig. 20.2 Key types used in the TextDocument example

There are three Marker traits that are used to indicate the roles played by the types in the application. These are the Product, Builder and Director traits:

```
trait Product

trait Builder

trait Director
```

The Document trait captures the semantics of a document product. That is any DocumentBuilder will provide the constituent parts required to create a Document. These parts will be requested by a DocumentDirector that will populate the document.

```
trait Document extends Product
```

The TextDocument represents a simple *textual* document. It holds a set of strings that make up the document in a ListBuffer. This trait can be mixed into any type that requires this basic text document data / behaviour.

```
trait TextDocument extends Document {
  private var _text = ListBuffer[String]()
  def reset: Unit = _text = ListBuffer[String]()
  def text = _text
}
```

The TextBuilder is a Builder that provides the constituent parts that comprise a document. That is, it can be used to create a title, a heading, a paragraph or an author element to add to a TextDocument. Note however, the Builder does not know about the TextBuilder; instead it provides elements that could be combined with different types of container (including a Text Document).

```
trait TextBuilder extends Builder {
  private var count = 0
  def title(t: String) = "title: " + t + "\n"
  def author(a: String) = "by " + a + "\n\n"
  def heading(h: String) = { count += 1; count + ". " + h + "\n" }
  def para(p: String) = p + "\n"

}
```

The TextDocumentDirector is a concrete case class that uses the functionality provided by the TextBuilder to build up a TextDocument. This could be done by instantiating a TextDocument object and a TextBuilder object and referencing them from the TextDocumentDirector (and this is the approach that might be used with a language such as Java). However, in Scala we can use the TextDocument trait and the TextBuilder trait and mix them into the TextDocumentDirector. This avoids the unnecessary construction of additional objects and provides a type safe, compile time, binding for the document and the builder behaviour.

```
case class TextDocumentDirector
               extends Director with TextDocument with TextBuilder {
  def addTitle(s: String): Unit = text += title(s)
  def addAuthor(s: String): Unit = text += author(s)
  def addHeading(s: String): Unit = text += heading(s)
  def addPara(s: String): Unit = text += para(s)
}
```

The simple Test application used with this example is shown below. This application obtains a new instance of the TextDocumentDirector and uses the various add methods to provide a title, an author, a heading and a paragraph for the document. It then retrieves the document from the director and converts it to a string for presentational purposes.

```
object Test extends App {
  val director = TextDocumentDirector()
  director.addTitle("Scala in Depth")
  director.addAuthor("John Smith")
  director.addHeading("Introduction")
  director.addPara("This is Scala.")
  println(director.text.mkString(" "))
}
```

The result of executing this application is shown below:

```
title: Scala in Depth
 by John Smith

 1. Introduction
 This is Scala.
```

20.9 Pros and Cons

The advantages of the Builder Pattern are:

- The construction of a product and its constituent parts are independent of each other. Allowing both to change independently (i.e. a different Director can be used and / or different builders can be used for the parts).
- The whole construction process is encapsulated from the client allowing the process to change without affecting the client.
- Builder provides finer grained control over the Factory pattern as the director has step-by-step control over the creation of the parts of the object to be constructed.

The drawbacks of the Builder Pattern include:

- There is added complexity and variability in the construction of the required objects that can make maintenance and debugging tasks harder.

20.10 Related Patterns

Composite The result of building an object is typically a composite (made up of the parts supplied by the builders).

Factory Object A Factory object is an alternative to the Builder pattern. However the Factory is expected to construct the required product itself and to know all the elements and how they are related.

Chapter 21
Adapter Pattern

21.1 Introduction

The Adapter pattern is one of the original GoF patterns from the original Design Patterns book. As such it has be described many times and implemented in numerous different languages.

An Adapter lets types work together that were not originally designed for such a purpose either because their interfaces are not compatible or because their interfaces are not known to each other.

One of the key advantages of the Adapter pattern is that it allows the functionality promised an interface to be provided without requiring the implementing type to have to implement that interface directly.

Note that the term interface is being used in the generic sense here as the adapter may convert one operation into another, may convert one data format into another or both.

21.2 Pattern Classification

GoF Structural Pattern

21.3 Intent

To convert the interface of one type into the interface that the client expects. Thus the adapter pattern allows types to work together that could not otherwise inter operate.

J. Hunt, *Scala Design Patterns: Patterns for Practical Reuse and Design*,
DOI 10.1007/978-3-319-02192-8_21, © Springer International Publishing Switzerland 2013

21.4 Context

There are numerous scenarios in which the adapter pattern may be relevant, for example:

- When converting the data format from one version of a service to another
- When converting some type that provides required functionality but whose interface names do not directly align with the clients expectations (and the source of the provider cannot be modified possibility because it is not available).
- When allowing types that were not originally designed to work together to cooperate.

As a concrete example, let us assume that a client was written to work with version 1 of some service. As part of the interface the client invokes a method that is given an XML document in a particular format. This format has a field name that is comprised of a users first name and surname. However, in version two of the service the XML format has been modified such that there are now two fields in the XML document, one for firstname and one for surname. The client is no longer compatible with the new service data requirements.

However, a different team to the service provider has implemented the client and there is no budget available to upgrade the client. One option in this situation is to provide both the old and the new service. However, the old service may have budgetary or resource overheads associated with it, may have fundamental issues with performance or its implementation (i.e. bugs) or it may just be that the team do not want to support two versions of the same service.

In this situation one option is to provide an adapter. The adapter sits between the client and the new version of the service and receives all requests. If the request contains version 1 XML format data, then it first translates the XML document into the new format and then invokes the updates operation on the new service.

When the new service returns a result, the same operation can be performed in reverse. That is, the new format result data (containing for example a separate firstname and surname can be converted back into a single name field) and the old format data returned to the client.

In this way the client is buffered from changes made to the service and does not require any modification.

Another common example is where the operations or function names of one type do not align with the expectations of a client (although semantically they are the same). In such a case an adapter can map the expected names to the actual names.

A third scenario is where the client expects a type that implements some abstract concept (which depending upon the implementation language may be an interface, a trait, an abstract class etc.) but the concrete implementation does not actual implement or extend that concept. However, the functionality expected by the client is provided by the concrete type – and thus at a functional level they are compatible from the type system perspective they are incompatible.

21.5 Forces/Motivation

You want to achieve the following:

- To link together to types in which the operations are semantically the same but are not named the same.
- To link together two types in which are functionally the same but where they are not related in the type system.
- To link together two types in which the data formats required are transformable but not directly compatible.
- Some combination of the above.

Where link together may relate to static or dynamic association and may involve structural or invocation based associations.

21.6 Constituent Parts

The solution to the problem addressed by the Adapter pattern involve

- **The Adapter**. An object or a type that converts the interface expected by a client into the interface offered by the Adaptee.
- **The Adaptee**. An object or type that offers an interface that will be invoked by the Adapter.
- **The Client**. An object or type that requires the functionality provided by the Adaptee but expects that interface exposed by the Adapter.

These roles and their relationships are illustrated in Fig. 21.1.

21.7 Implementations

Scala offers a number of ways in which the Adapter Pattern can be realized. These can be categorised into Object based, Class based, Trait based and Function based solutions.

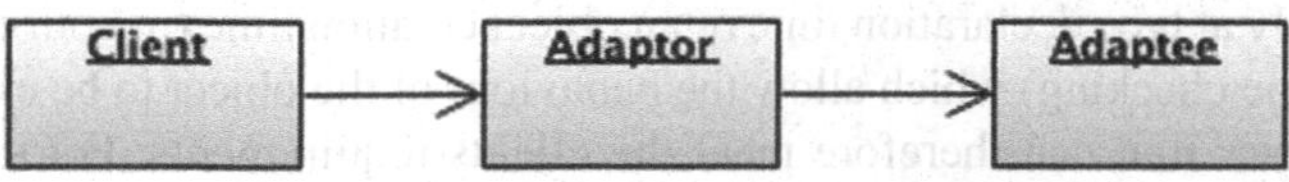

Fig. 21.1 Constituent Parts in the Adapter pattern

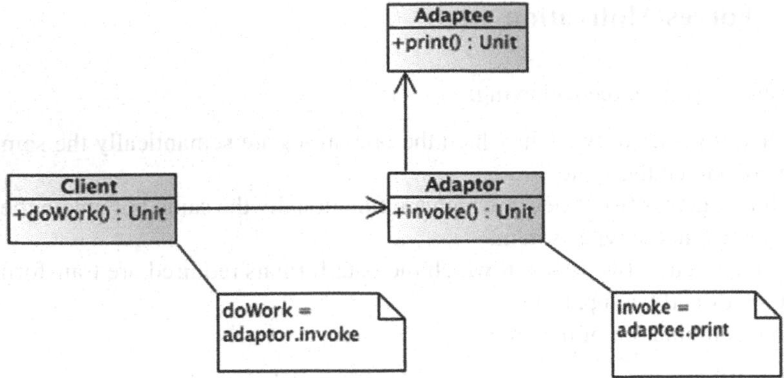

Fig. 21.2 Object based Adapter pattern implementation

21.7.1 Object Based Solution

In this type of implementation of the adapter pattern, the Adapter contains a reference to the Adaptee object (see Fig. 21.2). In this model the Adapter object invokes functionality on the Adaptee converting any data formats or function calls as required.

In Scala this approach can be combined with implicit functions to hide the creation of the Adapter object from the developer. In this case the adapter can be *implicitly* instantiated and provided to the client simplifying the code process for the developer.

21.7.2 Class Based Solution

This approach exploits inheritance to allow an Adapter to extend the Adaptee and to provide the link between the Client's expectations and the Adaptees implementation (see Fig. 21.3). This is done by invoking the Adaptees (inherited) methods from within the operations provide by the Adaptor which meet the clients requirements.

21.7.3 Trait Based Solution

Scala Traits provide a third approach. This allows a Trait to be mixed into a type either directly at type declaration time or an object creation time (in both cases ensuring static type checking) which allow the behaviour of the object to be extended.

An Adapter trait can therefore meet the clients requirements. For example the trait can be mixed into a new type the extends the Adaptee and provides a named type that can be reuse whether the clients interface requirements are found. Alternatively the trait could be mixed into the object when instantiating the Adaptee.

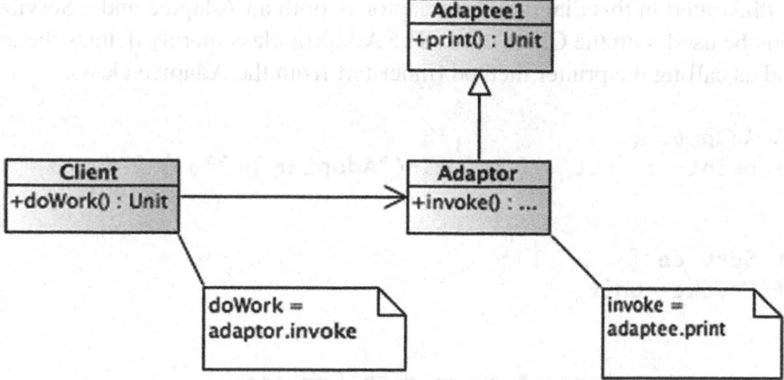

Fig. 21.3 A class-based implementation of the Adapter

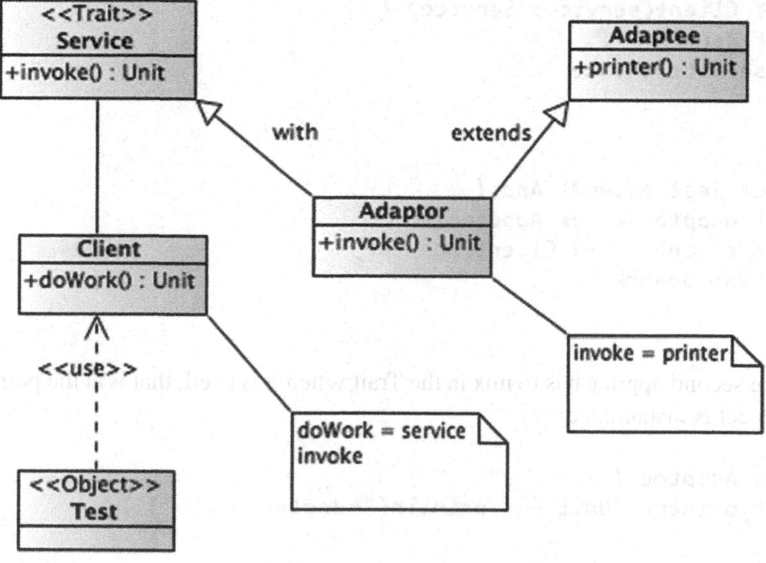

Fig. 21.4 A Trait based implementation of the Adapter pattern

The two approaches are described below.

In this scenario the Client class has been developed to work with classes that implement the Service trait. The Service trait specifies one method invoke which is called by the Client's doWork method. However, the Adaptee class does not mixin the Service trait and is therefore incompatible with the Client. Assuming that we do not have access to the Adaptee source (or for some reason do not want to change that source) we can use the Adapter pattern to *adapt* the Adaptee to a Service object.

The first approach is to create a new class Adaptor that extends the Adaptee and mixes in the Service Trait. This is illustrated in Fig. 21.4.

As illustrated in this diagram the Adaptor is both an Adaptee and a Service and cab thus be used with the Client class. The Adaptor class merely defines the invoke method as calling the printer method (inherited from the Adaptee class).

```
class Adaptee {
  def printer: Unit = { println("Adaptee Hello") }
}

trait Service {
  def invoke: Unit
}

class Adaptor extends Adaptee with Service {
  def invoke = printer
}

class Client(service: Service) {
  def doWork = {
    service invoke
  }
}

object Test extends App {
  val adaptor = new Adaptor()
  val client = new Client(adaptor)
  client doWork
}
```

The second approach is to mix in the Trait when it is need; that is at the point that the object is instantiated:

```
class Adaptee {
  def printer: Unit = { println("Adaptee Hello") }
}

trait Service {
  def invoke: Unit
}

trait Adaptor extends Service {
    self: Adaptee =>
    def invoke = printer
}

class Client(service: Service) {
  def doWork = {
    service invoke
  }
}
```

```
object Test extends App {
  val adaptor = new Adaptee() with Adaptor
  val client = new Client(adaptor)
  client doWork
}
```

In this scenario the Adaptee class does not provide the required invoke method as specified by the Service trait; indeed it does not implement the Service trait. However, the Client class expects to work with a Service type and that the provided object will implement the invoke method. In this case a new Trait Adapter is defined that does extend the Service trait and provides an implementation of invoke. This method calls the printer method of the Adaptee. It is linked to the Adaptee through the use of the explicit self type statement that will tie this trait an object of type Adaptee when the object is instantiated.

The actual weaving of the Adaptee class and the Adaptor trait is done in the Test object allowing the Adaptee to be passed to the Client and the printer method to be run when the *doWork* method is called on the client.

The advantage of this approach is that the Adaptee class has not been modified in any way; which is useful if the source code for the Adaptee is not available etc. The drawback is that by looking at the class Adaptee in isolation, it is not obvious that it can be used with the Client class.

21.7.4 Function Based Solution

In the function based approach new functions can be created from existing functions to meet the operational requirements of the clients. This can be done using anyone of a number of the functional features in the Scala language. Such as composing a new function form existing functions, using partially application to alter the number of parameters expected by a client or currying to create new functions from existing (multiple argument) functions.

Examples of how these language features can be used to implement the Adapter Pattern are provided below.

The simplest way in which a functional approach can be used to adapt one interface to meet the requirements of another is to directly assign one function to another named function using an Object, thereby allowing the first to be invoked via another name (effectively creating an alias for the original function). This avoids the need to create a class merely to link the Adaptor and the Adaptee together and also makes the invoke function directly reference the printer function.

```
class Adaptee {
  def printer: Unit = { println("Adaptee Hello") }
}

trait Service {
  def invoke: Unit
}

class Client(service: Service) {
  def doWork = {
    service invoke
  }
}

object Adaptor extends Service {
  val adaptee = new Adaptee()
  val invoke = adaptee printer
}

object Test extends App {
   val client = new Client(Adaptor)
   client doWork
}
```

Alternatively, if the client expects a single method which would be the equivalent of combining two methods together in sequence in an Adaptee, this can be met using the compose syntax in Scala. This allows two existing functions to be composed into a single function that can be invoked directly.

```
class Adaptee(title: String, name: String) {
  def func1(s: String) = s + " " + name
  def func2(s: String) = s + " " + title
}

object Adapter extends Adaptee("Dr", "Who") {
  val addAndPrint = func1 _ compose func2 _
}

object Client extends App {
   println(Adapter.addAndPrint("->"))
}
```

In the above example, the Client expects to be provided with an object that has a addAndPrint. However, the Adaptee class only has the methods func1 and func2. The Adapter object combines these together in an AddAndPrint function that is

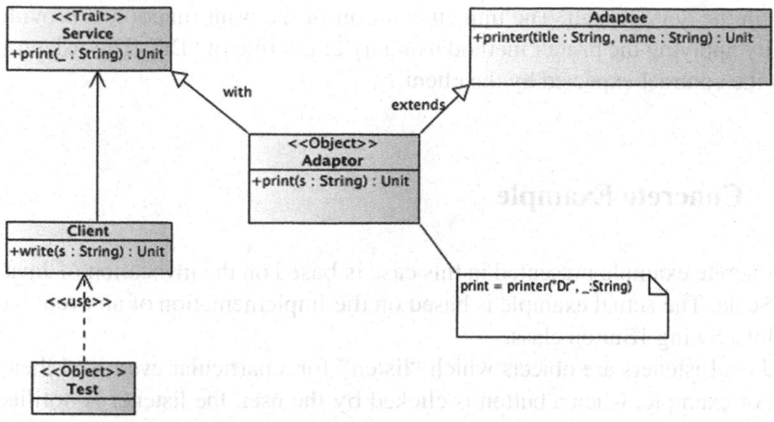

Fig. 21.5 Implementing the Adapter Pattern using partially applied functions

created by composing func1 and func2 together. Alternatives would also include using Partial Functions and combining them together using andThen or orElse.

The final example in this section illustrates how partially applied functions can be used to match the interface requirements of a Client. The approach is illustrated in the following diagram (Fig. 21.5):

The Scala code for this example is shown below:

```
class Adaptee {
  def printer(title: String, name: String) = println(title + " " + name)
}

trait Service {
  val print: String => Unit
}

class Client (service: Service) {
  def write(s: String) = service.print(s)
}

object Adaptor extends Adaptee with Service {
  val print = printer("Dr", _: String)
}

object Test extends App {
  val c = new Client(Adaptor)
  c.write("Who")
}
```

In this example, the Adaptee class defines a method printer that takes two parameters title and name (both of type String). However the Client expects a Service that defines a function print that takes a String and return Unit. To allow the Adaptee to work with the Client an Adaptor object is defined that extends the Adaptee and mixes in the Service trait. The implementation of the print function is provided by partially applying the printer method using a default title of "Dr". The Adaptor now meets the contract expected by the client.

21.8 Concrete Example

The concrete example presented in this case is based on the invocation of Java code from Scala. The actual example is based on the implementation of an event handler for a Java Swing JButton class.

In Java Listeners are objects which "listen" for a particular event and then react to it. For example, when a button is clicked by the user, the listener is notified and decides what action to take. This approach is known, in Java, as the *Event Delegation Model* because the responsibility for handling an event, which occurs in one object, is held by another object. Within this model an event handler is essentially a piece of *functionality* that will be invoked when the button is pressed.

This Event Delegation model is used throughout the Swing GUI classes provided with Java. The general model is that for a graphical component, there is:

- an appropriate event class (such as ActionEvent)
- And appropriate listen interface that an event handler must implement (for example ActionListern)
- An appropriate method on the graphical component that allows instances of the handler class to be registered with the component (e.g. addActionListener on the JButton class)

As our example will explore providing an event handler for a JButton component.

One way to implement this in Scala is to essentially write the Java version but using Scala syntax. For example:

```
val b = new JButton()
b.addActionListener(
  new ActionListener {
    def actionPerformed(e: ActionEvent) {
      println("pressed")
    }
  })
```

However this does not feel very Scala like (as in fact it isn't). It is just Java written using Scala syntax and would look very familiar to any Java programmer (albeit with some ';' etc. missing).

However, what essentially is being done here is that some functionality (what happens when a user presses the button) is being defined and passed to the button to invoke when required. This is a very functional oriented behaviour and one that should be ideally suited to implementation using Scala functions.

This However, if you tried to write this without considering the fact that Java does not (currently) have any concept of a first class function in the language you would get a compilation error:

```
object Test extends App {
  val b = new JButton()
  b.addActionListener( (e: ActionEvent) => println("pressed") )
}
```

The actual compilation error will inform you that you have a type mistmatch. The above code makes available a single parameter function that return Unit while the receiving method expects to be given an ActionListener.

One option here is to provide an Adapter that will adapt a (ActionEvent) => Unit function into an Action Listener. The following AdapterManager object provides a function func2ActionListener that creates an anonymous an Adapter object that implements the required ActionListener interface and invokes the provided function when the actionPerformed method is called.

```
object AdapterManager {
  def func2ActionListener(f: ActionEvent => Unit) =
    new ActionListener {
       def actionPerformed(e: ActionEvent) = f(e)
  }
}
```

This Adapter can then be used to convert the Scala function into the interface required by the JButtons addActionListener method:

```
object Test2 extends App {

  import AdapterManager._

  val b = new JButton
  b.addActionListener(
      func2ActionListener(
         (_: ActionEvent) => println("pressed")
      )
  )

}
```

In this case I am importing the AdapterManager however I could just as easily have used AdapterManager.func2ActionListener within the addActionListener method call.

However, this does look a bit awkward and may not be the easiest code to read (although it is explicit and makes it clear that the Scala function is being adapted into the ActionListener interface). However, Scala provides the ability to implicitly apply methods when necessary. This allows the Adapter pattern to be applied without the developer necessarily being aware of it.

We can mark the func2ActionListener method in the AdapterManager as implicit. This means that Scala will apply it in situations where

```
object AdapterManager {
  implicit def func2ActionListener(f: ActionEvent => Unit) =
    new ActionListener {
      def actionPerformed(e: ActionEvent) = f(e)
  }
}
```

This means that we can now write

```
object Test3 extends App {

  import AdapterManager._

  val b = new JButton()
  b.addActionListener((_: ActionEvent) => println("pressed"))

}
```

Which now allows a far more natural Scala syntax to be used and one which semantically states what is being done. When the user clicks the button the function ActionEvent => Unit will be called to print the message pressed.

The fact that the function literal is underlined indicates (in Eclipse Scala IDE) that an implicit conversion is taking place. The issue here may be that in a complex application, with many imports, it may not be obvious what conversion is actually being performed.

21.9 Pros and Cons

The primary advantages of the Adapter are:

- The client and Adaptee classes remain independent of each other.
- The adapter can dynamically determine which of the Adaptees operations to invoke allow for both flexibility but yet further complexity n the solution.

The main disadvantage of the Adapter is:

- The Adapter pattern introduces an additional indirection into the program (for example if *implicits* are used it may not be immediately obvious to the developer what is going on) and may contribute to the complexity in understanding the implementation.

21.10 Related Patterns

Bridge The Bridge pattern's structure can be similar to that of the adapter pattern, however the semantics of the bridge pattern are different. The bridge pattern aims to separate the client-facing *interface* for a concept from the *implementation* of that concept. This allows the implementation to be varied depending upon the needs of the situation. In contrast the adapter pattern aims to change the *interface* it presents to client code for an *existing* type.

Façade A Façade provides a standardised (often simplified) client-facing *interface* to multiple objects/types. An Adapter presents the interface for a single object and is oriented around making that interface suit the needs of the client.

Proxy A Proxy provides an intermediate object that appears to be the actual object, but which is in fact a surrogate for that object. As such it has the same client-facing *interface* as the actual object.

Decorator The aim of the decorator pattern is that it introduces new functionality to an object where as the adapter pattern merely aims to present the functionality that already exists via a new client-facing *interface*.

Strategy The structure of the Strategy pattern is similar to that of the Adapter pattern, however the semantics/intent of the two patterns are completely different. The aim of the Strategy pattern is to allow different implementations for a client-facing *interface* to be provided. The aim of the Adapter pattern is to change the client-facing *interface* of an *existing* type to meet the needs of a given client.

Delegation Delegation is closely linked to the way in which the Adapter delegates responsibility for the implementation onto another function/type.

Dependency Injection Dependency Injection can be used in support of the Adapter pattern when injecting the Adaptee into the Adapter as required.

Chapter 22
Decorator

22.1 Introduction

The Decorator Design pattern extends the behaviour of an object without using sub classing. This decoration of an object is transparent to the decorators' clients.

As the Decorator pattern is one of the original Gang Of Four patterns it is very well understood and widely used.

22.2 Pattern Classification

Gang Of Four Structural Pattern

22.3 Intent

To dynamically attach additional behaviour to an object (without the use of subtyping).

22.4 Context

In some cases it is necessary to add additional behaviour to specific objects rather than to an entire class of objects. For example, we might want to add different embellishments to a basic window depending on how we are going to use (as a main window, as a pop up dialog, as a menu etc.).

One way to add such additional behaviour is to decorate the objects created with types that provide the extra functionality.

J. Hunt, *Scala Design Patterns: Patterns for Practical Reuse and Design*,
DOI 10.1007/978-3-319-02192-8_22, © Springer International Publishing Switzerland 2013

22.5 Forces/Motivation

The Decorator pattern can be used when

- it is necessary to add behaviour to an individual object dynamically and transparently to the client, without affecting other objects.
- this behaviour may also need to be withdrawn in some cases.
- extension by sub classing is not possible (such as with Java's final classes).
- there are very many possible decorations which may need to be selected depending upon the situation.

22.6 Constituent Parts

The constituent parts of the Decorator pattern are:

Service An abstraction representing the concept to be decorated.
Concrete Service A concrete implementation of the service concept.
Decorator The abstract type defining the behaviour to be added to an object.
Concrete Decorator A concrete implementation of the Decorator that provides the extended behaviour to be added to the services.
Client A client that requires the behaviour added to the service.

These are illustrated in Fig. 22.1.

22.7 Implementation Issues

There are a number of issues to consider when implementing the Decorator pattern in Scala. For example, the most basic question is how to implement the Decorator. One approach is to use a very object oriented style in which the decorators are

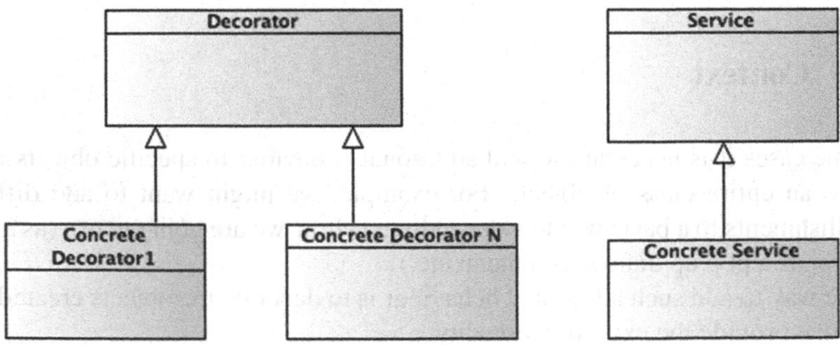

Fig. 22.1 Constituent parts of the Decorator pattern

objects that have the same interface as the main service with the addition of any new behaviour. The decorator then delegates to the service for the behaviour it already provides and directly implements the new behaviour. This is the approach that is usually adopted in languages such as Java and can certainly be used with Scala. Its primary advantage in the Scala world is that the decorator can be dynamically added to the service object as a runtime configuration and this may have significant advantages.

However, an alternative approach is to define the Decorators as traits and to mix these traits in to the object at the point of instantiation. This has both the advantage of being a static compile time construct (with the inherent compilation verification and validation) and the disadvantage that it is a compile time configuration (and thus less flexible).

Which approach should be adopted will depend on your own situation and requirements. For example, if you need to dynamically change the decorators used with an object, during its lifetime, then the runtime approach of fronting the service object with separate decorator objects may well be your best option. However, if this is not required I would generally stick with the trait-based approach as my default.

22.8 Concrete Example

The application used in this section is based on decorating a simple FileReader object with further readers that provide additional behaviour (in this case buffering and synchronization of the data reading process).

The structure of these types is illustrated in Fig. 22.2.

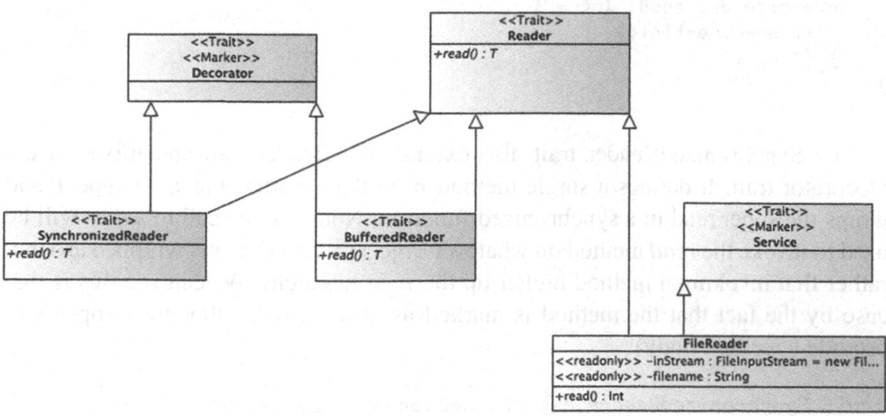

Fig. 22.2 The types used in Decorator the FileReader

The types in this application are described below:

The Decorator trait is a marker trait indicating the role of any sub type or object using this trait.

```
trait Decorator
```

The Service trait is a marker trait indicating the service role being played by any sub type or object using this trait.

```
trait Service
```

The Reader trait is a trait defining the abstraction representing the Reader concept. It defines a *read* method that returns a value of type T. Note that in this case rather than using generics to create a parameterized class we are using the type declaration mechanism in Scala to allow the type to be returned to be specified by a sub type of Reader. Both generics and this approach could have been used and this example merely provides an alternative to the generic approach.

```
trait Reader {
    type T
    def read: T
}
```

The FileReader class mixes in the Reader trait and the Service trait. It defines the type T as being *Int* resulting in the *read* method returning objects of type Int. It also creates a scanner val member that holds a reference to a Scanner (containing a FileInputStream) that is used in the read method.

```
class FileReader(file: String) extends Reader with Service {
   private val scanner = new Scanner(new FileInputStream(file))
   type T = Int
   override def read: Int = {
     scanner.nextInt()
   }
}
```

The SynchronizedReader trait also extends the Reader trait and mixes in the Decorator trait. It defines a single method *read* that returns objects of type T and wraps the super.read in a synchronized function. Note that the call to *super* will be used to invoke the *read* method on whatever object this decorator is wrapped around, rather that invoking a method higher up the type hierarchy. We can see this is that case by the fact that the method is marked as abstract (even though it appears to provide a method body).

```
trait SynchronizedReader extends Reader with Decorator {
    abstract override def read: T = synchronized(super.read)
}
```

The BufferedReader, like the SynchronizedReader, is a decorator that also provides an abstract override read method that could buffer reads before returning a result.

```
trait BufferedReader extends Reader with Decorator {
    abstract override def read: T = {
        //buffering code
        super.read
    }
}
```

The simple Test application used with these types is shown below:

```
object Test extends App {
  //Now we can mix in stuff that we need
    //Create a FileReader
    val f = new FileReader("Test.txt")
    println(f.read)
    //create a fileReader which is synchronized
    val syncReader = new FileReader("Test.txt") with SynchronizedReader
    println(syncReader.read)
    //create a fileReader which is synchronized and buffered
    val bsReader = new FileReader("Test.txt")
                                with BufferedReader
                                with SynchronizedReader
    println(bsReader.read)
}
```

This test application creates a FileReader, a FileReader decorated with a Synchronized Reader and a FileReader decorated with a Synchronized Reader and a Buffered Reader.

22.9 Pros and Cons

The advantages of the Decorator Pattern are:

- **More flexibility than sub type inheritance**. As a Decorator can be added to a wide range of objects as required it provides a very flexible approach to extending the behaviour of a type. This can be done when that behaviour is needed rather than permanently defined as part of the (less flexible) static type hierarchy.
- **Avoids feature-laden types** by enabling lightweight types with rich interfaces. A problem with simple type inheritance is that it can result in types higher up the hierarchy possessing large amounts of functionality that may or may not be required by types further down the hierarchy. This is done to ensure the rich interfaces that might be required by potential clients but results in bloated type definitions. The use of decorators allows the type hierarchy to be lightweight

(in terms of the behaviour defined within the type hierarchy) but expressive in terms of the concepts represented by the types. By using Decorators the final interface offered by a type can still be both rich and functional
- **Fewer types**. By using different combinations of a few different kinds of Decorators, it is possible to create many different combinations of behaviour. The equivalent using traditional sub typing would require more types to be defined.

The drawbacks of the Decorator Pattern include:

- **Flexibility of decorators can lead to problems**. For example, it is possible to combine the decorators with service objects in ways that do not make sense or are cause confusion.
- **Additional objects**. Depending upon the implementation approach adopted, the decorator pattern can result in additional objects being created. For example, if each decorator is treated as a separate object (rather than as a Trait) then each decoration added to a service object results in an additional object being created with additional links and method invocations.
- **Limitations on use of object identity**. If an object-based approach is used to the addition of decorators; object identity for the underlying service may be lost and thus cannot be used to uniquely reference that service. This is not a problem with the trait-based approach.
- **More complexity**. Due to the way in which decorators are added to objects as required, it may become difficult to maintain or extend a system which makes extensive use of decorators.

22.10 Related Patterns

Adapter An adapter alters the interface of one object to meet the client's requirements, where as the Decorator pattern adds behaviour to meet the client's requirements.

Composite The Composite pattern is oriented around object aggregation whereas the Decorator pattern is focussed on adding new behaviour to an existing object.

Strategy A Decorator allows the external interface of an object to be extended where as the Strategy Pattern allows the internal implementation to be changed.

CAKE Pattern for Dependency Injection This pattern uses a similar structure to allow objects to be combined at the point of use rather than via the type hierarchy. Although the end result may be similar the semantics of the intention is different.

Chapter 23
Façade

23.1 Introduction

This pattern allows a (simplifying) object to unify a (potentially more complex) interface to a set of objects. The Façade can often be viewed as an *interface* to a subsystem. It has the effect of simplifying the interface between the clients and the subsystem objects. This is illustrated in Fig. 23.1 where a client only has to deal with a single Façade object. The Façade object then deals with the interactions with multiple subsystem objects.

23.2 Pattern Classification

Gang Of Four Structural Pattern

23.3 Intent

To simplify access to a related set of objects, by providing one object that all client objects outside the set, can use to interact with that set.

23.4 Context

A recurring theme in applications is the need for client code to interact with a set of other objects in order to achieve some goal. This may be because it is necessary to construct a complex structure, or because numerous objects must be invoked to achieve the end result (sometimes in a specific sequence).

J. Hunt, *Scala Design Patterns: Patterns for Practical Reuse and Design*,
DOI 10.1007/978-3-319-02192-8_23, © Springer International Publishing Switzerland 2013

Fig. 23.1 The Facade pattern

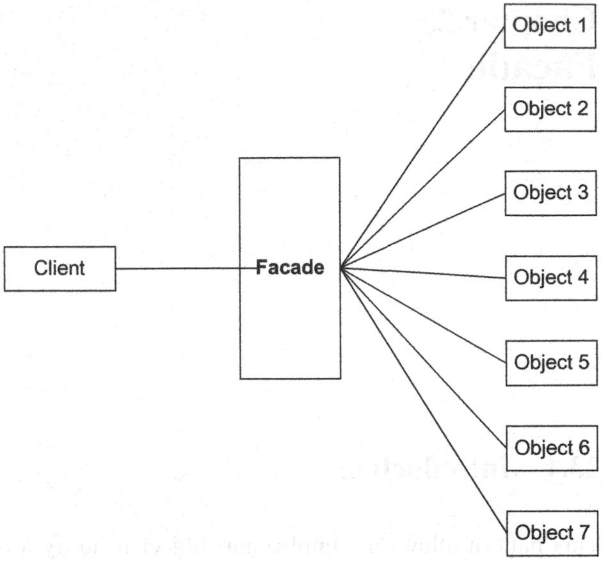

Without a Façade each client would need to interact with all of the individual elements resulting in numerous interaction paths and potential complex dependencies.

A common example used with Facades is that of creating an email message. An Email message is comprised of several entities that all need to be constructed and linked together in an appropriate manner. For example, as well as the Message Body there is a Message Header that combine together to form a Message. The Message may have attachments and there may also be security related information. Once the message has been created a Message Sender must be used to actually send the message.

Any Messaging sending client code must therefore interact with six different types with at least six entities (more if there are multiple attachments etc.) and must connect these entities together in an appropriate way.

By using a Message Facade it is possible to simplify the clients' view of the world to a single object with a simplified interface. The Message Façade then interacts with the additional six types and knows how to construct the email message and how to send it.

23.5 Forces/Motivation

Situations which motivate the use of the Façade pattern include:

- Clients with many dependencies on other types that must be instantiated, configured or invoked in potentially complex ways.
- The dependencies between the client and the implementing types add significantly to the complexity of the client code.

- The interactions present in one client are repeated in several additional classes resulting in the complexity being propagated.
- Packaging a set of classes behind a Façade decouples those classes and their implementations from the their clients, thereby allow for future development, enhancement and modification of the implementing classes.

23.6 Constituent Parts

The constituent parts of the Façade Pattern are the client of the Façade, the Façade itself and the set of objects that the Façade encapsulates. This is illustrated in Fig. 23.2 and are described below.

Client The client object (typically) only interacts with the Façade and knows nothing about the set of objects behind the Façade.

Façade The Façade object provides links to the actual implementing objects and provides a suitable (typically simplified) interface to the client.

Façade members Members of the set of objects behind the Façade. These objects (typically) are unaware of the Façade and may or may not have been developed at the same time as the Façade.

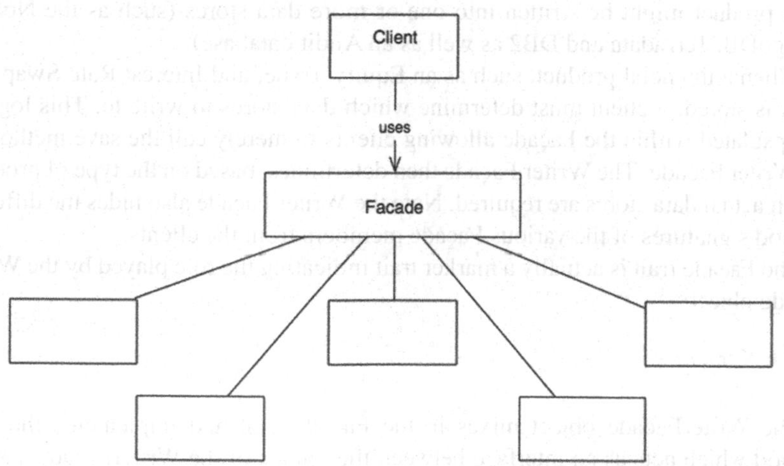

Fig. 23.2 Client and Facade relationships

23.7 Implementation Issues

It is not necessary for the Façade to be an impenetrable barrier for clients. In some cases it may be better for the Façade to be a default access mechanism but to allow clients to access the set of classes *internal* to the Façade when required (for example for exceptional behaviour or situations).

The Façade may be a Scala class or a Scala object. If the Façade is a singleton object then the use of a Scala Object is preferred. However, this presumes a singleton instance and limits the ability to sub class the Façade itself.

In some cases the actual objects that are used behind the façade may change depending upon the implementation requirement. For example, a different set of classes might be used behind a Data Access layer Façade for DB2, than for a NoSQL database such as MongoDB or for a data store such as Terradata.

The Façade class may mix in one or more traits to provide a generic Façade concept that is implemented by concrete Façade classes.

23.8 Concrete Example

The code example presented in this chapter is based on the idea of creating a Façade that handles writing different types of financial product to appropriate data stores. Each product might be written into one or more data stores (such as the NoSQL MongoDB, Terradata and DB2 as well as an Audit database).

When a financial product, such as an Equity Trade, and Interest Rate Swap or a Loan is stored, a client must determine which data stores to write to. This logic is encapsulated within the Façade allowing clients to merely call the save method on the Writer Facade. The Writer Façade then determines, based on the type of product, which actual data stores are required. Note the Writer Façade also hides the different method signatures of the various Façade members from the clients.

The Façade trait is actually a marker trait indicating the role played by the Writer Façade object:

```
trait Facade
```

The WriterFacade object mixes in the Façade trait and implements the save method which acts as an interface between the clients of the WriterFacade and the members of the façade.

```
object WriterFacade extends Facade {
  def save(product: Product) = product match {
    case trade: EquityTrade => { MongoDBWriter.write(trade); TerradataWriter.save(trade) }
    case irs: InterestRateSwap => { TerradataWriter.save(irs); DefaultWriter.write(irs) }
    case loan: Loan => DB2Writer.store(loan)
    case _ => DefaultWriter.write(product)
  }
}
```

When a financial product is passed to the save method, pattern matching is used to determine the actual type of the parameter and to decide the action required. For example, if the product parameter is actually an Equity Trade it must be written into the MongoDB and Terradata data stores. However, if the product is actually an Interest Rate Swap then it is written to the Terradata and Default data stores. Whereas if it is a loan it is only written into the loan specific DB2 datastore. Any other type of financial product is written to the Default data store.

The Four different types of data store are represented here by four Scala Objects that merely print out a message. The four Façade members are listed below:

The basic Default Writer:

```
object DefaultWriter {
  def write(p: Product): Unit = println("Default writer: " + p)
}
```

The MongoDB Writer:

```
object MongoDBWriter {
  def write(trade: EquityTrade): Unit = println("MongoDBWriter.write: " + trade)
}
```

The Terradata Writer:

```
object TerradataWriter {
  def save(product: Product): Unit = println("TerradataWriter.save: " + product)
}
```

The DB2 Writer:

```
object DB2Writer {
  def store(loan: Loan): Unit = println("DB2Writer.store: " + loan)
}
```

The financial products used with this application are modelled using a trait Product and three case classes that mix in that trait. Again the trait is a marker trait. The Product and the three classes are presented here:

```
trait Product
case class EquityTrade(val id: String,
                       val stock: String,
                       val quantity: Double) extends Product
case class InterestRateSwap(val id: String,
                            val nominal: Double,
                            val fixedRate: Double,
                            val floatIndex: String) extends Product
case class Loan(val id: String,
                val borrower: String,
                val facility: Double) extends Product
```

The simple test client for this Façade is shown below:

```
object Test extends App {
  val trade = EquityTrade("1", "IBM", 100)
  val irs = InterestRateSwap("2", 10000, 1.4, "LIBOR")
  val loan = Loan("3", "John", 1000)
  WriterFacade.save(trade)
  WriterFacade.save(irs)
  WriterFacade.save(loan)
}
```

The result of running this application is:

```
MongoDBWriter.write: EquityTrade(1,IBM,100.0)
TerradataWriter.save: EquityTrade(1,IBM,100.0)
TerradataWriter.save: InterestRateSwap(2,10000.0,1.4,LIBOR)
Default writer: InterestRateSwap(2,10000.0,1.4,LIBOR)
DB2Writer.store: Loan(3,John,1000.0)
```

23.9 Pros and Cons

The advantages of the Façade Pattern are:

- Clients of the Façade do not need to know anything about the objects behind the façade.
- There is a single dependency between the client and the façade.
- Changes can be made to the objects behind the Façade with little or no impact on the client.

The drawbacks of the Façade Pattern include:

- The Façade must be able to deal with at least the typical range of interactions required by clients.
- Client may need to *get behind* the Façade for edge case or exception scenarios.

23.10 Related Patterns

Delegate A Delegate can be viewed as a Façade with a single object behind the Façade.

Chapter 24
Flyweight

24.1 Introduction

The Flyweight pattern allows a large number of similar objects to be reduced in number to a small set of shared objects. This has benefits in terms of memory overheads, object creation, object destruction etc. However, the state of the shared objects may need to be analysed to determine which parts of the state can be shared (and permanently stored internally to the object) and which parts of the state need to be externalized and provided by a client of the shared object each time it accesses that object.

24.2 Pattern Classification

Gang Of Four Structural Pattern

24.3 Intent

To allow fine-grained objects to be shared, avoiding the expense of multiple instances.

24.4 Context

If an application does not consider how and where it is using objects then it may be dynamically creating essentially the same object many times. These objects may be referenced briefly and then discarded. The impact on the runtime environment could be massive with significant additional memory requirements additional garbage collection processing and overall reductions in performance.

J. Hunt, *Scala Design Patterns: Patterns for Practical Reuse and Design*,
DOI 10.1007/978-3-319-02192-8_24, © Springer International Publishing Switzerland 2013

If these objects are essentially the same, and particularly if they share state information and are immutable, it may not have been necessary to create multiple copies of the same data. If a framework was provided that allowed these objects to be easily shared significant benefits may be obtained. This is the intention of the Flyweight pattern.

Note that in Java (and thus in Scala) strings are immutable objects that are treated as flyweights, that is one string "John" is shared between all the references to that string by the JVM.

24.5 Forces/Motivation

The Flyweight pattern can be used where

- Applications use a large number of similar objects.
- The application may benefit from reducing the number of objects created and garbage collected.
- Storage costs are high due to the quantity of objects created.
- The context associated with the object is enough to represent the object, that is no unique reference or object identity is required.

24.6 Constituent Parts

The primary roles in the Flyweight pattern are illustrated in Fig. 24.1.
The roles in the Flyweight pattern are described below:

Flyweight This represents the core Flyweight concept. It may define how the extrinsic state of the object is received and acted upon (or it may simply be a marker trait).

Shared Concrete Flyweight A Concrete implementation of the Flyweight concept that is inherently designed to be a shared object.

Unshared Concrete Flyweight In situations it may not be possible to share the flyweight objects, for these situations an unshared Concrete Flyweight object can be used. However, to gain the maximum benefit from the Flyweight pattern, the unshared flyweights should be kept to a minimum.

Flyweight Factory The client of a Flyweight is not responsible for creating the Flyweight. Instead a factory object is used to manage the creation and supply of flyweights. In this way the Factory is able to ensure that flyweights are shared amongst clients in an appropriate manner.

Client The Client obtains flyweights form the Flyweight Factory and (may set their intrinsic sate) and uses the functionality provided by the flyweight as required. It may or may not maintain a reference to that flyweight.

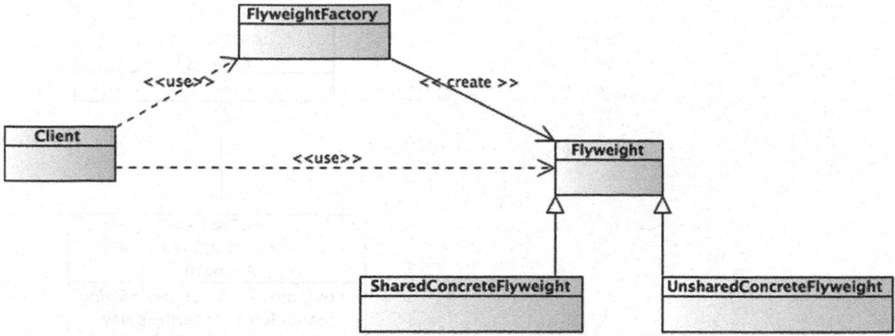

Fig. 24.1 Constituent elements in the Flyweight pattern

24.7 Implementation Issues

It may be necessary to consider what should be viewed as the internal (intrinsic state) of the shared object. Here state refers to the values held in the properties of the object between its use by one client and another client. By externalising some of that state we may be able to increase the scope of the shared objects.

Thus, the state used by the flyweight is characterised as either intrinsic or extrinsic. The client of the flyweight must provide the extrinsic state.

It is also necessary to decide how the factory will manage the flyweights and under what circumstances it shares objects (and when it does not). It may also be necessary to decide how and when a client releases that flyweight (or how it returns it to the factory for reuse).

24.8 Concrete Example

The simple scenario used in this section illustrates how account information, required by multiple trade objects, can be shared using flyweight accounts.

Figure 24.2 illustrates the structure of the application:

The Flyweight trait is a marker trait used to indicate the Flyweight role in the application.

```
trait Flyweight
```

The Account trait defines the abstract read only properties *number, counterparty* and *valid*. The Account represents the account for a counter party involved in various trades. As the account used for any number of trades by a counter party is the same account it can be shared amongst all the trades. Note that the account is immutable as it represents information about an account (such as the counter parties name,

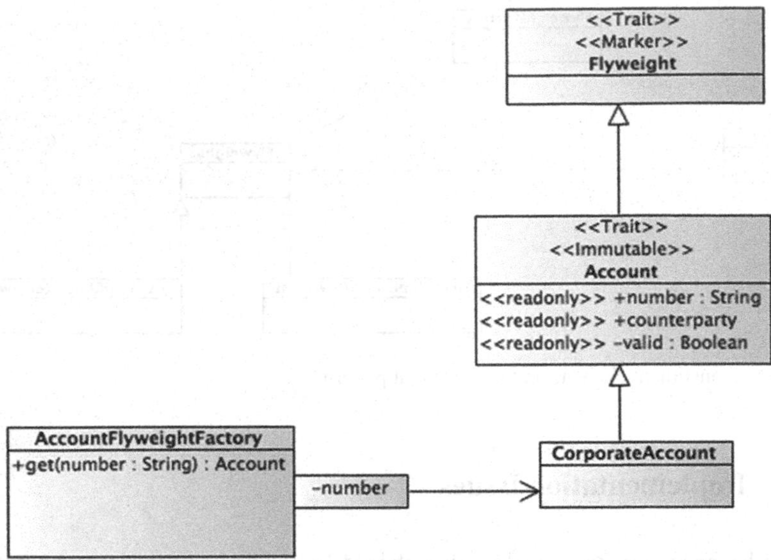

Fig. 24.2 The structure of the trade account application

their account number and whether the account is valid or not). It is not the actual account and thus does not have a balance or set of transactions associated with it.

```
trait Account extends Flyweight with Immutable {
  val number: String
  val couterparty: String
  val valid: Boolean
}
```

The Account trait extends the Flyweight trait and mixes in the Immutable (marker) trait. This illustrates both its role and the semantics of the Account.

The Corporate Account case class mixes in the Account trait and defines three read only properties for the (account) number, the counterparty name and the valid indicator (which is defaulted to true). A println is used to show when a Corporate Account is created.

```
case class CorporateAccount(val number: String,
                            val couterparty: String,
                            val valid: Boolean = true) extends Account {
  println("Creating Corporate Account: " + number)
}
```

The AccountFlyweightFactory is a singleton object that is used to provide Account objects on demand. If the account object has already been requested then that flyweight object is reused for the new request. Thus multiple clients can use the same Account object.

```
object AccountFlyweightFactory {
  val map = HashMap[String, Account]()
  def get(number: String): Account = {
    return map.getOrElseUpdate(number,
                               CorporateAccount(number,
                                                retrieveName(number)))
  }
  private def retrieveName(number: String): String = {
    return "John" + number
  }
}
```

The simple Test application used to illustrate how this framework is used is shown below:

```
object Test extends App {
  val a1 = AccountFlyweightFactory.get("111")
  println(a1)
  val a2 = AccountFlyweightFactory.get("222")
  println(a2)
  val a3 = AccountFlyweightFactory.get("111")
  println(a3)
  // Check for referential equality
  println(a1.eq(a3))
}
```

The result of running the sample application is listed below:

```
Creating Corporate Account: 111
CorporateAccount(111,John111,true)
Creating Corporate Account: 222
CorporateAccount(222,John222,true)
CorporateAccount(111,John111,true)
true
```

This shows that although three requests were made to the factory for account objects, only two were instantiated (as the 111 account was reused).

24.9 Pros and Cons

The advantages of the Flyweight Pattern are:

- Reduces the storage requirements of the application
- Reduces the number of object creations and destruction that occur and may therefore improve performance of an application.

The drawbacks of the Flyweight Pattern include:

- It introduces additional runtime costs, as the clients may need to set the extrinsic state of the objects.
- There is additional complexity in the application, as the Flyweight Factory must manage the sharing of flyweights.
- Debugging and maintenance may be made more difficult as any one object may be shared amongst several clients.

24.10 Related Patterns

Marker Trait Flyweights may be indicated via a marker trait.
Factory The Flyweight Factory is an example of the Factory pattern.
Singleton The Flyweight Factory may be a singleton object.
Composite This may be combined with the Flyweight pattern to represent complex hierarchical structures.
Immutable The shared flyweight objects are often designed to be immutable.

Chapter 25
Proxy

25.1 Introduction

The Proxy pattern uses a placeholder whose interface resembles the actual object and that is used by clients rather than the client directly accessing the actual object. The Proxy may manage access to the actual object.

The Proxy pattern may be used in a number of situations. It may be used because

- the actual service is expensive to create and should only be done so lazily when required (known as a Virtual Proxy),
- the actual service requires protection, for example, via access controls for security reasons (known as a Protection Proxy),
- the actual service is remote and we wish local clients to access the proxy as a local object and for the proxy to handle the complexities of remote access (known as a Remote Proxy).

It may be argued that Scala's built in ability to lazily initialise objects means that the Virtual Proxy version of the Proxy pattern is no longer required. However, the key here is that if you rely on just the language feature, you must ensure that everyone who accesses the service, must do so appropriately. If you expect them to all access the service lazily then you must ensure that this is done by all the clients, just one piece of code accessing it without the keyword lazy may defeat your purpose. So how can you ensure this? You can of course provide documentation, comments, wiki pages for developers to read and you can arrange for code reviews to check that client source code access the service in prescribed ways etc. But can you guarantee that no one makes a change that overrides your intended actions? This is also an issue for the Protection and remote versions of the Proxy pattern.

25.2 Pattern Classification

Gang Of Four Structural Pattern

J. Hunt, *Scala Design Patterns: Patterns for Practical Reuse and Design*,
DOI 10.1007/978-3-319-02192-8_25, © Springer International Publishing Switzerland 2013

25.3 Intent

To make use of a surrogate or placeholder for another object allowing controlled access to that object or for that object to be created lazily.

25.4 Context

Utilizing the Proxy pattern allows standardised access to the service ensuring that all client code accesses the service in the appropriate manner. Scala can certainly make this easier (using the lazy keyword and by limiting the visibility of the actual Service implementation) but this does not inherently deprecate the pattern.

25.5 Forces/Motivation

The Proxy Pattern can be used where it is

- Time consuming to instantiate objects.
- Expensive in terms of system resources (such as memory) to instantiate very many objects
- Instantiating an object per client is unnecessary as target objects do not hold state.
- The apparent performance of the application may be improved by reducing the number of objects created and destroyed.
- Avoiding placing the responsibility/burden on client code to determine whether to lazily instantiate the service or not.

25.6 Constituent Parts

The primary roles within the Proxy pattern are:

Service This role representation the abstract (or generic concept) that is implemented by the service implementation and whose *interface* is mirrored by the proxy.

Service Implementation The concrete implementation of the service concept.

Proxy Implementation The concrete implementation that provides the operations in the Service by utilizing the behaviour in the Service implementation. May lazily instantiate the Service Implementation or may protect access to the service implementation etc. as required.

Client Uses the proxy to access the service implementation. Should not have direct access to the service implementation.

These roles are illustrated in Fig. 25.1.

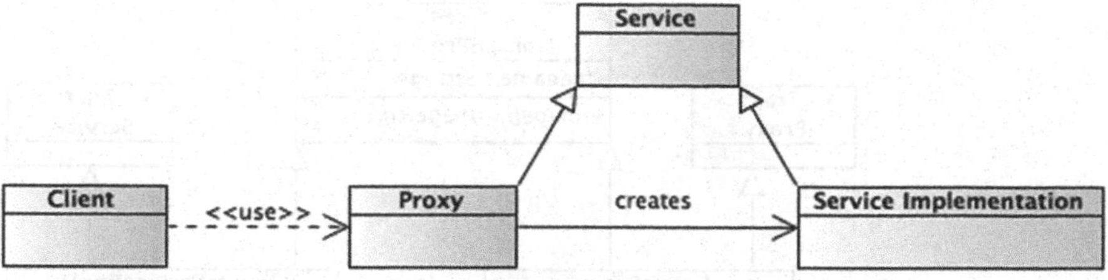

Fig. 25.1 Constituent parts in the Proxy pattern

25.7 Implementation Issues

It may be argued that in Scala there is no need for the proxy pattern as the language inherently provides the *lazy* keyword to allow for lazy (on demand) instantiation of objects. However, this misses the point of the Proxy pattern. It allows the proxy to handle the creation of and/or access to the actual service implementation as appropriate. For a Protection and Remote proxies, the lazy keyword is no help. Even for the Virtual Proxy the lazy keyword merely makes it easier to implement the Proxy pattern rather than replacing it.

Client code must be also be restricted from accessing the service directly, ideally using the language constructs to ensure that the service type is not visible to the client code.

25.8 Concrete Example

The simple application used to illustrate the Proxy pattern provides a proxy that lazily loads an image when the contents of that image is actually required, rather than when the Proxy is created. Thus the cost of reading the image file, loading the image data into memory and creating an image object is avoided unless the image is actually used.

The structure of the application is shown in Fig. 25.2.

The Proxy trait is a marker trait used to indicate the role of the relevant types.

```
trait Proxy
```

The Service trait is another marker trait used to indicate the role of types implementing a service.

```
trait Service
```

The ImageProvider trait is a *interface* oriented trait used to define the behaviour of classes supplying an image (i.e. they must implement the image method). It also

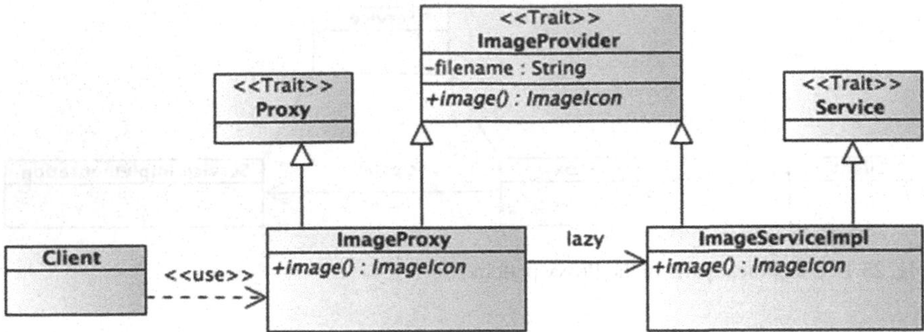

Fig. 25.2 Structure of the Proxy pattern example application

defines an abstract read only property *filename*. It is mixed into the ImageProxy and the ImageServiceImpl.

```
trait ImageProvider {
  val filename: String
  def image: ImageIcon
}
```

The Image Proxy is a class that defines a lazily initialized ImageService and delegates access to that object when required. Note that as far as a client of the ImageProxy is concerned it *is* the service that will supply the image.

```
case class ImageProxy(filename: String) extends Proxy with ImageProvider {
  println("Creating ImageProxy")
  private lazy val service = new ImageServiceImpl(filename)
  def image: ImageIcon = service.image
  override def toString = "Proxy for: " + filename
}
```

The ImageServiceImpl is a class that implements the functionality required to load an Image as specified by the ImageService trait. It is private to the package and is thus not visible outside of the Proxy package. It possesses a private member _ image which is used to hold the ImageIcon created to represent the required image. This object is returned as the result of the image method.

```
private class ImageServiceImpl(val filename: String)
                        extends Service with ImageProvider {
  println("Creating ImageServiceImpl")
  private val _image = new ImageIcon(filename)
  def image: ImageIcon = _image
}
```

The simple Test application written to illustrating the use of the Proxy pattern.

```
object test extends App {
  val proxy = ImageProxy("help.jpg")
  println(proxy)
  val image = proxy.image
  println(image)
}
```

The application first creates an ImageProxy and prints out the proxy. It then accesses the image itself and prints out the image.

The result of running this application is shown below:

```
Creating ImageProxy
Proxy for: help.jpg
Creating ImageServiceImpl
help.jpg
```

As you can see form this example, the ImageServiceImpl is only created when the image is actually required.

25.9 Pros and Cons

The advantages of the Proxy Pattern are:

- Standardised access to the service, e.g. all clients instantiate the service lazily or provide common secure access to the service.
- Clients do not need to be aware of the use of lazy initialization, or secured access etc.

The drawbacks of the Proxy Pattern include:

- There is an extra level of indirection between the client and the actual service.

25.10 Related Patterns

Facade The Façade pattern can be used to reduce the number of Proxy classes required if there are numerous services to be invoked.

Adapter An adapter fronts a target object but does so in order to change the published interface of that object to match the requirements of the client.

Decorator The Decorator also fronts a target objects but does so in order to add additional functionality not originally defined in the target.

Chapter 26
Filter

26.1 Introduction

The Filter Design pattern describes how objects can intercept requests for a target object and carry out some activity before the target object receives that request. In general a Filter will pass the request onto the next object in the filter chain. If that object is another filter this object can also perform some processing on the request etc. until the target object is reached. In this pattern the target object is unaware of the presence of the filters. Once the target object returns a response, that response may also be processed by the filters in the chain (in reverse order).

In some situations a Filter may veto the processing of the rest of the filter chain if some condition is not met, for example a Security filter is an example of such a filter.

Note that the Filter pattern is not a Gang Of Four pattern; it is included here as it is similar in nature to the GoF patterns and is also widely used. It was described originally in (Buschmann et al. 1996).

26.2 Pattern Classification

Bushmann et al. Structural Pattern

26.3 Intent

To provide pre and post processing of a request/invocation on a target object.

J. Hunt, *Scala Design Patterns: Patterns for Practical Reuse and Design*,
DOI 10.1007/978-3-319-02192-8_26, © Springer International Publishing Switzerland 2013

26.4 Context

There may be situations where it is useful to wrap a target object in one or more Filter objects. These objects may be used to provide logging, auditing, performance, or security operations. Such operations in general do not change the data being passed in or the results being returned. In some cases it may also be useful to provide transformational Filters that provide some processing of the input data or results (for example to covert from one data format to another). The Filter Pattern provides a way of structuring such objects.

26.5 Forces/Motivation

The Filter pattern can be used when

- A target object's input and output data must be pre or post processed without changing that object.
- Where some pre or post processing operations/behaviour is required and either access to the target objects source is unavailable or changes to that source are undesirable.

26.6 Constituent Parts

There are four constituent parts to the Filter Pattern; these are the Abstraction representing the *interface* presented to the client, the Client, the Target and one or more Filters. This is illustrated in Fig. 26.1.
An explanation of these roles is presented below:

Abstraction The *interface* to be presented to the client by the target and the filters that will sit in front of the target.

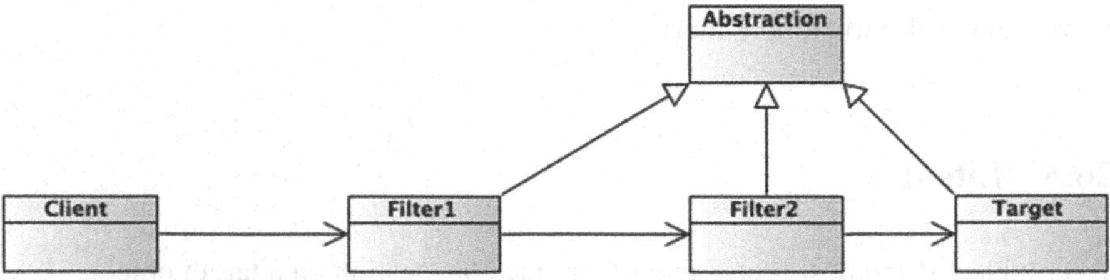

Fig. 26.1 Participating types in the Filter pattern

Target The eventual target object, around which the filters are organised.

Filter One or more objects that will sit in front of the Target and will pre and post process any operations that can be invoked on the target.

Client The client invokes behaviour that will be pre and post processed by the Filters. The Client may be responsible for constructing the Filter Chain or may be unaware of the fact that the target is filtered.

26.7 Implementation Issues

The application must be structured around the client invoking behaviour on a target object which can be wrapped in Filters either statically at compile time or dynamically at runtime. The use of traits in Scala to provide Filter behaviour provides a static, compile time, form of Filtering, while the Scala Spring approach based on XML configuration files provides a runtime based approach.

Filter objects that do not maintain internal state can be dynamically replaced at runtime. The stateless nature of the filters thus allows the system to adapt dynamically to the runtime requirements.

The Filter objects should be designed without knowledge of how the target object is implemented (or indeed in many cases of the actual concrete target object which they will filter).

Filter objects should also not communicate directly with each other; rather they should be designed to work entirely independently.

26.8 Concrete Example

The example used in this section provides two filters that can be added to a DAO (Data Access Object). This simplified DAO allows a type to be saved, retrieved and deleted. The Filters provide for logging of method invocation and monitoring of the time taken to execute a method.

In this implementation we have chosen to use Traits to implement the filters. This allows the filters to be mixed in either to a type when it is declared or when an instance of a class is created. Both of which represent a form of static application of the filters thus guaranteeing strict typing.

The implementation of this simple application is presented below. A Market trait is used to represent those elements playing the role of a Filter. This trait, the Filter trait, is not required by the design pattern but provides a semantically useful addition:

```
trait Filter
```

The DAO trait represents the Abstraction being implemented. This trait is a generic trait that can save, delete and get (retrieve) objects of the generic type T.

```
trait DAO[T] {
  def save(a: T): Unit
  def delete(a: T): Unit
  def get(id: String): Option[T]
}
```

Defining this *interface* trait ensures that the filters as well as the concrete target object all implement the same set of methods.

The type that will be used with the example is a simple Person class that contains an id, a name and an age property. The id and name properties are read only properties.

```
case class Person(val id: String, val name: String, var age: Int)

class PersonDAO extends DAO[Person] {
  private val data = HashMap[String, Person]()
  def save(p: Person) = { println("PersonDAO.save"); data.put(p.id, p) }
  def delete(p: Person) = { println("PersonDAO.delete"); data.remove(p.id) }
  def get(id: String): Option[Person] = {
    println("PersonDAO.get");
    data.get(id)
  }
}
```

The PersonDAO class is a concrete implementation of the generic DAO class where the parameterized type of the DAO has been set to Person. The actual implementation of the PersonDAO holds the Person objects provided to it in memory in a HashMap. The id of the object is used as the key for the map. The save method adds the object to the HashMap, the delete removes it form the HashMap and the get retrieves it form the HashMap. The actual value returned by the get method is an Option that wraps around the value None or an instance of the class Person. This allows clients to test for the presence of a Person object etc.

Two filters have been implemented. The first is the DAOLoggerFilter. This is a generic trait which extends the Filter trait and mixes in the DAO trait. It overrides the save, delete and get methods of the DAO trait. Each method prints a logging message and then calls the method on the *super* keyword. Note that the methods are all marked as *abstract override*. This indicates that they are only partial implementations of the method, something else must be provided to complete the implementation. This is indicated by the call to super. <method name>. This invocation causes any other wrapped traits to be invoked (or if no further traits are available) the target object. It is thus this feature that implements the filter chain behaviour of the Filter Pattern in this example.

```
trait DAOLoggerFilter[T] extends Filter with DAO[T] {
  abstract override def save(a: T) = {
    println("Logger save: " + a);
    super.save(a)
  }
  abstract override def delete(a: T) = {
    println("Logger delete: " + a);
    super.delete(a)
  }
  abstract override def get(id: String): Option[T] = {
    println("Logger get: " + id);
    super.get(id)
  }
}
```

The DAOPerformanceFilter trait also extends the Filter trait and mixes in the DAO trait. As with the DAOLoggerFilter it overrides the three methods in the DAO trait with abstract override methods. These methods record the start time of the methods, then pass the method invocation down the filter chain (using super.<method name>) and the print out the execution time for the method using the (private) printDuration method.

```
trait DAOPerformanceFilter[T] extends Filter with DAO[T] {
  abstract override def save(a: T) = {
    println("Starting save performance monitoring")
    val start = System.nanoTime;
    super.save(a);
    printDuration(start)
  }
  abstract override def delete(a: T) = {
    println("Starting delete performance monitoring")
    val start = System.nanoTime;
    super.delete(a);
    printDuration(start)
  }
  abstract override def get(id: String): Option[T] = {
    println("Starting get performance monitoring")
    val start = System.nanoTime;
    val obj = super.get(id);
    printDuration(start);
    return obj
  }
  private def printDuration(start: Double) = {
    val diff = (System.nanoTime - start) / 1000;
    println("Performance " + diff + " microseconds")
  }
}
```

The printDuration method calculates the difference between the start time and the current time and prints a message stating the number of microseconds the method invocation took.

The simple Test application used with this example is presented below:

```
object Test extends App {
  val dao = new PersonDAO
                  with DAOPerformanceFilter[Person]
                  with DAOLoggerFilter[Person]
  dao.save(Person("1", "John", 49))
  val p = dao.get("1")
  if (p.nonEmpty) dao.delete(p.get)
}
```

This application first creates a *dao* object. This object is an instance of the class PersonDAO with the DAOPerformaneFilter and the DAOLoggerFilter mixed in. This means that the methods invoked on the *dao* object can be viewed as a chain in which the outer most method is called first before the invocation is passed on towards the target. In this case it means that the DAOLoggerFilter's methods are called before the DAOPerformanceFilter's methods, after which the PersonDAO methods are invoked.

Therefore, when the save method is called on the *dao* with a new instance of the class Person, the save method on the logger is first executed, before the performance monitor method is called before the actual save method get to run.

```
Logger save: Person(1,John,49)
Starting save performance monitoring
PersonDAO.save
Performance 167.936 microseconds
Logger get: 1
Starting get performance monitoring
PersonDAO.get
Performance 102.144 microseconds
Logger delete: Person(1,John,49)
Starting delete performance monitoring
PersonDAO.delete
Performance 83.968 microseconds
```

26.9 Pros and Cons

The advantages of the Filter Pattern are:

- Allows a program to provide transformations and analysis on data for a target object without requiring modification of that target object.

The drawbacks of the Filter Pattern include:

- The Filters are intentionally independent of each other and of the target object, therefore any interactions between the filters must inherent be handled via the passing of data into and out of each filter.
- The processing stream is linear; that is it is not possible to skip some filters depending upon the scenario.

26.10 Related Patterns

Composite The Composite pattern is an alternative to the Filter pattern when the objects involved do not have a consistent interface and can be composed statically.

Delegate The Delegate pattern provides an object that sits in front of a target object and delegates requests onto that target. In this case the Delegate is similar to a Filter Pattern with only one Filter in it.

Decorator The Decorator pattern also places an object in front of a target, however the Decorator pattern adds additional functionality.

Chain of Responsibility This is a series of objects that are expected to process the request. Structurally an implementation may resemble that of the Filter Pattern but semantically they have very different meanings.

Reference

Buschmann, F., Meunier, R., Rohnert, H., Sommerlad, P., & Stal, M. (1996). *Pattern-oriented software architecture – A system of patterns*. New York: Wiley. ISBN 0-471-95869-7.

Chapter 27
Bridge

27.1 Introduction

The Bridge pattern provides an intermediary between an abstraction and its implementation. This is particularly useful when there is a hierarchy of abstractions and another (corresponding) hierarchy of implementations. Rather than combine the two into many distinct classes, the Bridge Pattern implements the abstractions and implementations as independent types that can be combined dynamically.

27.2 Pattern Classification

Gang Of Four Structural Pattern

27.3 Intent

To separate those types that represent an abstraction (concept) from those types that provides the implementation for the abstraction.

27.4 Context

In some situations a concept may be complex enough (or due to the nature of the domain may lead to) multiple types representing that concept. In addition a separate type hierarchy may best support the way in which these different versions of the concept are implemented. The resulting implementation is a combination of the concept (and its interface) presented to the client and an underlying implementation.

J. Hunt, *Scala Design Patterns: Patterns for Practical Reuse and Design*,
DOI 10.1007/978-3-319-02192-8_27, © Springer International Publishing Switzerland 2013

27.5 Forces/Motivation

The motivating conditions behind the Bridge Pattern include:

- When hierarchies of abstractions and hierarchies of their implementations are combined into a single type hierarchy, classes that use those classes become too closely linked to a specific implementation of the abstraction. Changing the implementation used for an abstraction should not require changes to the classes that use the abstraction.
- The logic in difficult implementations of an abstraction is repeated in each implementation. It would therefore be useful to make this logic reusable by encapsulating it into a trait or collaborator class.
- This also allows the common logic to be reused when a new implementation of the abstraction is produced.
- In some cases multiple abstractions should share the same implementation.
- Where extending the common logic of an abstraction is required, and the implementation should be reused as widely as possible.

27.6 Constituent Parts

The roles that comprise the Bridge Pattern are illustrated in Fig. 27.1 and described below:

The Abstraction This element represents the top level of the Abstraction hierarchy and that the concept represented by the two hierarchies in the Bridge Pattern. For example, if the concept being implemented represents type of financial products then the Abstraction would express the generic Product concept (and the implementation hierarchy would represent different ways of implementing that financial product). Where as if the concept being implemented represented a UI Window then the abstraction would be a Window and the implementation a type of Window (e.g. OSX Window, X Window, Microsoft 8 Window etc.). The Abstraction role is also expected to manage the linkage between the Abstraction and the Implementor.

Specialization of the Abstraction Extends the concept of the Abstraction as a subtype of the Abstraction. There may be many refinements of the Abstraction as required. For example, for financial Products, there may a Derivatives refinement or a type of Option, such as a Swaption, refinement. For a UI Window abstraction there may be IconWindow, FramelessWindow.

Implementor This role provides an implementation of the Abstraction concept. There may be one or many implementation for the Abstraction.

Specialized Implementor These classes provide different implementations of the Specialization of the Abstraction.

Multiple Bridge Classes In Scala the combination of the Abstraction and the Implementor may be combined in one or more concrete classes that represent the combination of the two aspects of the Bridge Pattern.

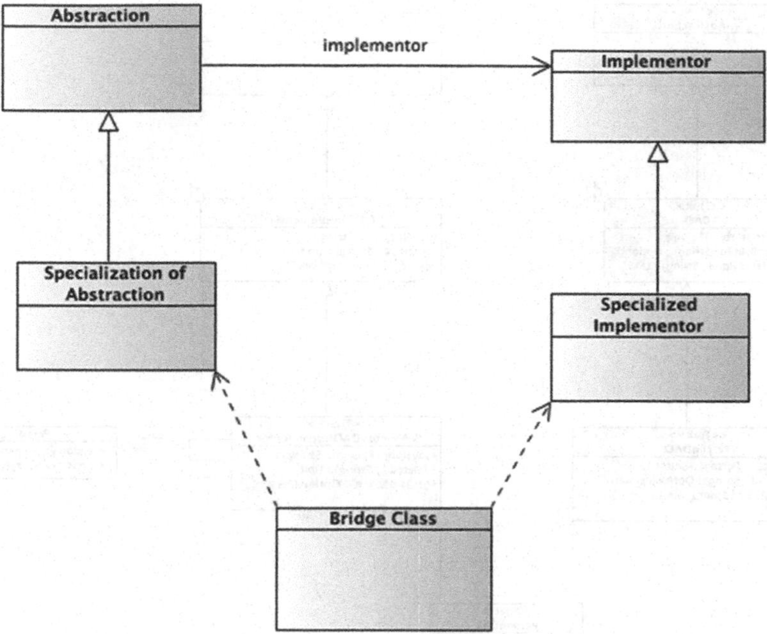

Fig. 27.1 Primary Bridge pattern roles and their relationships

27.7 Implementation Issues

In Scala the abstraction and the implementation hierarchies could both be represented by a set of Scala classes rooted on a single abstract class. However, Scala traits offer a much cleaner way of implementing the Bridge Pattern. In Scala both the *abstraction* hierarchy and the *implementation* can be represented by traits. These traits can then be mixed together in a concrete class that provides the wrapper that is accessed by the client. The client only needs to know about the root of all types (the trait representing the concept being implemented) and/or the concrete class.

27.8 Concrete Example

The example application we will look at is oriented around the creation of a Data Access Object framework for Person objects. The domain entity is the case class Person. Instances of this class are persisted via an appropriate DAO (Data Access Object). The Data Access Object concept is implemented using the Bridge Pattern. There is therefore the DAO abstraction hierarchy comprised of the generic DAO and

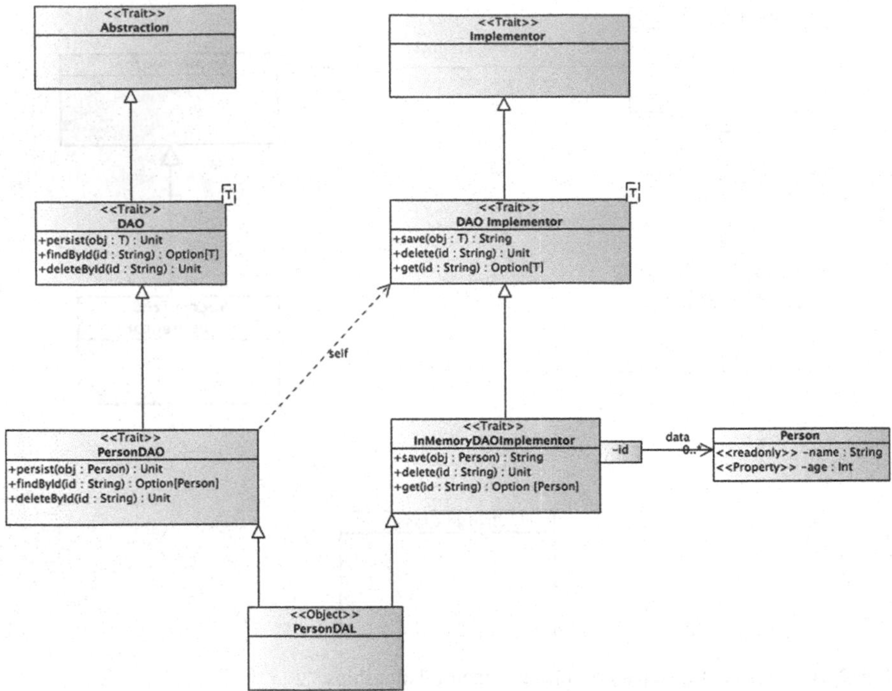

Fig. 27.2 Sample DAO application types based on the Bridge pattern

the more specific PersonDAO and the DAO Implementor. The Implementor also has a hierarchy allowing for different concrete implementations, in this case one is provided; an InMemoryDAOImplementor for persisting Person objects to memory (although others based on relational databases, NoSQL databases, Hibernate etc. could be provided).

Figure 27.2 illustrates the Scala Traits, Class and Object comprising this example implementation.

From the diagram you can see that there are two hierarchies one for the Abstraction and one for the Implementor. These are brought together in the PersonDAL (Person Data Access Layer) that provides the linkage between the DAO Abstraction and the DAO Implementor. Note that the PersonDAO trait uses a self type reference to link it to the DAO Implementor – this is a Scala language facility that allows the PersonDAO trait to refer to methods and functions defined in the DAOImplementor (for which an implementation must be provided before an object is created). It is *logically* the equivalent of having a reference from the PersonDAO to the DAO Implementor; but is clearer and is based on the concept of mixing together different traits.

The implementation of this Bridge Pattern based application is described below:

The two traits Abstraction and Implementor are essentially Marker traits merely being used to indicate the role of the two hierarchies:

```
trait Abstraction

trait Implementor
```

The DAO Abstraction hierarchy is defined by two traits, the generic DAO trait (which is parameterized by the type T) and its sub trait PersonDAO that specifies the Person class as the type being managed and provides the self type reference to the DAOImplementor. These two traits are listed here:

```
trait DAO[T] extends Abstraction {
  def persist(obj: T): Unit
  def findById(id: String): Option[T]
  def deleteById(id: String): Unit
}

trait PersonDAO extends DAO[Person] {
  self: DAOImplementor[Person] =>
  def deleteById(id: String): Unit = this.delete(id)
  def findById(id: String): Option[Person] = this.get(id)
  def persist(obj: Person): Unit = this.save(obj)
}
```

Note that in the PersonDAO trait the references to the methods *this.delete*, *this.get* and *this.save* indicate that the DAOImplementor (or a sub type of that trait) will provide the implementation for these methods. Also note that for this example I have changed the method names used between the DAO and the Implementor; merely to show that you can; the same method names could be used.

The two implementor types are the generic DAOImplementor and the Person specific InMemoryDAOImplementor. The DAOImplementor trait defines the methods that must be provided by any DAOImplementor. The InMemoryDAOImplementor provides implementations for the DAOImplementor methods that rely on storing the Person objects in a HashMap keyed on the id generated for each Person. This data is held in the private readonly property data. The private property count is used to maintain a unique id for each new Person object stored. The two traits are shown below:

```
trait DAOImplementor[T] extends Implementor {
  def save(obj: T): String
  def delete(id: String): Unit
  def get(id: String): Option[T]
}
```

```
trait InMemoryDAOImplementor extends DAOImplementor[Person] {
  private val data = HashMap[String, Person]()
  private var count = 0
  def save(obj: Person): String = {
    count += 1
    val id = "p" + count
    data.put(id, obj)
    return id
  }
  def delete(id: String) = data.remove(id)
  def get(id: String): Option[Person] = data.get(id)
}
```

The Person class itself is a simple case class with a read only *name* property and a variable *age* property:

```
case class Person(val name: String, var age: Int)
```

Finally the PersonDAL Object brings the two hierarchies together. Note a class could also have been used an instance created which would be necessary if multiple instances of the implementation are required, however the in memory data storage mechanism should be shared across all parts of the application so a singleton object is being used instead. The implementation of this Object is trivial in that it is defined purely to mix together the two trait hierarchies in the form of the PersonDAO trait and the InMemoryDAOImplementor:

```
object PersonDAL extends PersonDAO with InMemoryDAOImplementor
```

The Test Application for this example is shown below:

```
object Test extends App {
  println("Create Person")
    val p1 = Person("John", 49)
    println(p1)
    println("Person Person")
    PersonDAL.persist(p1)
    println("Retrieve Person by ID")
    val p2 = PersonDAL.findById("p1")
    println(p2)
    println("Delete Person")
    PersonDAL.deleteById("p1")
    println("Try to find again by ID")
    val p3 = PersonDAL.findById("p1")
    println(p3)
}
```

The application first creates a new Person object. This person object is then persisted to via the PersonDAL object. The PersonDAL object is then used to obtain a new reference to the Person object using the ID "p1". The Person object is then deleted from the PersonDAL object. Finally to validate that the Person object has been deleted an attempt is made to re-reference it by retrieving it from the PersonDAL object.

The result of running this test application is presented below:

```
Create Person
Person(John,49)
Person Person
Retrieve Person by ID
Some(Person(John,49))
Delete Person
Try to find again by ID
None
```

27.9 Pros and Cons

The advantages of the Bridge Pattern are:

- The abstraction and its implementations are organized into separate hierarchies. It is therefore possible to extend each hierarchy without directly impacting the other.
- It is also possible to have multiple concrete implementations for an abstraction type or multiple abstraction types using the same implementation.
- Clients of the abstraction are unaware of the implementation types.
- An abstraction can change its implementation without any impact on the client.

The drawbacks of the Bridge Pattern include:

- There is added complexity in the implementation of an abstraction with respect to its implementation.
- It is not obvious from the client perspective what the implementation type is and thus it may make maintenance and future extension more complex.

27.10 Related Patterns

Abstract Factory The Abstract Factory Pattern can be used within the Bridge Pattern to help encapsulate the instantiation of the concrete implementation class, thereby buffering the abstraction from the implementation.

Delegate Pattern Simple version of the Abstraction can be viewed as being an example of the Delegate Pattern as they merely delegate the request onto the Implementor. However, this is merely the simplest example, the Abstraction may well have additional functionality of its own.

Adapter Pattern This pattern is oriented around making unrelated types work together. The Abstraction may adapt the interface of the Implementor to meet the expectations of the client. However, in general Adapter is used to link together an existing client with an apparently incompatible type where as bridge is used at design/implementation time to provide flexibility.

Chapter 28
Chain of Responsibility

28.1 Introduction

When using the Chain of Responsibility Pattern; one object (the sender) can send a request for some behaviour to a chain of handlers, without knowing what the contents of the chain is and without knowing which of the handlers will process the request. The basic idea is illustrated in Fig. 28.1.

Thus the Chain of Responsibility pattern allows an object to send a request without knowing what will handle that request. It thus decouples the sender from the receiver(s). Members of the chain (the handlers) may handle the request, may pass the request on to the next handler or may do both (depending upon the requirements).

28.2 Pattern Classification

Gang of Four Behavioural Pattern

28.3 Intent

Allows a sender to be decoupled from the receiver(s) who are organised in to a sequence where each member of the sequence has a chance to process the request.

28.4 Context

In situations where a sending object needs to invoke some behaviour, but it is not clear (until runtime) which of a set of request handlers are available or which of the request handlers should handle that request. In such situations the Chain of

J. Hunt, *Scala Design Patterns: Patterns for Practical Reuse and Design*,
DOI 10.1007/978-3-319-02192-8_28, © Springer International Publishing Switzerland 2013

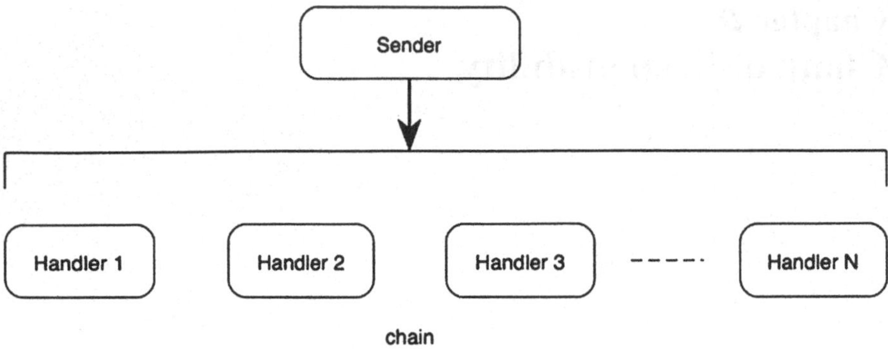

Fig. 28.1 The core chain of responsibility concept

Responsibility pattern provides a very flexible mechanism for managing how requests get processed.

28.5 Forces/Motivation

The Chain of Responsibility Pattern can be used when

- More than one element should handle a request, but those elements are not known *a priori*.
- The sender may not be aware of, or should not know, the handlers that will process the request.
- The set of handlers for the request may be determined dynamically at runtime rather than static at compile time.
- More than one handler should process a request but the sender can only send a single request.

28.6 Constituent Parts

There are a number of roles that can be identified in the Chain of Responsibility pattern, these are:

Handler This role is an abstraction representing the generic aspect of handling a request.

Concrete Handler One or more concrete handlers that are offered the chance to process the request in turn. The combination of the Concrete Handlers forms the chain.

Chain A container that manages the handlers, and allows the client to submit a request to the chain thereby ensuring that the sender is independent of the handlers (or indeed the technology used to manage the chain).

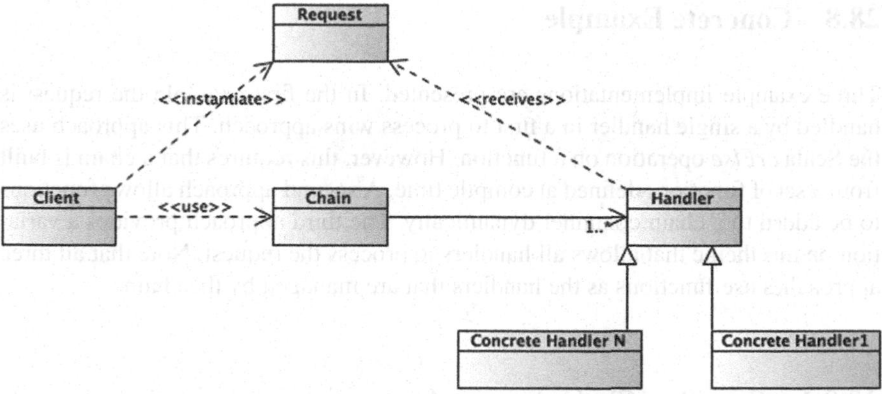

Fig. 28.2 Main roles and their relationships in the Chain of Responsibility pattern

Request This role is played the type used to represent the command sent to the handlers by the sender. It may be as simple as an existing type (such as an Integer) or it may be an object encapsulating the operation required and the parameters used with that operation.

Client/Sender Objects playing this role acts as the sender of the request to the chain.

When a Client issues a request it does so to the Chain. The chain then ensures that each handler in the chain has a chance to process the request.

These roles are illustrated in the following diagram (Fig. 28.2)

28.7 Implementation Issues

There are a number of questions to consider. These question include:

- **Do all handlers process the request?** Do all the handlers in the chain get to handle the request or is the first to accept the request the one that gets to handle it? We will look at both strategies later in this chapter.
- **How should the chain be implemented?** This could be done by hold each handler in sequence in a list or other ordered data structure. It could hold references to Scala functions, or wrappers could be used to hold each handler in a form of linked list.
- **How should requests be represented?** How the actual request is represented needs to be considered. It could be that the request is as simple as a parameter passed to the chain or the request could be a wrapper object holding the data to be presented to each handler or the Request could be a formal object representing some request for behaviour.

28.8 Concrete Example

Three example implementations are presented. In the first example the request is handled by a single handler in a first to process wins approach. This approach uses the Scala *orElse* operation on a function. However, this requires that a chain is built from a set of functions defined at compile time. A second approach allows functions to be added to a chain container dynamically. The third approach provides a variation on this theme that allows all handlers to process the request. Note that all three approaches use functions as the handlers that are managed by the chain.

28.8.1 Function Chain Approach

The first approach presented relies on Scala's ability to chain partial functions together with *orElse*. Partial Functions are a very flexible and a useful feature in the Scala language. A Partial Function is one that is only defined for a subset of the possible values that its argument can take. The term *partial* here comes from mathematics and is to distinguish it from a *total* function that can handle all values that its argument takes. For example, a function that takes an *Int* may be partial if it only deals with positive integers and total if it deals with all values of integers.

In Scala Partial Functions can be chained together using the *orElse* operator. If a Partial Function deals with the range of values passed in (as expressed by a case statement) then the Partial Function handles the invocation. If it does not handle the value passed it then it can be passed onto the next Partial Function in the partial function chain by the *orElse* operator.

In the following example, three Partial Functions are defined, HandleEvents, handleOdds and handlePalindrome. The body of each is defined by a single case statement that has a conditional if statement to determine whether the function will deal with the parameter passed in (thus making them Partial Functions). Finally to keep the syntax clean we have also defined a Handler type as being a Partial Function that takes a Request parameter and return Unit.

```
object ChainController {
  type Handler = PartialFunction[Request, Unit]

  val handleEvens: Handler = {
    case Request(x) if x % 2 == 0 => println("Handling even value " + x)
  }

  val handleOdds: Handler = {
    case Request(x) if x % 2 == 1 => println("Handling odd value " + x)
  }
```

```
  val handlePalindrome: Handler = {
    case Request(x)
        if x.toString.reverse.toString == x.toString
                                    => println("Handling palindrome " + x)
  }
  // Create the chain
  val handlerChain = handlePalindrome orElse handleEvens orElse handleOdds

}
```

Each of the Partial Functions are combined together into a partial function chain using the *orElse* operator and are stored in the *handlerChain*. This allows Request objects to be submitted to the chain of partial functions (as shown in the Example application).

A Request case class, that acts as a wrapper for the values to be processed, defines the actual parameter passed to the chain.

```
case class Request(value: Int)
```

The simple test application used to illustrate using the handler chain is shown below (note we could have created an implicit function to automatically convert an Int into a Request but this was deemed unnecessary in this case).

```
object Exmaple extends App {
  ChainController.handlerChain(Request(21))
  ChainController.handlerChain(Request(121))
  ChainController.handlerChain(Request(12))
}
```

The result of executing this application is shown below:

```
Handling odd value 21
Handling palindrome 121
Handling even value 12
```

28.8.2 Chain Manager Approach

The second approach adopted to illustrate the Chain of Responsibility pattern allows for runtime configuration of the handlers in the chain. In this case each of the handlers is a Scala Objects object. We could have implemented the handlers an objects whose classes implemented the Handler trait that could provide greater flexibility for future extension, but for efficiency reasons Scala Objects were chosen.

The Handler is a trait indicting that each element in the chain should be able to determine if it should accept the request as well as being able to handle the request. In this case the request is merely the parameter to be processed although an explicit

Request wrapper could again have been used. Note that the Handler trait is a generic trait parameterized by the type T.

```
trait Handler[T] {
  def accept(obj: T): Boolean
  def handle(obj: T): Unit
}
```

The ChainController itself is a class that holds a group of Handlers in a ListBuffer. A new handler can be added to the chain of handlers using the add method. Note that the add method returns a reference to the ChainController itself so that invocations of the *add* method can be linked together to simplify the construction of the chain, for example:

```
controller.add(p1).add(p2).add(p3)
```

The Chain Controller defines an apply method that takes some object and first identifies which members of the chain will accept that data. From this it takes the first member of this set and calls the handle method on that member. If none accept the data then a message "Can't handle" is printed out.

```
case class ChainController[T] {
  private val chain = new ListBuffer[Handler[T]];
  def add(h: Handler[T]) = { chain += h; ChainController.this }
  def apply(obj: T) = {
    val handler = Option(chain.filter(n => n accept obj) head)
    handler match {
      case Some(chainElement) => chainElement handle obj
      case None => println("Can't handle")
    }
  }
}
```

The two objects that extend the Handler trait are the Printer1 and Printer2 objects. They define the accept and handle methods. Printer1 accepts the request to handle the data if the data String is "John" where as Printer2 accepts the request to handle the data if the string is not "John". The handle methods then print out an appropriate message. The definition of these two objects is shown below:

```
object Printer1 extends Handler[String] {
  def accept(obj: String) = obj equals "John"
  def handle(obj: String) = println("HI John")
}

object Printer2 extends Handler[String] {
  def accept(obj: String) = obj != "John"
  def handle(obj: String) = println(obj)
}
```

The sample application, Exmaple2, is shown below. This application creates a new ChainController (parameterized by the type String) and adds the two handler objects to the chain. It then invokes the apply method passing in the strings "John" and then "Bob". Note that we are using both syntaxes for the invocation of apply (with round brackets and curly brackets). This illustrates how the invocation of the chain behaviour can be made to look like part of a language construct.

```
object Example2 extends App {
  val controller = ChainController[String]
  controller.add(Printer1()).add(Printer2())
  controller apply { "John" }
  controller apply ("Bob")
}
```

The output from this application is illustrated below:

```
HI John
Bob
```

28.8.3 Processing Chain Approach

This third example, illustrates how the Chain Of Responsibility pattern can be modified to allow all the handlers in the chain to handle the data passed in. In this case the Handler trait only has one method, handle (no accept method is now required).

```
trait Handler[T] {
  def handle(obj: T): Unit
}
```

The ChainController class still has an add method and a chain property holding the handlers. However the apply method now merely applies the data to all the members of the chain via the handle method.

```
case class ChainController[T] {
  private val chain = new ListBuffer[Handler[T]];
  def add(h: Handler[T]) = { chain += h; ChainController.this }
  val apply = (obj: T) => {
    chain.foreach(_ handle obj)
  }
}
```

In this case the handlers are instances of two classes (that extend the Handler trait) rather than two objects, however this is merely to illustrate some of the options available. The Adder handler merely adds the "+" string to the data passed in. The Subtractor handler in turn adds the "–"string to the data. Both print out the result.

```
case class Adder extends Handler[String] {
  override def handle(obj: String) = println("+" + obj)
}

case class Subtractor extends Handler[String] {
  override def handle(obj: String) = println("-" + obj)
}
```

The sample application used to illustrate this version of the controller is shown below. It is the same as that used for the previous example, illustrating how the controller encapsulates the behaviour of the chain of handlers.

```
object Test extends App {
  val controller = ChainController[String]
  controller.add(Adder()).add(Subtractor())
  controller apply { "John" }
  controller apply ("Bob")
}
```

The output from this application is shown below:

```
+John
-John
+Bob
-Bob
```

28.9 Pros and Cons

The advantages of the Chain of Responsibility Pattern are:

- Reduces the coupling between sender and receiver. The sender of the message is unaware of the receiver or the receivers of the message. This can therefore simplify object interactions.
- Flexibility in responsibilities. As each object in the chain is responsible for determine whether it accepts the request or not it is possible to change the object in the chain without affecting the client at runtime.

The drawbacks of the Chain of Responsibility Pattern include:

- Although the order in which the request is processed may be guaranteed, the order in which the chain is constructed may differ from one run to the next, which may result in different results being generated.
- No guarantee of being handled. As it is up to each of the handler sin the chain to decide if they will handle the request, there is no guarantee that the request will be handled at all!

28.10 Related Patterns

Composite One way of viewing the chain is as a composite made up of many elements.

Command A Command is an object representing the behaviour to be executed and the parameters associated with that command. A request in the Chain of Responsibility represents the parameters to be used but the members of the chain represent the operation to be performed.

Chapter 29
Command

29.1 Introduction

The Command Pattern presents a way of encapsulating an operation into an object that can be passed around between objects, managed, sequenced, scheduled and executed as required. It insulates an operation from the execution of that operation and thus also allows operations to be persisted, resurrected as well as offers the option of executing operations remotely.

In the Command Pattern, an object creates a new instance of a Command and passes it to a Command Executor that actually performs the execution of that command.

29.2 Pattern Classification

Gang of Four Behavioural Pattern

29.3 Intent

Encapsulates behaviour into an object so that it can be selected, sequenced, queued, done and undone, submitted to clients for execution (locally or remotely) and otherwise manipulated.

J. Hunt, *Scala Design Patterns: Patterns for Practical Reuse and Design*,
DOI 10.1007/978-3-319-02192-8_29, © Springer International Publishing Switzerland 2013

29.4 Context

In some situations it is necessary to represent an operation to be executed explicitly rather than implicitly as a method or function on an object, class or trait. This might occur if it is necessary to store and rerun these operations, or if an undo/redo framework to where operations may be executed remotely (in a separate JVM).

A classic example of where such a requirement occurs is in user interfaces where a set of user configurable menus can be created and a series of operations can be undone and redone by the user. In such systems the Menu operations and toolbar buttons are often represented by *commands* which can be placed onto menus and toolbars, passed around, stored in undo frameworks etc.

29.5 Forces/Motivation

The Command Pattern can be used when

- Specifying an action to perform for a client object.
- Specifying, queuing and executing requests at different times, or selecting amongst requests based on some criteria.
- You wish to be able to undo and redo operations.
- Supporting the logging of operations so that they can be reapplied if a system crashes or is otherwise corrupted.
- Providing the semantics of a set of high-level operations that can be combined in an appropriate manner and that are built on lower level primitive operations.

29.6 Constituent Parts

There are four main roles within the Command Pattern:

Command This type represents the abstract concept of the Command.

Concrete Command This type implements a particular command that can be submitted by a client (invoker) and submitted to a Command Executor.

Command Executor This type is responsible for managing the collection and execution of Commands. That is the executor knows how to execute Commands.

Invoker The Invoker is responsible for creating Commands and submitting them to the Command Executor. There may be any number of invokers.

This is illustrated in Fig. 29.1.

The Invoker creates Concrete Command objects and submits them to the Command Executor. The Command Executor then executes the Commands.

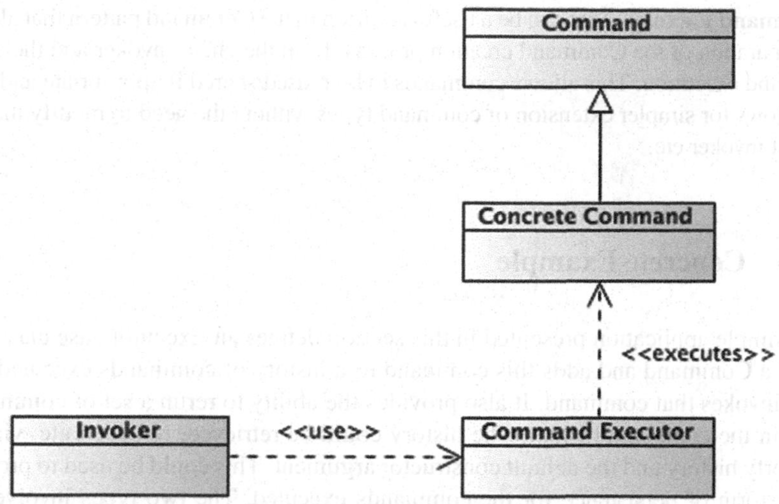

Fig. 29.1 Key roles and their relationships in the Command pattern

29.7 Implementation Issues

Implementation questions to consider when implementing the Command Pattern:

How intelligent should the command be? A Command could be a simple holder for an operation to perform. In this scenario it is the responsibility of the Command Executor to handle all the aspects of determining whether to execute the command and how to execute the commend etc. At the other end of the scale a Command can provide all of the facilities need to determine how and when to execute itself and the Executor is in that context merely a holder of commands.

How should the Command be implemented? Scala offers both traits and functions as types beyond that made available in languages such as Java. As a Command is essentially an encapsulation of some functionality that will be executed at some point in the future, it may appear that Scala functions are the obvious implementation vehicle. In many cases this will be true, however as it may also be necessary to persist and recreate commands if they are being logged etc. it may be necessary t adopt another approach. Consideration needs to be given to the requirements of the Pattern command in a particular context and determine the approach to adopt.

Provision of undo/redo operations Commands can be used as part of a undo/redo framework. However, the operation may perform side effects that change the state of other objects. To ensure that the undo/redo operation results in the original state/same new state each time they are applied it may be necessary to hold state information in the Command as well as the functionality inherent included.

Command Factory This can be a useful addition to the Command pattern that allows separation of the Command creation process, from the client invoker and the command execution. This allows commands to be reused/shared if appropriate and also allows for simpler extension of command types without the need to modify the client invoker etc.

29.8 Concrete Example

The simple application presented in this section defines an Executor case class that takes a Command and adds this command to a history of commands executed and then invokes that command. It also provides the ability to rerun a set of commands held in the command history. The history could be retrieved, reloaded etc. via the property history and the default constructor argument. This could be used to provide some form of persistence for the commands executed. The two types involved in this example are shown in Fig. 29.2:

The implementation defines a type Command that is, in this case, defined to be a function that takes no parameters and returns no value (Unit). This is defined in the package object used with the example:

```
package object command {
  type Command = () => Unit
}
```

We could have used a Trait to define the abstraction of a Command containing the operation to be executed. This would allow state information to be stored along with the operation. However, in the example being developed here, it was considered unnecessary.

```
case class Executor(
    val history: ListBuffer[Command] = ListBuffer[Command]())
{
  def rerun = history.foreach(_())
  def execute(cmd: Command) = { history.append(cmd); cmd() }
  override def toString = "Executor: " + history
}
```

The Executor class presented above has a *history* read-only property that contains a ListBuffer that holds Commands. The three methods implemented allow a Command to be submitted via the execute method (which also recorded the command in the history); to rerun any previously submitted commands and an override of the toString that prints out the command history.

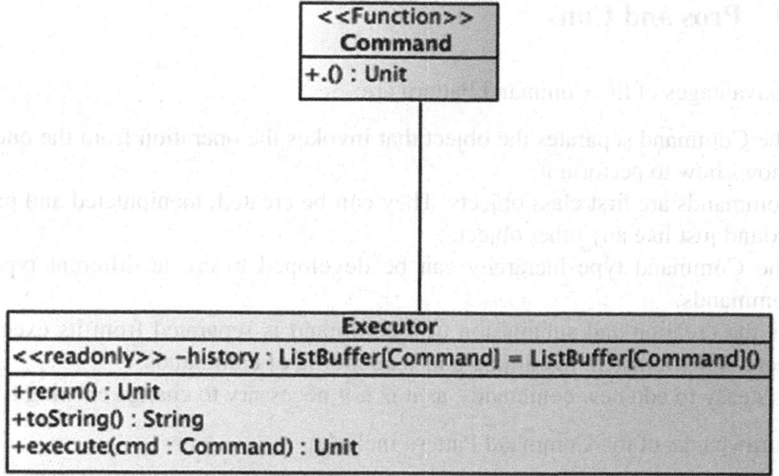

Fig. 29.2 Key types in sample application

The simple Test application creates a new instance of the Executor. It then creates two zero parameter functions which are run via the Executor. The executor is then printed out and the commands submitted are rerun:

```
object Test extends App {
  val exec = Executor()
  val sayHello = () => println("Hello")
  exec.execute(sayHello)
  val x = 10
  exec.execute(() => println(x * 3))
  println(exec)
  exec.rerun
}
```

The output from this application is illustrated below:

```
Hello
30
Executor: ListBuffer(<function0>, <function0>)
Hello
30
```

29.9 Pros and Cons

The advantages of the Command Pattern are:

- The Command separates the object that invokes the operation from the one that knows how to perform it.
- Commands are first class objects. They can be created, manipulated and passed around just like any other object.
- The Command type hierarchy can be developed to create different types of commands.
- As the creation and submission of a command is separated from its execution there is flexibility in the timing and sequencing of commands.
- It is easy to add new commands, as it is not necessary to change existing types.

The drawbacks of the Command Pattern include:

- The object that requires the operation represented by the Command is no longer directly invoked in its invocation and this can make debugging and maintenance more difficult.

29.10 Related Patterns

Factory Method This pattern can be used to encapsulate the command invoker from the command type hierarchy and the command creation process.

Marker Trait This can be used to indicate Commands, Command that can be undone/redone, those that can be persisted etc.

Composite The Composite Pattern can be used to handle Commands made up of simpler Commands (often referred to as Macro Commands).

Memento A Memento can be used to capture the state of some objects to which the command is applied, for undo/redo operations.

Chapter 30
Strategy

30.1 Introduction

If you are developing a body of work where the implementations available for a particular operation can be changed then there are a number of options regarding how you might implement this. It could be that you might implement a type hierarchy with a generic or abstract method at the root of the hierarchy and sub types providing alternative implementations of that method as required. It would then be possible to select between completing implementations based on the type that is instantiated.

However, in some cases it may be necessary to alter the implementation of an operation without changing the type (or the identity) of the encompassing object. In this situation instantiating a whole new object would lose the identity and may result in additional, unnecessary objects being created.

The Strategy pattern provides an approach to this problem that allows the implementation of an operation can be changed dynamically at runtime.

30.2 Pattern Classification

Gang of Four Behavioural Pattern

30.3 Intent

To allow the algorithmic implementation of some behaviour to be selected as required (and to be changeable over time).

J. Hunt, *Scala Design Patterns: Patterns for Practical Reuse and Design*,
DOI 10.1007/978-3-319-02192-8_30, © Springer International Publishing Switzerland 2013

30.4 Context

Being able to plug in different implementations for an operation is a common requirement in a number of different situations. For example, being able to use different encryption and decryption algorithms, or different algorithms for breaking a stream of text into lines, or different algorithms for calculating tax payments or pension rights etc.

30.5 Forces/Motivation

The Strategy Pattern can be used when

- An application must be able to change the implementation of an operation at runtime or must be able to change it based on some selection criteria.
- The differences in implementation (algorithm) can be encapsulated into the strategy and there is a consistent approach to accessing these different implementations.
- Clients do not need to know anything about how the operations are implemented.
- Switching between different instances of different classes would lose identity integrity.

30.6 Constituent Parts

There are a number of roles in the Strategy Pattern. These are:

Client The invoker of the behaviour implemented by the strategy.

Strategy The abstract concept represented by the implementations of this strategy; may be given a name to provide semantic meaning to the strategy (such as a name indicating the purpose of the strategy). In Scala may be defined as a function indicating the number and type of parameters expected and the return type generated.

Concrete Strategy One or more implementations of the operation(s) indicated by the Strategy abstraction (in Scala this may be one or more functions that implement the function specification provided by the Strategy).

The Context A container for the concrete strategy. This may be an encapsulating Object, Class or Trait.

When a client requires the operation indicated by the strategy it invokes it on the *context*. The context then uses the appropriate concrete strategy to provide the implementation of the operation. The client is unaware of the strategy and is hidden from the different implementations.

The roles and their relationships are illustrated in Fig. 30.1.

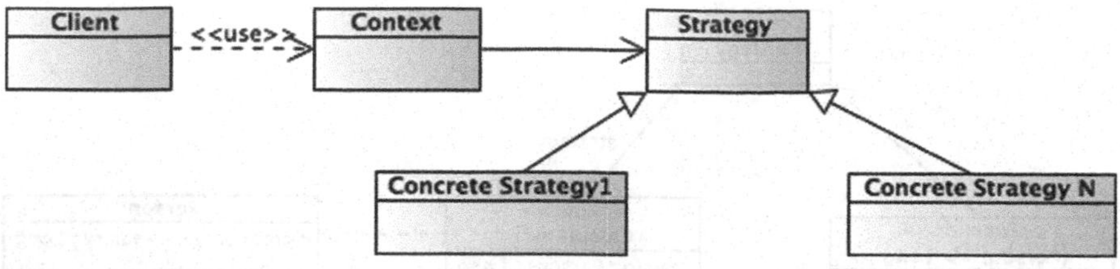

Fig. 30.1 Constituent types in Strategy pattern

30.7 Implementation Issues

Scala implementations of the Strategy pattern have a number of issues that should be considered, including:

Defining the Strategy What from should the strategy take? It could be a trait that defines some function such as *apply* or it could be a type declaration specifying the signature of a function to be made available.

Strategy to Context interface The interface between the Strategy (and its concrete implementations) and the Context that holds that strategy must be rich enough to give the strategy access to all the information it needs.

Linking the strategy to the context In Scala this could be done in several ways including by providing a trait that meets the dependency implied by the *this* self-type annotation or by providing a function etc. In the example in the next section this latter approach is adopted as it feels very natural in Scala and allows for runtime changes to the strategy. However, if a compile time approach was acceptable then the use of stacked traits may well provide an alternative solution.

30.8 Concrete Example

The simple example of the Strategy pattern used in this section defines a TaxCalculator class that can be given different strategy implementations that are used to determine the tax to be paid by a given Person. Each Person object has an associated salary and the strategy uses the person's salary information to generate the tax they must pay. However, the tax rate may differ depending upon a number of factors and must therefore be set as appropriate.

The key elements that make up this implementation example are presented in Fig. 30.2.

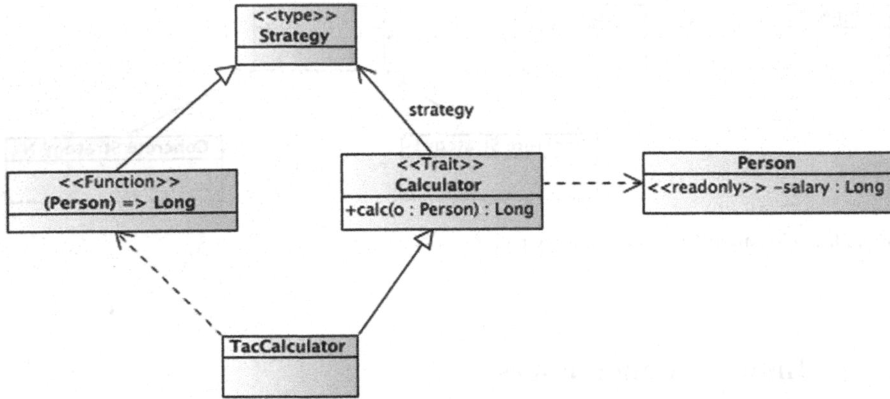

Fig. 30.2 Types used in TaxCalculator example application

A Strategy type is defined in the package object indicating that a Strategy in this implementation is a function that takes a Person as an argument and returns a Long result.

```
package object strategy {

  type Strategy = Person => Long

}
```

We also define the case class Person to represent a tax payer and the salary they have.

```
case class Person(val salary: Long)
```

A trait Calculator is defined. This is a reusable trait that can be used wherever a Strategy is used to perform some calculation on a Person i.e. Strategy is a function applied to a Person object. Note that there is nothing specific to taxes in this trait.

```
trait Calculator {
  private[strategy] var strategy: Strategy
  def calc(o: Person): Long = strategy(o)
}
```

The Tax Calculator class mixes in the Calculator trait and defines the strategy property to be a simple function that calculates the tax to be paid as 30 % of the person's salary.

```
case class TaxCalculator extends Calculator {
  var strategy = (e: Person) => Math.ceil(e.salary * .3).toLong
}
```

Note that the strategy can be reset (it is a var not a val) and thus the strategy to apply can be altered during the lifetime of a TaxCalculator object.

The text application Test1 creates a Person object and a TaxCalculator object. It then uses the tax calculator to 'calc' the tax due. The result of this calculation is printed out. It then resets the tax calculator's strategy such that the new function calculates that the tax to be paid is 50 % of the person's salary. It then reruns the 'calc' method and prints out the new result.

```
object Test1 extends App {
  val p = Person(24000)
  val tc = TaxCalculator()
  println(tc.calc(p))

  tc.strategy = (e: Person) => Math.ceil(e.salary * .5).toLong
  println(tc.calc(p))
}
```

The result of executing this example application is shown below.

```
7200
12000
```

30.9 Pros and Cons

The advantages of the Strategy Pattern are:

- The Strategy Pattern allows the behaviour of clients to be determined dynamically, at runtime, potentially on a per invocation basis.
- Client objects can be simplified, as they do not need to be responsible for the selection of the appropriate behaviour.

The drawbacks of the Strategy Pattern include:

- It may not be clear at compile time which strategy will be employed and this may make debugging and maintenance tasks harder.

30.10 Related Patterns

Adapter An adapter *delegates* some of its behaviour to an *adaptee* object, however the semantics of the adapter pattern differ from that of the Strategy pattern.

Flyweight The Flyweight pattern can be used as the basis for the sharing of strategies between contexts.

Chapter 31
Mediator

31.1 Introduction

This pattern is based on that presented in the Gang Of Four design patterns book as the Mediator Pattern (Gamma et al. 1995), however it is very widely used in a range of programming languages and technologies.

Every object-oriented system involves multiple objects exchanging data, and requests for behaviour, in some form. Each object maintains a reference to those objects with which it is collaborating. Using these references it can invoke appropriate behaviour or make data available. In Scala this may be extended to include references to functions defined within the context of some type.

As a simple example, Fig. 31.1 illustrates three objects each of which needs to communicate with the other two objects:

Due to the way in which references are implemented in language such as Scala this results in six references, each of which must be maintained if one of the objects is replaced etc.

This situation becomes more complex and difficult to maintain as the number of objects involved increases. For example, the following illustrates the situation for five objects. There are now 20 references required to connect all 5 objects together (see Fig. 31.2). Each time a new object is added this number increases and the new object must be connected to all of the previous objects and those objects need to reference the new object. This requires each object to maintain a list of references and for the system as a whole to have some way of holding onto the objects so that they can be linked to new objects etc.

If the number of objects involved in the communication becomes large this becomes unmanageable!

The Mediator pattern provides a solution to this problem by introducing an intermediary object that is responsible for controlling and coordinating the communication of other objects. In this architecture each object need only communicate

J. Hunt, *Scala Design Patterns: Patterns for Practical Reuse and Design*,
DOI 10.1007/978-3-319-02192-8_31, © Springer International Publishing Switzerland 2013

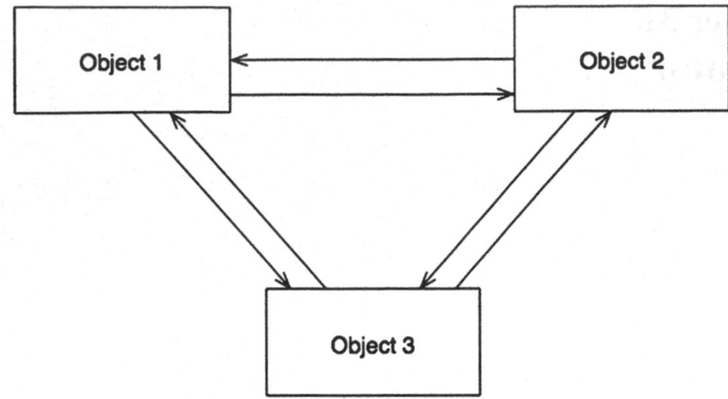

Fig. 31.1 Three cooperating objects

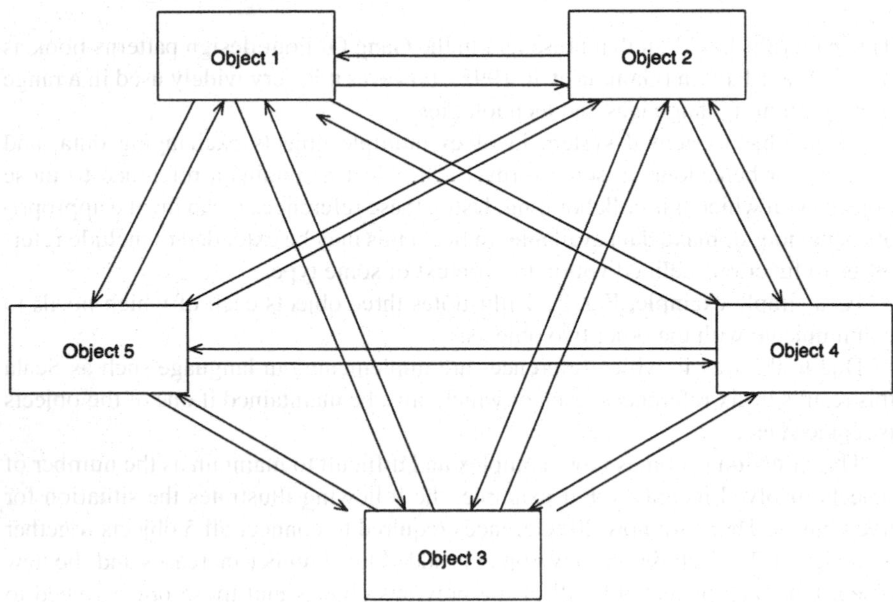

Fig. 31.2 Five cooperating objects

with the mediator and thus only needs to maintain a single reference. The Mediator is then responsible for maintaining references to all those objects that wish to communicate.

This structure is illustrated in Fig. 31.3.

When an object now needs to communicate with other objects it only needs to send a message to one other object, the Mediator. It is then the responsibility of the Mediator to determine who to send the request or data onto etc.

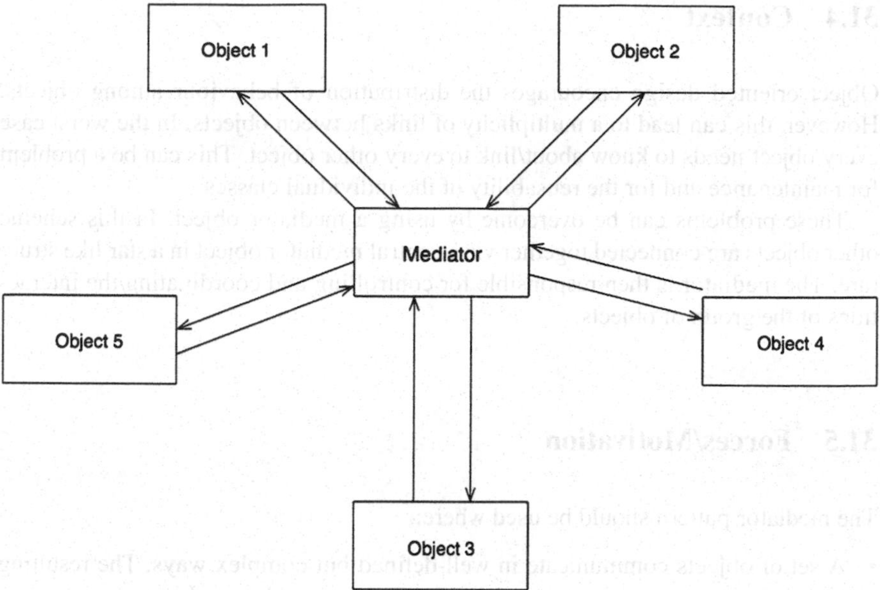

Fig. 31.3 Using a Mediator to connect five objects

Although the terminology used above has referred to objects in Scala there are a range of technologies that could be used to implement this design pattern including traits, functions and objects. Also note that the communication mechanism may be based on method and function invocation but may also utilize other technologies such as Message Queues, socket communications and web services etc.

31.2 Pattern Classification

Gang of Four Behavioural Pattern.

31.3 Intent

To define an object that represents a common communication mechanism, that allows a set of objects to interact, without those objects needing to maintain links to each other. It therefore promotes a loosely coupled, but high cohesive communication infrastructure without each object need to maintain a reference to all the other objects.

31.4 Context

Object oriented design encourages the distribution of behaviour among objects. However, this can lead to a multiplicity of links between objects. In the worst case every object needs to know about/link to every other object. This can be a problem for maintenance and for the reusability of the individual classes.

These problems can be overcome by using a mediator object. In this scheme other objects are connected together via a central mediator object in a star like structure. The mediator is then responsible for controlling and coordinating the interactions of the group of objects.

31.5 Forces/Motivation

The mediator pattern should be used where:

- A set of objects communicate in well-defined but complex ways. The resulting interdependencies are unstructured and difficult to understand.
- Reusing an object is difficult because it refers to, and uses, many other objects.
- A particular behaviour is distributed amongst a number of classes and we wish to customize that behaviour with the minimum of sub-typing.

31.6 Constituent Parts

A class diagram for a Scala based mediator is illustrated in Fig. 31.4.

The primary participants in the mediator pattern are:

Mediator trait abstractly defines behaviour that handles invocation of Colleague Callback functions for a client. Note that the notify method may or may not take a parameter. In this case it is shown as taking a reference to Any type of Scala object. Optionally the data to be notified to the colleagues by the Concrete Mediator could be of a specific type rather than Any.

ConcreteMediator maintains the list of Colleague callback functions and provides a concrete implementation for the notify method. Thus method determines how the callbacks are invoked (in this case when given some data by a client). This could be done by holding a list buffer of callback functions and then applying the data to each callback using a foreach function. The Concrete Mediator may be a class or an object (an object may be used if only one such mediator is required).

Colleague trait. This is a marker trait used to indicate the role of the concrete colleagues in the design pattern. It is optional as there is no abstract or concrete members in this trait and the trait is not used as a parameter to any function or method nor to specify any collection etc.

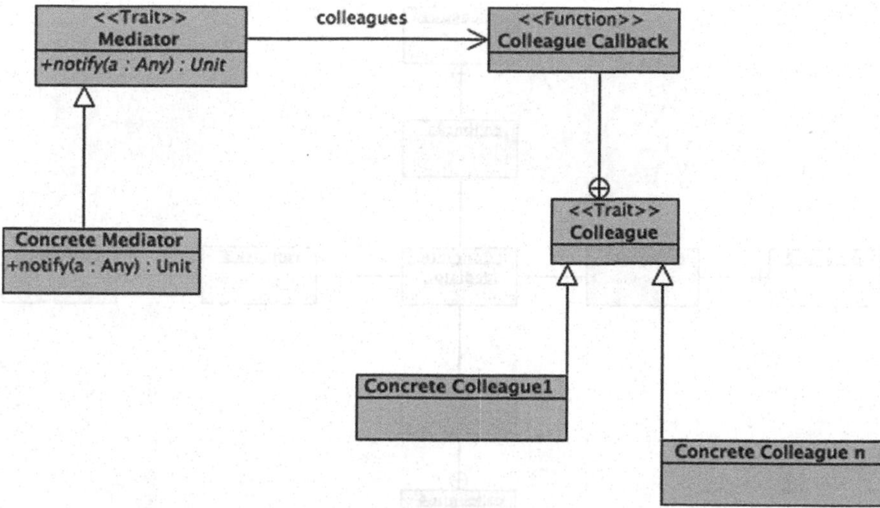

Fig. 31.4 Mediator class diagram

Concrete Colleague classes Each colleague must provide a CallBack function that can be invoked by the mediator when required. It must register this function with the mediator in order to be included in any particular notification process. Colleagues may have a reference to the Concrete Mediator (or mediators) although they may access the mediator through a singleton object.

Collaborations: The mediator object receives messages from clients (which may or may not be colleagues) and relays them to all colleagues as appropriate.

A typical object diagram for a mediator is illustrated in Fig. 31.5.

31.7 Implementation Issues

The following implementation issues are relevant to the mediator pattern:

Omitting the abstract Mediator type. If there is only to be one mediator type there is no reason to define an abstract version.

Colleague mediator communication. The colleagues need to tell the mediator when something interesting happens to them that they wish to relay to their colleagues. This could be handled via a dependency mechanism (see the Observer pattern) or by direct communication by the object. For example the colleague could tell the mediator that something has changed and then allow the mediator to interrogate it to find out what. This is the approach taken in the sample code example.

Communication implementation. Many different technologies could be adopted to implement the communication between colleagues and the mediator. It could be based on in memory method or function invocation or could use a form of

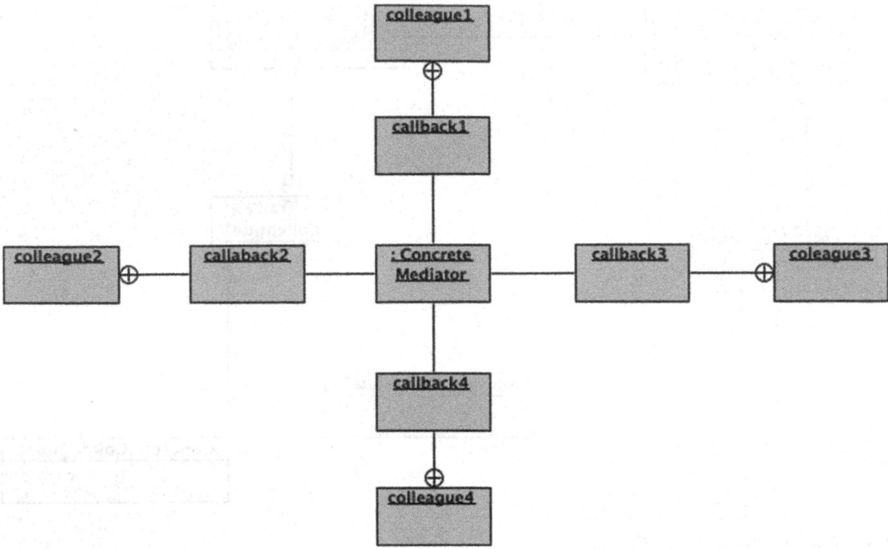

Fig. 31.5 A mediator object diagram

messaging utilizing a message queue (such as Apache MQ) and the java Message Service. It could also be implemented using Actors and the inherent message passing mechanism used with such Actors (e.g. either Scala or Akka Actors).

Mediator as a separate object. The Mediator could be a separate type that is instantiated as required. The various objects that need to communicate could then access this Mediator object. It could also be a Scala Object in which case it represents a singleton Mediator (which is not an uncommon way to implement the mediator). It could also be a trait that is mixed into each of the objects that need to communicate providing the infrastructure necessary for that communication. Each of these is a viable option in Scala.

31.8 Concrete Example

The sample implementation we will look at builds upon the use of a Mediator Trait and a Colleague marker trait. These are shown below:

```
trait Mediator {
  type ColleagueCallback
  var colleagues = ListBuffer[ColleagueCallback]()
  def notify(any: Any): Unit
}

trait Colleague
```

The Colleague marker trait can be easily mixed into any type (class, object or trait) to indicate its role within the mediator pattern.

The Mediator trait defines a colleague's property based on a ListBuffer that holds a group of Colleague Callback functions. The actual format of these callbacks is not defined in the Mediator trait; instead this is defined as an abstract type that must be provided by a subtype of the Mediator trait. It also defines an abstract method, *notify*, that will be used to pass data to all the colleagues via the callback functions.

A concrete subtype of the Mediator must define both the ColleagueCallback function and the notify method.

31.9 Event Manager Sample Code

To illustrate the use of the Mediator and Colleague traits we will explore a typical UI scenario. In this scenario various different GUI elements need to communicate. For example, when a change is made in a form, the overall frame needs to change its display to show that a save is required, the save button may need to be enabled and the logger may need to record the user activity for future audit trails etc.

We have decided to use the Mediator pattern to simplify the communication between these different components. We have also chosen to use an Event class as the basis of the data exchanged. The Event takes a reference to the object that created the event and the data provided as the payload of the event (in this case a string).

```
class Event(val source: Colleague, val description: String)

case class ActionEvent(s: Colleague, d: String) extends Event(s, d)
case class SaveEvent(s: Colleague, d: String) extends Event(s, d)
case class MouseEvent(s: Colleague, val x: Int, val y: Int, d: String)
                                                   extends Event(s, d)
```

This Event class is then subclassed into specific types of event such as ActionEvent, SaveEvent and MouseEvent. MouseEvent adds information about the x and y coordinates of the mouse when it was clicked.

The concrete Mediator class is then defined with respect to the Event class:

```
case class EventMediator extends Mediator {
  type ColleagueCallback = Event => Unit
  def notify(e: Any) = e match {
    case event: Event => (colleagues clone) foreach(_(event))
    case _ => throw new RuntimeException("Invalid Mediator type")
  }
}

object EventMediator {
  val instance = EventMediator()
}
```

The concrete EventMediator extends the Mediator trait and provides a concrete implementation of the ColleagueCallback type and the notify method. The ColleagueCallback type is defined as a function that takes an event as a parameter and return Unit (that is it does not return a value). The notify method uses pattern matching to valid the type of the parameter passed in (which should now be an Event type) and invokes each of the functions in the colleagues list buffer passing in the event as a parameter to those functions.

Note that because the ListBuffer defined in the Mediator pattern is defined to hold only ColleagueCallbacks, this means that when mixed into the EventMediator it will hold functions that take an Event and return Unit. Therefore we are able to invoke each function, passing in the event to that function within the foreach.

Also note that we could have used asInstanceOf to convert the parameter e into an Event, however we have used pattern matching as this is consider more idiomatic Scala.

A companion object is used to provide simple access to the singleton instance of the EventMediator that will be used in this example. This is a design choice, there is no specific reason why the EventMediator should be a singleton object other than it makes this example straight forward to work with. There could equally be separate instances of the EventMediator that are used with different parts of the GUI thus allowing controlled communication between them. For example, there could be an EventMediator for the Admin oriented components and a separate one for the Update oriented components. These components would then need to access the EventMediator they are expected to work within the appropriate way.

We can now define a set of components that can play the role of a group of communicating Colleagues: LogPanel, Form and Frame.

The LogPanel object is intended as a simple output only panel that displays messages indicating what is happening within the application. This might be useful both for debugging purposes and for user notification uses. In this sample application the LogPanel merely prints a message to the console whenever the log method is called. The log method takes an event, return Unit and prints the event as part of the log message. The LogPanel also extends the Colleague marker trait.

```
object LogPanel extends Colleague {
  def log(e: Event): Unit = println("Logger: " + e)
}
```

As such the log method meets the contract specified by the ColleagueCallback type and thus can be used with the EventMediator.

Note that we have chosen to use objects for the actual Colleague instances; this is a choice; we could have used classes or further traits and instantiated them when required.

The Form object also extends the Colleague trait and defines three methods. One method, *receive*, meets the contract specified by the ColleagueCalback type in the EventMediator and so can be registered with the mediator. The other two methods take no parameters and instead perform logic associated with the Form and then notify the EventMediator that something has happened. In the case of the Update method it prints a message (simulating some user activity) and then publishes an ActionEvent to the EventMediator. It access the EventMediator using the component objects *instance* property.

```
object Form extends Colleague {
  def receive(e: Event) = println("Form Received event:" + e)
  def update = {
    println("Input changed")
    EventMediator.instance.notify(ActionEvent(this, "Updated doc"))
  }
  def save = EventMediator.instance.notify(SaveEvent(this, "Saved"))
}
```

Finally, the frame object is shown below. This object also extends the Colleague trait. It posses two methods, handleEvent which meets the ColleagueCallback contract of the EventMediaotr and a zero parameter input method. The input method notifies the mediator of a MouseEvent. It also possess a *requiresSave* property that is changed from true to false (and back again) depending upon the activity of other colleagues.

```
object Frame extends Colleague {
  var requiresSave = false
  def handleEvent(e: Event): Unit = e match {
    case e: MouseEvent if e.source == this => println("Do nothing event from self")
    case _: MouseEvent => println("Some other MouseEvent")
    case _: ActionEvent => requiresSave = true; println("Frame Requires save")
    case _: SaveEvent => requiresSave = false; println("Frame Save reset")
    case _ => println("Frame recieved 'Other' Event")
  }
  def input = EventMediator.instance.notify(MouseEvent(this, 10, 10, "Clicked"))
}
```

The handleEvent method is worth examining in some more detail. In this case the method is a little more sophisticated than those shown above. Specifically, the handleEvent method takes different actions depending upon whether the event type received is a MouseEvent, an ActionEvent a SaveEvent or some other yet to be defined Event type. It does this using pattern matching which is a common code oriented pattern in Scala. If an ActionEvent is received it sets the requiresSave property to true. If a SaveEvent is received it sets the requiresSave property to false.

In addition the Frame object also distinguishes between MouseEvents sent by itself, which it ignores, and those sent by other Colleagues in which case it takes appropriate action. This is why the source of the event was included in the event class; it allows Colleagues to determine whether the event was raised by themselves and ignore if they wish.

The Test application, which constructs the mediator and its colleagues, is presented below. The mediator registers each of the ColleagueCallback compliant functions provided by the three colleagues with the mediator by appending them to the mediator. Notice that although we are using the term method and function interchangeably here as the method (which is essentially a function tied to the object) also meets the interface specification defined by the ColleageCallback type in the EventMediator.

```
object Test extends App {
  val mediator = EventMediator.instance
  mediator.colleagues.append(LogPanel.log)
  mediator.colleagues.append(Frame.handleEvent)
  mediator.colleagues.append(Form.receive)
  Frame.input
  Form.update
  Form.save
}
```

Note that in this example, for simplicity, the Colleagues are registered with the mediator in the wrapping application (in this case Test). However, the Colleagues could have registered themselves with the mediator as part of the setup process.

Once all mediator and the colleagues are set up, the Test application calls the input method on the Frame, and the update and save methods on the Form. When these methods are invoked communication between the colleagues is started. The output from running this program is shown below:

```
Logger: MouseEvent(com.jeh.scala.pattern.mediator.Frame$@799318fa,10,10,Clicked)
Do nothing event from self
Form Received event:MouseEvent(com.jeh.scala.pattern.mediator.Frame$@799318fa,10,10,Clicked)
Input changed
Logger: ActionEvent(com.jeh.scala.pattern.mediator.Form$@417c6323,Updated doc)
Frame Requires save
Form Received event:ActionEvent(com.jeh.scala.pattern.mediator.Form$@417c6323,Updated doc)
Logger: SaveEvent(com.jeh.scala.pattern.mediator.Form$@417c6323,Saved)
Frame Save reset
Form Received event:SaveEvent(com.jeh.scala.pattern.mediator.Form$@417c6323,Saved)
```

31.10 Pros and Cons

The mediator pattern has the following benefits and drawbacks:

- It limits sub-typing to the mediator (e.g. by changing the routing algorithm in mediator you can change the systems behavior).
- It de-couples colleagues.
- It simplifies object protocols from many to many down to one to many.
- It abstracts how objects cooperate.
- It centralizes control.

31.11 Related Patterns

Façade Facade differs from Mediator in that it abstracts a subsystem of objects to provide a more convenient interface. However its protocol is unidirectional where as mediator is multi-directional.

Observer Colleagues can communicate with a mediator using the Observer pattern.

Command The Command pattern can be used to represent the behaviour to be invoked on appropriate colleagues.

Proxy The proxy pattern also places an intermediate object between a client and the object providing the required service. However, this is a one to one mapping and still requires the client to maintain links to each of the proxies with which it is working.

Reference

Gamma, E., Helm, R., Johnson, R., & Vlissades, J. (1995). *Design patterns: Elements of reusable object-oriented software*. Reading: Addison-Wesley.

Chapter 32
Observer

32.1 Introduction

The observer pattern provides a way of ensuring that a set of objects is notified whenever the state of another object changes. It has been widely used in a number of languages (such as Smalltalk and Java) and can also be used with Scala. However, numerous commentators have dismissed the Observer pattern in favour of other patterns such as the Mediator pattern as the communication involved is more obvious and easier to following, maintain and debug. This does not mean that the Observer pattern is without merit and there are situations in which it can be used successfully; it is therefore useful to be aware of this pattern and how it might be realised in Scala.

32.2 Pattern Classification

Gang Of Four Behavioural Pattern

32.3 Intent

To manage a one to many relationship between an object and those objects interested in the state and in particular state changes of that object. Thus when the objects state changes, the interested (dependent) objects are notified of that change and can take whatever action is appropriate.

J. Hunt, *Scala Design Patterns: Patterns for Practical Reuse and Design*,
DOI 10.1007/978-3-319-02192-8_32, © Springer International Publishing Switzerland 2013

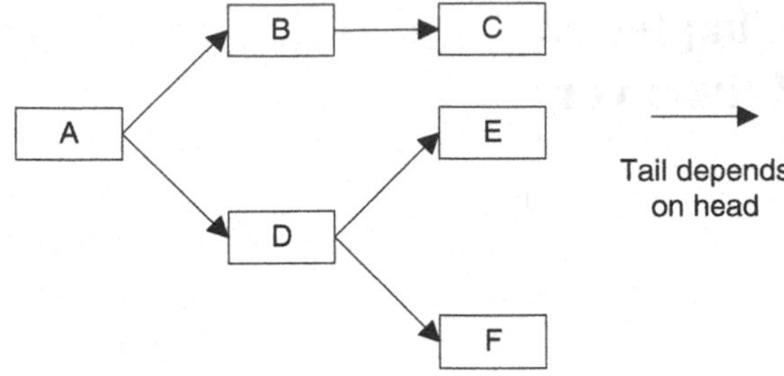

Fig. 32.1 Dependency between objects

32.4 Context

A common side effect of organising an application in terms of cooperating objects is that when the state of on object changes, other related objects (possible in different parts of the application) need to be notified of this change. This relationship, where the state or behaviour of one object is dependent on the state of another object, occurs again and again in applications. For example, in Fig. 32.1 the arrows indicates that there is a set of dependency relationships between the objects A to F. Object A is dependent on some aspect of objects B and D. In turn object B is dependent on some aspect of object C and so on.

The reasons for such dependencies are all down to *change*. We wish to communicate the fact that an object has changed its value to another object that may be interested in either the fact of the change or the new value effected by the change. The Observer Pattern provides a mechanism for communicating such changes in a generic, implementation independent, manner.

An obvious question is "why not just get the object to send messages to those interested in it?" The answer is that if you know the objects that are interested; then you can send messages to them. However, if all you know is that sometime, at a later date, some object may need to know something about the state of an object (but you do not know what that other object might be) then you cannot arrange to send messages to it.

The Observer Pattern mechanism allows any Observable object to act as the source of a notification. Any object that is an `Observer` can act as the dependent object.

32.5 Forces/Motivation

The Observer Pattern may be applicable in situations such as:

- Two, otherwise independent types, are related by the changes in the state of one (which need to be notified to the other).
- Where a change in the state of one object needs to be notified to zero or more other objects and where the number or actual objects may change or are not known until runtime.

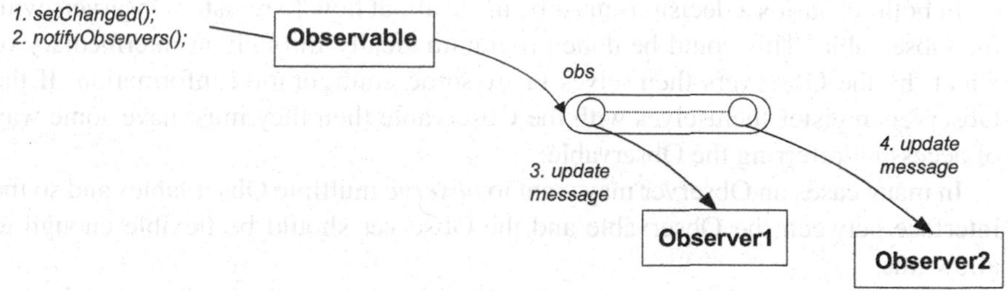

Fig. 32.2 Interactions in the Observer pattern

32.6 Constituent Parts

There are two key roles within the Observer Pattern, these are the Observable and the Observer roles.

Observable This is the object that is responsible for notifying other objects that a change in its state has occurred

Observer An Observer is an object that will be notified of the change in state of the Observable and can take appropriate action (such as triggering a change in their own state or performing some action).

State This role may be played by an object that is used to share information about the change in state that has occurred within the Observable. This might be as single as a String indicating the new state of the Observable or it might be a data oriented object that provides more detailed information.

These are illustrated in Fig. 32.2. In this figure, the Observable object must sent itself the setChanged() method followed by the notifyObservers() method. This then causes an update message to be set to all the objects currently registered with the Observable object. These Observer objects can then update themselves as required.

32.7 Implementation Issues

There are numerous options available for how the Observable object communications with the Observer objects. One option is to have a sequence of Observers held in a list that the Observable iterates down invoking an appropriate update or changed method or function on the Observers. In this implementation the Observer may be an interface only trait that specifies a method to be invoked by the Observable.

Alternatively the Observers may make a function available to the Observer that takes a state as a parameter and returns Unit. This means that the Observable does not need to maintain a link to the Observers directly and the only association between them is via a function specification.

In both scenarios a decisions must be made about how to register Observers with the Observable. This could be done programmatically through an intermediary or client, by the Observers themselves or by some configuration information. If the Observers register themselves with the Observable then they must have some way of accessing/referring the Observable.

In many cases an Observer may want to *observe* multiple Observables and so the interface between the Observable and the Observer should be flexible enough to allow this.

When an observer is de-referenced within its own area of the application, it must also be de-referenced from the Observable; otherwise it will not be available for garbage collection.

The State may or may not be provided as part of the notification mechanism to Observers. It may be enough merely to notify the Observers that the Observable has changed state.

32.8 Concrete Example

The application used to illustrate the Observer pattern is a simple Share Price Watcher application. A SharePriceWatcher is an object the monitors the price for a given share (for example "Google", "IBM" or "Apple"). When the price changes the SharePriceWatcher notifies any interested parties of the change in its state.

Within this implementation the SharePriceWatcher is an Observable and the Logger is an Observer (that is notified whenever the price changes).

The Observable trait defines the *changed* method that can be invoked by classes mixing in the trait to notify any observers of a change in the Observables state. Each Observer is actually a callback function that matches the type defined by the ObserverCallback type (which is a function that takes an ObservableEvent and returns Unit). An ObservableEvent is a simple case class that holds a reference back to the source of that event; the Observable object.

```
trait Observable {
  type OberverCallback = ObservableEvent => Unit
  val observers = ListBuffer[OberverCallback]()
  def changed = {
    val event = ObservableEvent(this)
    observers.foreach(_(event))
  }
}
```

The other trait in this example is the Observer trait, which is a Marker trait indicating the role of the object or class that mixes in this trait.

```
trait Observer
```

The SharePriceWatcher case class holds a reference to an identifier indicating the share being monitored and mixes in the Observable trait. It uses the long hand form for defining a property *value* so that we can implement the setter method for the value such that having reset the _value member we can call the *changed* method ensuring that Observers are notified of the change via their call back function.

```
case class SharePriceWatcher(val share: String) extends Observable {
  private var _value : Double = 0.0
  def value=_value
  def value_=(value: Double):Unit = {
    _value=value
    changed
  }
  override def toString(): String = "curent value: " + _value
}
```

The logger class is a simple case class that implements the Observer marker trait and implements a single method that takes an ObservableEvent and returns Unit (which thus meets the contract specified by the ObserverCallbakc function type):

```
case class Logger extends Observer {
  def printer(e: ObservableEvent) = println(e)
}
```

A simple test application has been written to illustrate the use of the SharePriceWatcher observable and the Logger Observer classes:

```
object Test extends App {
  val watcher = SharePriceWatcher("Google")
  val logger = Logger()
  watcher.observers.append(logger printer)
  watcher value = 32.0
}
```

This test application creates a new SharePriceWatcher for *Google* shares and a Logger instance. It registers the logger's printer method with the watcher and then sets the value of the watcher to 32.0.

The result of executing this simple application is that when the value is set to 32.0 the Loggers printer method is invoked and the ObservableEvent is printed out:

```
ObservableEvent(curent value: 32.0)
```

32.9 Pros and Cons

The advantages of the Observer Pattern are:

- **Loose Coupling**. The pattern allows an object to deliver notifications of changes to other objects without the objects being directly aware of each other's types. All that an Observable is aware of is that it might have a list of Observers.

All an Observer is aware of is that some operation has been invoked notifying it of some change.
- **Support for broadcast mechanisms**. Due to the nature of the association between the Observable and its Observers a single change notification can be broadcast to multiple Observers. In addition the actual mechanism for this communication is hidden behind the notification functionality and thus could use different implementation approaches depending upon the context (such as method invocation, the use of message queues, Actors etc.).

The drawbacks of the Observer Pattern include:

- **Unpredictable notification times**. Notification of changes to Observers can be a time consuming process. It is also unpredictable from the Observers point of view as it does not know what Observers may be registered with it and how long the behaviour invoked as part of the notification process will take. One way to handle this is to use the Actor model in Scala to notify each Observer in its own thread.
- **Cyclic Dependencies**. When the state of an Observable changes it *notifies* its Observers of that change. These Observers may in turn be Observables for other Observers. It is possible that a cyclic chain exists which results in the original Observable being an Observer of a downstream object resulting in it being notified of a change that originated within itself. This can result in stack overflow issues and may not come to light until runtime when all the component parts of a system are actually connected together. One way to overcome this issue is to record the origin of a notification and check for that origin before acting upon a notification.

32.10 Related Patterns

Adapter This pattern may be used to allow objects that do not meet the Observer requirements to be notified of Observable changes.

Mediator This pattern can be used as an alternative to the Observer pattern.

Singleton The Observable may be a singleton.

Chapter 33
State

33.1 Introduction

The State Design pattern encapsulates the states that an object can be in, as a discreet set of objects, each belonging to a separate sub type of an abstract state type.

33.2 Pattern Classification

Gang Of Four Behavioural Pattern

33.3 Intent

To allow an object to alter it behaviour when its internal state changes; the end result is that the object will appear to change its type.

33.4 Context

Some objects are required to have behaviour that is dependent upon their state. Such objects are referred to as stateful objects. The states associated with such objects are typically predefined and may changes as the result of external events.

For example, a cruise control system can be on, off and suspend. While the cruise control is off then changing the speed setting of the cruise control has no affect at all. When the cruise control system is on then changing the speed setting changes the speed of the vehicle. If the cruise control system is suspended then changing the speed has no immediate effect, but may result in a different speed being maintained

J. Hunt, *Scala Design Patterns: Patterns for Practical Reuse and Design*,
DOI 10.1007/978-3-319-02192-8_33, © Springer International Publishing Switzerland 2013

once the system is resumed. Thus the behaviour of the cruise control system is dependent on its state as well as the effect of changing the speed setting.

33.5 Forces/Motivation

The State pattern can be used when

- An object's behaviour depends on its state and it must change its behaviour at runtime depending upon that state.
- The logic to be implemented to manage the states of an object may become large and complex as the number of states grows.

33.6 Constituent Parts

There are two constituent parts to the State Pattern; these are the Context (which can be in a number of states) and the State (which represents a state of the Context), as illustrated in Fig. 33.1.

An explanation of these roles is presented below:

Context The Context is an object that exhibits stateful behaviour. That is the behaviour of the Context differs depending upon its state. Contexts determine their current state by keeping a reference to an instance of a concrete type of state. The Context delegates state-specific requests to the current Concrete State.

State The root type of the state hierarchy used to represent the states of the Context. Typically the State provides operations such as

- An *init* operation to handle any initializations required by the state (it is only called once just after the state object is originally created).
- A *handle* operation that takes an indicator of an event that has occurred and returns the appropriate new state generated as a result of transitions from the current state to the new state via the event.

The state may also provide two additional methods related to the state lifecycle:

- An *entry* operation that is invoked when the state is entered into (and after the *init* method has been invoked). If the state is reused this operation may be called each time the state is reused.
- An *exit* operation that is invoked just before the state is exited.

Finally, the state type will define a set of operations that may be invoked on each state (which will provide state specific behaviour).

Concrete States The concrete subtypes, of the abstract State, that are used to represent the states of the Context. These subclasses must implement the handle operation and any state based operations.

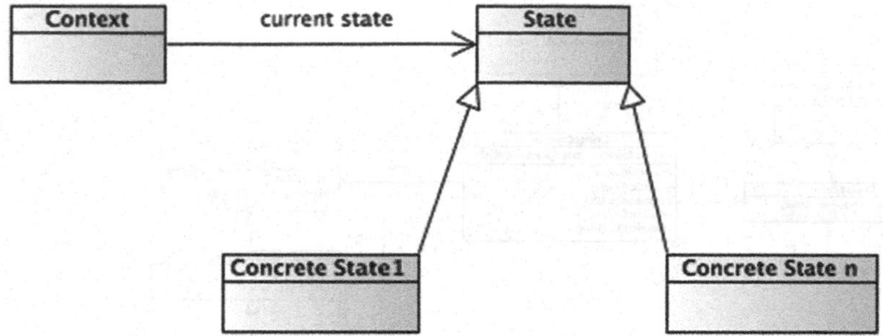

Fig. 33.1 Roles and relationships in the State pattern

33.7 Implementation Issues

The Context may pass itself as an argument to the State object handling the request. This lets the State object access the context if required.

The Context is the primary interface for clients. However, clients may or may not be aware of the state based behaviour of the context. For example, a Context may completely encapsulate the fact that internally its behaviour is state based; alternatively it may allow a client to initialise the Context based on some initial state!

Each concrete state needs to know which next states to transition to when an event occurs. However, the way in which this is configured may be hard coded, programmatic or may be handled by registering event transitions with a state.

It is necessary to identify what should happen when a state receives an event that it has no transition for.

33.8 Concrete Example

The simple application we will use to explore the State Pattern example is a simplified Cruise Control system. This system can be in one of three states, *On*, *Off*, and *Suspended*. It is possible to move from the *On* state to the *Off* or the *Suspended* state. It is possible to move from the *Off* state to the *On* state. It is also possible to move from the *Suspended* state to the *On* or *Off* state.

The structure of this application is illustrated in Fig. 33.2.

There are two traits used to define the core concepts Context and State. The Context defines a private (to the package) property state. This property holds a reference to an object of type State.

```
trait Context {
  private[state] var state: State
}
```

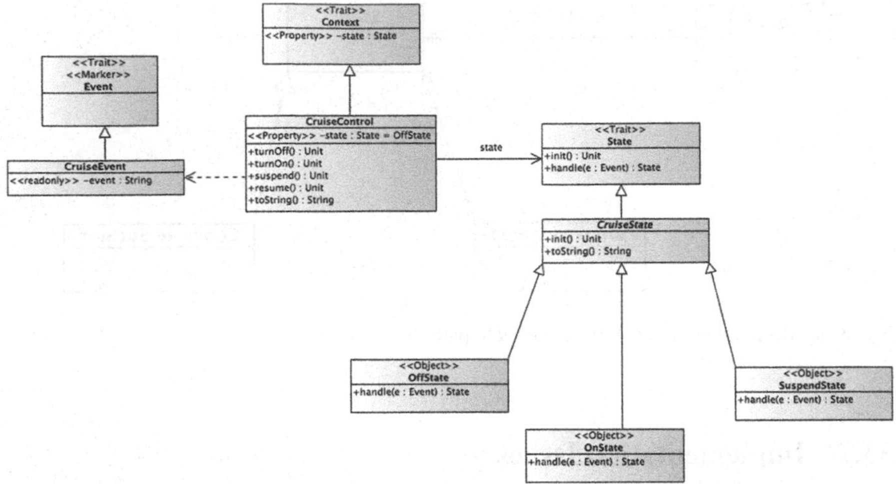

Fig. 33.2 Types used in a Cruise Control system based on the State pattern

The State trait defines two methods *init* and *handle*. The handle method takes an event and returns the new State that is the result of the transition from the current state to the new State. The *init* method is invoked just after the trait is instantiated.

```
trait State {
  init
  def init: Unit
  def handle(e: Event): State
}
```

The third trait is the Event trait that is a marker trait for Event types.

```
trait Event
```

The main CruiseControl class is a Context that uses the state objects (described later in this section) to represent its state. It also defines a set of methods that allow the CruiseControl to be turned on, turned off, suspended and resumed.

```
case class CruiseControl extends Context {
  private[state] var state: State = OffState
  def turnOn: Unit = state = state.handle(CruiseEvent("on"))
  def turnOff: Unit = state = state.handle(CruiseEvent("off"))
  def suspend: Unit = state = state.handle(CruiseEvent("suspend"))
  def resume: Unit = state = state.handle(CruiseEvent("resume"))
  override def toString = "CruiseControl: " + state
}
```

The methods it defines invoke the *handle* method on the current *state* object, this method takes a CruiseEvent with an appropriate string indicating the type of CruiseEvent. The CruiseEvent is a simple case class that extends the Event trait and defines a readonly property event:

```
case class CruiseEvent(val event: String) extends Event
```

An abstract class CruiseState is used to define a class that mixes in the State trait and implements the init method. Each CruiseState has a label which is used with the init method and the overridden toString method.

```
abstract class CruiseState(label: String) extends State {
  def init = println("init " + label)
  override def toString = label
}
```

The CruiseState class can be extended by a class or object to define the behaviour of the handle method.

The three state objects are the OffState, the OnState and the SuspendState. These immutable singleton state objects can be reused throughout the Cruise Control application. Each one encapsulates the logic that determines the transitions from that state to any of the other states (via the handle method)

```
object OffState extends CruiseState("Off") {
  def handle(e: Event): State =
    e match {
      case CruiseEvent("on") => OnState
      case _ => throw new RuntimeException("Unsupported transition")
    }
}

object OnState extends CruiseState("On") {
  def handle(e: Event): State =
    e match {
      case CruiseEvent("off") => OffState
      case CruiseEvent("suspend") => SuspendState
      case _ => throw new RuntimeException("Unsupported transition")
    }
}

object SuspendState extends CruiseState("Suspend") {
  def handle(e: Event): State =
    e match {
      case CruiseEvent("resume") => OnState
      case CruiseEvent("off") => OffState
      case _ => throw new RuntimeException("Unsupported transition")
    }
}
```

Note that in this case we have decided to throw an exception if an attempt is made to pass in an invalid CruiseEvent.

The simple Test application used with this example is presented below:

```
object Test extends App {
  val cc = CruiseControl()
  println(cc)
  cc.turnOn
  println(cc)
  cc.suspend
  println(cc)
  cc.resume
  println(cc)
  cc.turnOff
  println(cc)
}
```

This application first creates a CruiseControl object. It then transitions this CruiceControl object to on, then suspends it, then resumes and final turns it off.

33.9 Pros and Cons

The advantages of the State Pattern are:

- **Localized state-specific behaviour**. It localizes the state-specific behaviour and partitions behaviour for different states. This is because the State pattern ensures that all the behaviour associated with a particular state is maintained/implemented by a particular object.
- **State Transitions are explicit**. When an object defines its current state solely in terms of internal data values, the transitions from one state to another are not obvious. However, explicitly representing each state and transitioning from one state to another makes this whole process far more explicit.
- **State Object Sharing**. State objects that represent non-parametric states can be shared, as they do not hold instance-specific data. This is because the state they represent is encoded entirely in their type. In this case the state object can be shared amongst Context objects.
- **Immutable States**. The very nature of the states lends itself to the immutable concept underling many aspects of the Scala language. The Context calls the states transition method (e.g. handle(e: Event)) and this method returns the context's new state. The original state is unchanged and is thus immutable (and can be reused, cannot be corrupted by any side effects and new states can be easily added).

The drawbacks of the State Pattern include:

- The Context must be able to maintain a reference to its current state and the interface it publishes must be able to invoke appropriate behaviour on the state objects. Unless additional behaviour is mixed into the Context it may be difficult to dynamically extend the Context behaviour as new states are identified.

- To understand the behaviour of the Context object at any one time, it is necessary to understand what its current state is. This adds to the complexity of the implementation and may result in greater difficulty in maintenance and debugging tasks.

33.10 Related Patterns

Immutable The states that the Context can take are typically considered Immutable.
Flyweight The Flyweight pattern can be used as the basis for the sharing of state objects.
Singleton The non-parametric approach to implementing a state can use the Singleton pattern.

Chapter 34
Visitor

34.1 Introduction

The aim of the Visitor pattern is to allow client objects to obtain state information about other parts of an application without having direct access to (or knowledge of) those parts. This is particularly useful in producing highly modular applications that are resilient to change but have high cohesion.

That is, the Visitor pattern represents a way of placing logic that would need to be distributed across a set of classes into one place. The Visitor object is then passed amongst objects of these classes and the Visitor can perform operations or extract data as it goes. This has the advantage of simplifying the participating classes, reducing the distribution of the logic amongst these classes as well as reducing the cross references that would otherwise be necessary.

34.2 Pattern Classification

Gang of Four Behaviour Pattern

34.3 Intent

The Visitor pattern represents an operation to be performed on each of the members of an object structure in turn, capturing the results of those operations for client code. Visitor lets you define a new operation without changing the classes of the elements on which it operates

J. Hunt, *Scala Design Patterns: Patterns for Practical Reuse and Design*,
DOI 10.1007/978-3-319-02192-8_34,

34.4 Context

The Visitor pattern can be implemented is many different ways and for many different purposes and as with any pattern, it is necessary to apply the pattern to your own design situation before implementing it.

34.5 Forces/Motivation

The Visitor pattern is useful in situations where

- There are a variety of operations that need to be performed on an object structure.
- The object structure is composed of objects that belong to different types.
- The types of objects that can exist in the object structure do not change often and they ways in which they are related are consistent and predictable.

34.6 Constituent Parts

The constituent parts in the Visitor pattern are actually very simple and are illustrated in Fig. 34.1.

It is comprised of two classes and an interface. The interface defines the method that all objects that wish to receive a *Visitor* object must implement. In turn the *Visitor* class provides facilities for creating one or more state descriptions. A state description is an object, typically used to represent the state of an object or group of closely related objects. Thus a *Visitor* may have several state descriptions associated with it to allow it to describe the state of various un-related objects (or groups of objects).

In this framework the state description is implemented as a *StateMap*, keyed on the map name. In terms of implementation this association can be implemented as a HashMap or similar.

To use this architecture, one object must create the *Visitor* object and pass the object to the *visitable* objects. These objects can then fill out the state information in the state map (for an example, see the simple application later in this article).

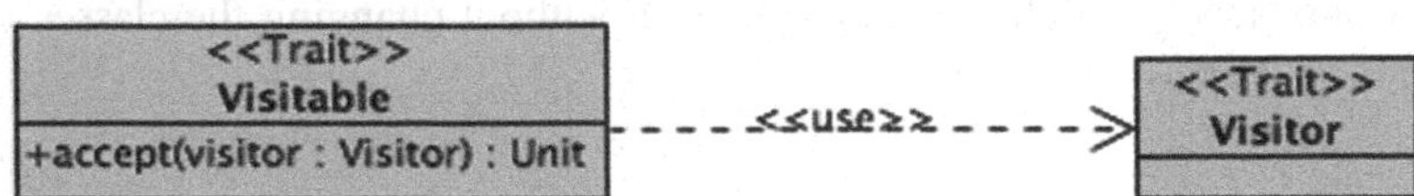

Fig. 34.1 Constituent parts of the Visitor pattern

34.7 Implementation Issues

Consideration must be given to where/how much of the logic defining how the visitor behaves can be placed within the Visitor itself. The more that the visitor is independent of the Visitable structure the more maintainable and comprehensible the Visitor will be. However, this may significantly increase the complexity of the interface between the Visitor and the Visitable. In contrast the higher the dependency between the Visitor and the Visitable the greater the need to update both if one changes. If behaviour is actually split between the Visitor and the Visitable then the line between the two may be blurred and maintenance become a far more significant task.

34.8 Concrete Example

The example explored in this section is for a document domain model. In this scenario a *Document* is comprised of a collection of *Chapters* and a *Table Of Contents*. The chapters each have a title and a set of headings. The Table Of contents is made up of a list of titles and headings, based on the chapters that comprise the document.

The challenge is to provide a way to generate the *Table Of Contents* without knowing the structure of the Document. To do this a Chapter Visitor is used. This is a visitor type (as indicated by the Visitor marker trait) that is used to visit each of the Visitable chapters and capture the information related to their title and headings. Once it has visited all the chapters it can generate the table of contents for the Document.

The types involved in this implementation are presented in Fig. 34.2.

The two traits, Visitor and Visitable are shown at the top of the diagram and are shown in Scala code below:

```
trait Visitor

trait Visitable {
  def accept(v: Visitor): Unit
}
```

The visitor is a marker trait and the Visitable trait defines a single method accept. This (abstract) method takes a Visitor as a parameter and return Unit.

The domain types, used to construct documents, are the Document, Chapter and Table of Contents types. These are presented below.

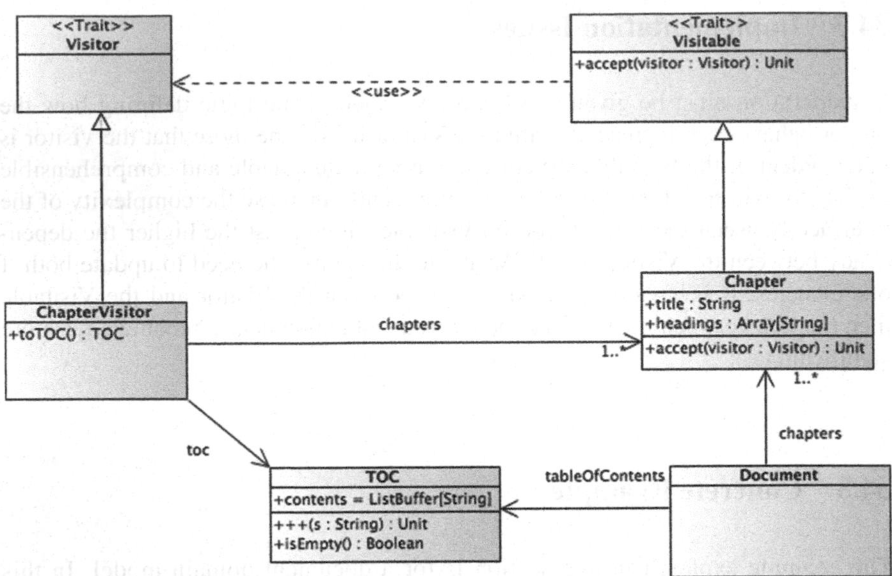

Fig. 34.2 Types used in the Table Of Contents visitor example

The Document type holds a list of chapters and can return a Table Of Contents on demand. The tableOfContents method uses the ChapterVisitor to generate the table of contents. To do this it passes a list of chapters into the ChapterVisitor constructor.

```
case class Document {
  val chapters = new ListBuffer[Chapter]()
  def tableOfContents: TOC = ChapterVisitor(chapters).toTOC
}
```

In this case Document is not an immutable object as chapters is a publically accessible list buffer (which keeps the example simple) however it could easily be modified to become immutable.

The Chapters case class is shown next. This class defines a chapter as having a title and a Set of headings. It also has the accept method required because it mixes in the Visitable trait which defines the abstract accept method. Internally to the accept method it checks to see that the actual type of the Visitor passed in is a ChapterVisitor. If it is then it adds its title and each of its headings, formatted appropriately to the ChapterVisitor.

```
case class Chapter(val title: String,
                   val headings: Set[String])
                                     extends Visitable {
  def accept(v: Visitor) = v match {
    case tocVisitor: ChapterVisitor => {
      tocVisitor.toc ++ (tocVisitor.count + ". " + this.title)
      var headingCount = 1
      headings.foreach(
          (heading: String) => {
            tocVisitor.toc ++ (tocVisitor.count +
                                 "." +
                                 headingCount +
                                 " " + heading);
            headingCount += 1 }
      )
    }
  }
}
```

The TOC case class represents the Table Of Contents. It allows strings to be added to the contents list it maintains. It also provides a isEmpty method to check to see if the table of contents exists yet and a toString to print out the contents list.

```
case class TOC {
  val contents = ListBuffer[String]()
  def ++(s: String) = contents append s
  def isEmpty = contents.isEmpty
  override def toString: String = "TOC: " + contents.toString
}
```

The ChapterVisitor case class holds a reference to all the chapters available and a count used to number each chapter (which is initialised to 1). It also holds a reference to an instance of the Table Of Contents class. When the toTOC method is invoked, if a Table Of Contents needs to be generated it invokes the accept method on each chapter passing itself in as a reference (and incrementing count for each chapter).

```
case class ChapterVisitor(chapters: ListBuffer[Chapter],
                          var count: Int = 1)
                                     extends Visitor {
  val toc: TOC = TOC()
  def toTOC: TOC = {
    if (toc.isEmpty) chapters.foreach(
        (c: Chapter) => { c.accept(ChapterVisitor.this); count += 1 })
    return toc
  }
}
```

The following Test application can be sued to execute this example. It first creates the Document object. It then creates two chapter objects and adds these to the document's list of chapters.

```
object Test extends App {
  val doc = Document()
  val c1 = Chapter("Introduction", Set("One", "Two", "Three"))
  val c2 = Chapter("Scala", Set("History", "Influences", "Sample"))
  doc.chapters.append(c1)
  doc.chapters.append(c2)
  println(doc.tableOfContents)
}
```

The result of running this test application is shown below:

```
TOC: ListBuffer(1. Introduction, 1.1 One, 1.2 Two, 1.3
Three, 2. Scala, 2.1 History, 2.2 Influences, 2.3 Sample)
```

34.9 Pros and Cons

34.9.1 Advantages

- The Visitor pattern makes it easy to (logically) add new operations to an object structure. Although a similar result could be achieved using Traits (by missing the traits into a set of objects) the visitor allows for run time dynamic binding of such operations.
- The Visitor represents the implementation of all the logic for some operation in one cohesive type, rather than spread across multiple types. This results in a simpler maintenance problem.

34.9.2 Drawbacks

- The concrete Visitable elements in the implementation must accept the visitor or allow access to enough of their state to allow the visitor access to the information required. This means that information may be exposed which should otherwise be hidden. This could be overcome by the use of a function that could be invoked only by visitors with a specific package or other controlled visibility.

34.10 Related Patterns

Composite The visitor pattern is often used with object structures that are organized based on the Composite pattern.

Chapter 35
Memento

35.1 Introduction

This pattern is used to obtain a snap shot of the state of an object without violating its encapsulation. It can be used to store the internal state of the object either for future reference (for example for auditing purposes) or to provide the ability to restore the state of the object if required (for example via an undo operation).

35.2 Pattern Classification

Gang Of Four Behavioural Pattern

35.3 Intent

This pattern provides the ability for client code to capture the state of an object without compromising or violating its encapsulation. In many cases this state can be restored at a later date if required.

35.4 Context

If it is useful to be able to return an object to a prior state, then it is necessary to record that prior state. It is also necessary to be able hold that state appropriately and to provide facilities to allow that state to be reused. The Memento pattern provides a design pattern for such a framework.

J. Hunt, *Scala Design Patterns: Patterns for Practical Reuse and Design*,
DOI 10.1007/978-3-319-02192-8_35, © Springer International Publishing Switzerland 2013

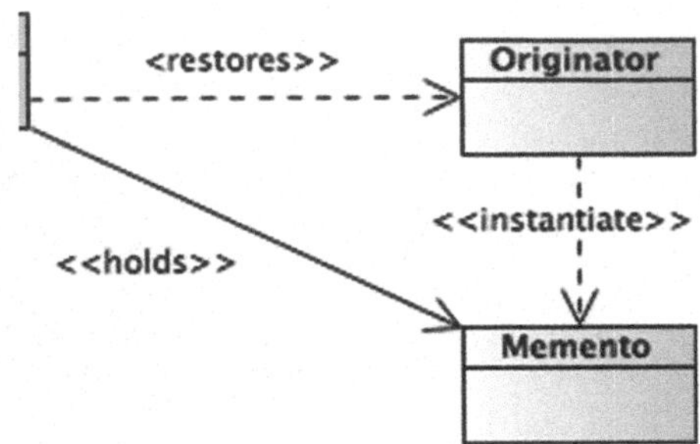

Fig. 35.1 Constituent parts in the Memento pattern

35.5 Forces/Motivation

Situations that motivate the use of the Memento pattern include:

- A client is about to perform one or more operations on an object and may need to be able to undo (rollback) the changes. The client can obtain a Memento of the current state of the object. If the changes being applied need to be undone then the client can use the Memento to reset the state of the object.
- If an undo/redo framework is being developed, a stack of Mementos can be used to recorded the state of an object and allow that state to be redone and undone as required.

35.6 Constituent Parts

The Consistent parts of the Memento Pattern are the originator and the caretaker plus the memento object itself. These roles are described in more detail below:

Originator This is an object that has internal state information that we wish to record in the memento. Using a Memento, the Originator itself can restore its own previous state.

Caretaker This is an object that record the mementos generated for the originator and that can restore the state of the originator using the stored memento information. The caretaker should not process the memento in anyway. It merely looks after the memento until such time as it is needed (the memento is said to be opaque to the Caretaker).

Memento An object representing the state of the Originator at a given point in time.

The relationships between these three constituent parts is illustrated in Fig. 35.1.

35.7 Implementation Issues

The Caretaker should not need to know anything about the Memento other than its existence and the operation to invoke on the Originator to obtain and supply a Memento.

The Memento should be opaque to the Caretaker.

The Originator should not affect the state of any other objects when its state is restored from the Memento. The Memento stores the state of a single object and restores the state of a single object.

Various methods can be used to store the state of an object; this could be done using Serialization, a class in the same scope as the Originator or via a Companion object.

35.8 Concrete Example

The example we will look at in this section provides a simple calculator with the ability to record and restore its state. The implementation makes use of traits to define not just the key roles in the Memento pattern but also to provide a generic implementation for the Memento pattern that can be easily mixed into a variety of classes.

The three traits are the Memento trait, the Originator trait and the Caretaker trait.

The generic Memento trait defines a protected property _state that holds an Option for a type *A* (initialised to *None*) and a getter method to return the current value of _state:

```
trait Memento[A] {
  protected var _state: Option[A] = None
  def state = _state.get
}
```

Thus the type of state being held by the Memento can be declared when appropriate (rather than being hard coded at this point).

The Originator trait declares a single abstract method createMemento which returns a Memento object. Again this is a generic trait with the type of state held by the memento left to be specified at a later date.

```
trait Originator[A] {
  def createMemento(): Memento[A]
}
```

The Caretaker trait defines a stack of Mementos that can be used to store additional Mementos or can be popped to retrieve previously stored Mementos. This trait can easily be mixed into concrete types to provide the basic Caretaker functionality.

```
trait Caretaker[A] {
  val mementos = Stack[Memento[A]]()
}
```

On top of these three generic traits we will build the Calculator application and its ability to backup and restore the state of the calculator.

The first aspect of the Calculator application is the definition of a CalcState type to be used with the Memento Pattern traits. This is defined in a package object for ease of access within the calculator application:

```
package object memento {
  type CalcState = Tuple4[Int,Int,String,Double]
}
```

A package object provides a convenient way of defining package level functions, types etc. The memento package object defines the CalcState type as a Tuple4; although a specific type such as a concrete class could have been used.

We can now define a concrete case class for the calculator specific Memento:

```
case class CalculatorMomento(s: CalcState) extends Memento[CalcState] {
  _state = Option(s)
}
```

This CalculatorMemento class mixes in the Memento trait using the CalcState type as the type of the state information used with the Memento.

The Calculator class itself mixes in the Originator trait (which requires the create Memento method) and the Caretaker trait that provides the stack based behaviour for recording and accessing Mementos:

```
class Calculator extends Originator[CalcState] with Caretaker[CalcState] {
  var first = 0
  var second = 0
  var operator = "+"
  var result = 0.0

  def calculate = operator match {
    case "+" => result = first + second
    case "-" => result = first - second
    case "*" => result = first * second
    case "/" => result = first / second
  }

  def createMemento = CalculatorMomento((first, second, operator, result))

  def backupOperation = mementos push createMemento

  def restoreOperation = {
    val state = mementos.pop().state
    first = state._1
    second = state._2
    operator = state._3
    result = state._4
  }

  override def toString() = result + " = " + first + " " + operator + " " + second

}
```

Note that the backOperation method pushes a Memento (produced by the create-Memento method) on to the mementos stack (obtained from the Caretaker trait) and the restoreOperation retrieves a Memento from the top of the stack and restores the fields in the Calculator.

The following test application illustrates the use of the Memento Pattern in the calculator example:

```
object Test extends App {
  val calc = new Calculator()
  calc.first = 10
  calc.second = 20
  calc.calculate
  println(calc)
  calc.backupOperation
  calc.second = 5
  calc.calculate
  println(calc)
  calc.restoreOperation
  println(calc)
}
```

The output from this example application is shown below:

```
30.0 = 10 + 20
15.0 = 10 + 5
30.0 = 10 + 20
```

35.9 Pros and Con

The advantages of the Memento Pattern are:

- Encapsulation of the Originator from a client is preserved as the Memento avoids exposing information that only the originator should be aware of.
- The Originator is simplified, as it is not responsible for managing the Mementos (although in out example we missed that behaviour into the Calculator it is was defined in the Caretaker trait and merely reuse din the Calculator).
- In Scala ensuring that only the Originator can access data from the Memento is possible through the use of package private operations.

The drawbacks of the Memento Pattern include:

- If the state of the Originator is complex and potentially large in terms of memory then creating multiple Mementos may be expensive.
- It is not clear when the Caretaker should delete a Memento it is holding.

35.10 Related Patterns

Command Commands can use mementos to maintain state for otherwise undoable operations.

Part V
Functional Design Patterns

Chapter 36
Functor

36.1 Introduction

Functor is a functional pattern in which a container references a group of objects and is provided with:

- The ability to apply a function to every object in the container (via a function *fmap*)
- Without altering the structure of the container
- Typically returns a new container (context) that contains the results of applying the function to the original contents of the container

In which the container provides the context for the function that is being applied (the container is often referred to as the context or as providing a *computational context* for the function).

Each Functor has a unique identity which represents its base value, for example the identity of integers is 0, or a for a string might be the empty string "".

There are a number of rules associated with Functors that affect their implementation, these rules are:

1. Applying the provided function to the Functors identity has no effect,
   This implies that fmap(id) == id. For example adding two 0 together results in 0, similarly the act of concatenating two empty strings together results in another empty string being created.
2. Functional combination applicability
   Combing two functions together and applying the combined function has the same effect as applying one function followed by a second function, that is fmap(g + h) == fmap(g) + fmap(h)

A functor is therefore a class, trait or object with usually only one method (or function) that applies another function to the objects held in the container (or context).

Functor objects can be created, passed as parameters and manipulated wherever it is useful to apply a function to a set of objects.

J. Hunt, *Scala Design Patterns: Patterns for Practical Reuse and Design*,
DOI 10.1007/978-3-319-02192-8_36, © Springer International Publishing Switzerland 2013

The collection classes provided by Scala exhibit Functor behaviour. In fact the more you look at the classes in Scala the more you will see examples of the Functor pattern.

36.2 Pattern Classification

Functional

36.3 Intent

To provide a container for a set of objects that allows a function to be applied to all elements within the container.

36.4 Context

There are many situation in which it is necessary to be able to apply some operation or functional to a set of objects. In languages such as Java or C++ such requirements are met by implementing some form of for loop. This for loop may use an index into the container or may be an iterator over the container, for example:

```
// Pseudo Java
Set set = new Set(1, 2, 3)
for (int i : set) {
     func(i)
 }
```

This is not a very functional approach. There is already some form of container available for the data and all that is required is to tell that container that a specific function should be applied to each element in turn. This results in a more expressive as well as more concise from of the above:

```
val c = Container(1, 2, 3)
c.fmap(func)
```

36.5 Forces/Motivation

The primarily motivating use case is the need to regularly apply a function to a group of data items.

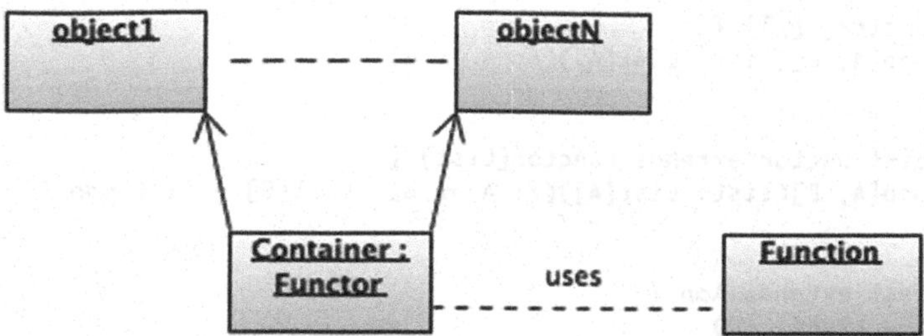

Fig. 36.1 Functor pattern roles and relationships

36.6 Constituent Parts

The constituent parts in a Functor are:

- The Functor container such as a List, Seq, ListBuffer or a custom container
- The ability to apply a function to all members in the container (usually represented as a function *fmap*)
- A one parameter function to apply to each element in the container

This is illustrated in Fig. 36.1.

In this diagram a container references a group of objects (object 1 to object n) and has an operation *fmap* that uses a function. It applies the function to the objects and creates a new group that is the result of applying the function to each.

36.7 Implementation Issues

There are a number of completing possible implementations within the Scala world for a Functor. The next section presents both a purely functional approach and a hybrid, more Scala oriented solution.

36.8 Concrete Example

36.8.1 Function Based Solution

The first implementation provided takes a purely functional approach. In this approach a Trait Functor is defined that specifies an fmap operation that takes a container of objects and a function to apply to that container. This can then be used to apply the fmap operation to any container.

```
trait Functor[T[_]] {
  def fmap[A, B](list: List[A])(f: A => B): List[B]
}

object ListFunctor extends Functor[List] {
  def fmap[A, B](list: List[A])(f: A => B): List[B] = list map f
}

object Test extends App {
  val l1 = List(1, 2)
  val result = ListFunctor.fmap(l1)((i: Int) => i + 1)
  println(result)
}
```

An example implementation of a Functor implementation is provided by the ListFunctor object. This object specifies that the container will be a List and that the result will be a List (where the type of the contents of the list will be determined at the point of use). Note that strictly speaking the List collection is already a Functor as it has a method map which performs the exact same role as the fmap function – however List is used here for simplicity and to illustrate the concept.

The object test then creates a List and applies the function to add a value 1 to each integer in the list. This results in a new list being created. For example:

```
List(2, 3)
```

36.8.2 Hybrid Solution

The version shown in the previous section illustrates that the Functor is a pattern and does not require a container to incorporate the Functor behaviour directly. However, it is not uncommon to want to develop a container that incorporates the Functor behaviour as a single concept. This version is illustrated in Fig. 36.2 and the source is presented below.

This revised implementation alters the previous implementation by providing a case class that will provide the implementation of the Functor behaviour and includes the concept of an *id* to which a function can be applied but will have no effect.

```
trait Functor[T[_], A] {
  def fmap[B](f: A => B): T[B]
  val identity: A
}

case class ListFunctor[A](val identity: A, list: List[A]) extends Functor[List,A]{
  def fmap[B](f: A => B): List[B] = list.map(f)
}

object Test2 extends App {
  val lf = ListFunctor[Int](0, List(1,2))
  println(lf.fmap(_ + 1))
}
```

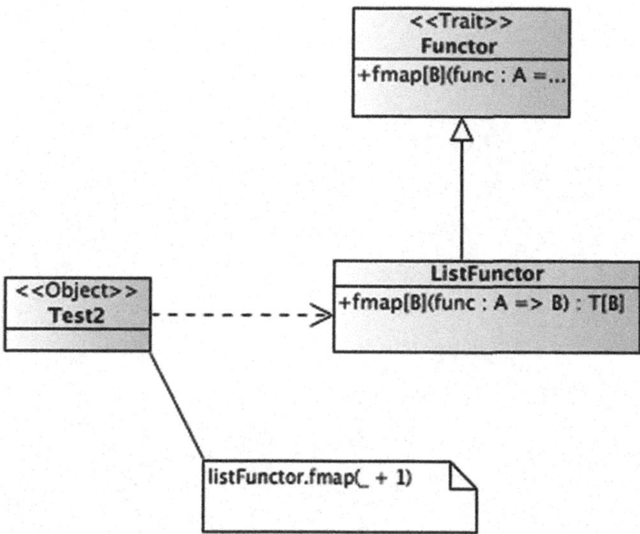

Fig. 36.2 Types used in the hybrid solution

Now in the Test2 application a new ListFunctor object is created for the List 1, 2 and that a function to add 1 to the objects in the ListFunctor container is applied using the *fmap* function. The result is as before

```
List(2, 3)
```

However, the ListFunctor now encapsulates both the data and the ability to apply the function to that data.

36.9 Pros and Cons

Functors greatly simplify the way in which a function can be applied to the contents of a container. However, whether that contents should be modified or (if as has been done here) the result of applying the function should be returned depends on whether the container should be mutable or immutable. This example has assumed immutability but that is not the only option.

36.10 Related Patterns

Applicative Functor This pattern extends the concept of a Functor.

Monad A Monad is an Applicative Functor and therefore also extends the basic concept of a Functor.

Chapter 37
Applicative Functor

37.1 Introduction

The Applicative Functor pattern builds on the Functor pattern described in the last chapter. This pattern adds two additional functions; one that places objects in to the container (or context) and one that applies functions held in a context to all the objects held in the container returning the result of applying each function in turn.

Note that the Applicative Functor *is a* Functor and thus everything that was said about the Functor pattern also holds true for the Applicative Functor Pattern.

The two operations added by the Applicative Functor pattern are typically called *pure* (to place things in context) and *apply* which is sometimes represented by <*>. These two operations are discussed below:

- **The pure operation**. This operation places objects in a context (or container). That is, it takes an object and wraps that object in its minimal context T (where T might for example be a List). It then returns that list containing just that element.
- **The apply operation**. This operation takes one or more functions, already in a context (such as a List) and applies them to the objects already in the context. The result that is generated is also in the context. The exact effect of applying the functions to the objects depends on the implementation. For example, a list of functions may be applied to a list of objects resulting a new list of the results being generated. The implementation may also ensure that the first function is applied to the initial objects in the list, subsequent functions are applied to the results generated by the previous function. The effect of the functions is thus culminative (however this is an implementation decisions).

J. Hunt, *Scala Design Patterns: Patterns for Practical Reuse and Design*,
DOI 10.1007/978-3-319-02192-8_37, © Springer International Publishing Switzerland 2013

37.2 Pattern Classification

Functional

37.3 Intent

To provide allow the construction of contained elements plus the ability to apply lists of functions.

37.4 Context

Being able to easily construct a container (or more generically a context) for a objects is generally useful. In addition being able to easily apply multiple functions in sequence to the contents of a container is also generally useful.

However, in isolation the Applicative Functor patterns contributes only a small amount to the Functor concept (however it is a building block on the way to Monoid).

37.5 Forces/Motivation

The motivating use case for Applicative Functors is the desire to either easily construct a container/context or to easily apply multiple functions to the contents of a container/context.

37.6 Constituent Parts

The constituent parts of the Applicative Functor are as for the Functor pattern, namely:

- The Functor container such as a List, Seq, ListBuffer or a custom container
- The ability to apply a function to all members in the container (usually represented as a function fmap)
- A one parameter function to apply to each element in the container

With the addition of:

- The *pure* operation to place objects in context
- The *apply* function to apply a list functions in context to objects in context. This is illustrated in Fig. 37.1.

In this diagram a group of objects are held in a list (context) and a group of functions are also held in a list (context). The Applicative Functor can then apply each function in turn to the objects using the *apply* operation.

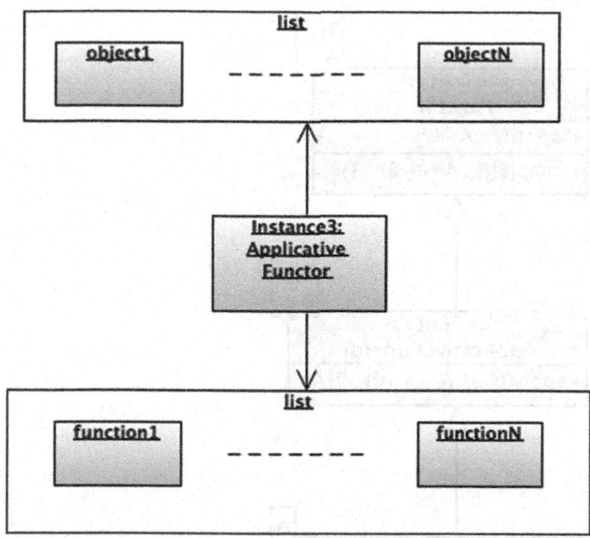

Fig. 37.1 The constituent parts of an Applicative Functor

37.7 Implementation Issues

The Applicative Functor can be implemented purely in functional terms as a type that has functional members that take a context such as a List and apply the Applicative Functor operations to the members of that list returning appropriate results.

However, in the example shown in the next section we have chosen to hold the objects being contained within the Applicative Functor and to apply the methods defining the Applicative Functor to that list.

37.8 Concrete Example

The example implementation builds on the hybrid Functor example illustrated in the previous chapter. It constructs a container that can hold lists of objects and can apply lists of functions to those objects. It also uses a companion object to provide an implementation of the pure operation that can place an object into context; in this case this means creating an instance of the container and wrapping the object provided.

The structure of the implementation is shown in Fig. 37.2.

The Functor trait is the same trait as was used in the previous chapter, illustrating that an Applicative Functor is also an example of the Functor pattern.

```
trait Functor[T[_], A] {
  def fmap[B](f: A => B): T[B]
  val identity: A
}
```

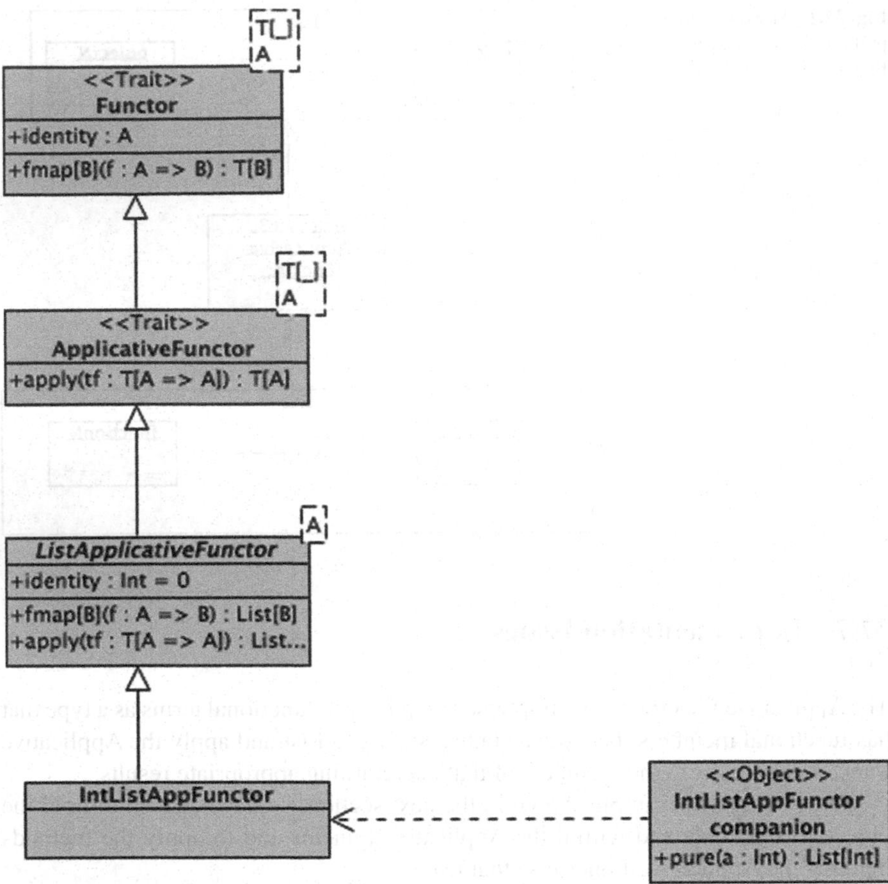

Fig. 37.2 The types used in the Applicative Functor example

The ApplicativeFunctor trait builds on this by adding the apply operation that takes a set of functions that are also in the same type of context as the objects held by the Functor, and returns the result of applying these functions in context.

```
trait ApplicativeFunctor[T[_], A] extends Functor[T, A] {
  def apply(tf: T[A => A]): T[A]
}
```

An abstract class, ListApplicativeFunctor, is provided that uses List as the *context* or container for the objects and the functions. The actual type of the list will be defined by subclass of ListApplicativeFunctor, we could there for have integer, String or Person List based Applicative Functors. Note that the ListApplicativeFunctor could be marked as immutable as it does not modify the change the list of objects held once created.

```
abstract class ListApplicativeFunctor[A](list: List[A])
                            extends ApplicativeFunctor[List, A] {
  def fmap[B](f: A => B): List[B] = list.map(f)
  def apply(tf: List[A => A]): List[A] = {
    var l: List[A] = list
    tf.foreach(f => l = l.map(f))
    return l
  }
}
```

The implementation of the *fmap* operation exploits the built-in map function of the underlying List implementation (note that this implies that lists are Applicative Functors).

The implementation of the apply operation takes each function and applies it in turn. The first function is applied the objects held by the Applicative Functor in the list. Subsequent functions are applied to the results returned by the previous function.

The concrete case class IntListAppFunctor merely provides the type to use with the ListApplicativeFunctor and defines the *identity* for integer list based applicative functors.

```
case class IntListAppFunctor(list: List[Int],
                             val identity: Int = 0)
                               extends ListApplicativeFunctor[Int](list)
```

The companion object for the IntListAppFunctor meets the other part of the Applicative Functor requirement by providing the pure method. It takes a single integer and returns that integer wrapped in a IntListAppFunctor. Note that as such the pure method is a factory method for the creation of IntListAppFunctors.

```
object IntListAppFunctor {
  implicit def pure(a: Int) = IntListAppFunctor(List[Int](a))
}
```

Finally the Test application for this implementation is presented below:

```
object Test extends App {

  val af = IntListAppFunctor(List(1, 2))
  val increase = (x: Int) => x + 1
  val double = (x: Int) => x * 2

  println(af.apply(List(increase)))
  println(af.apply(List(increase, double)))

  println(IntListAppFunctor.pure(23))

}
```

The Test application creates an IntListAppFunctor for the values 1 and 2 (held in a List). It then defines two functions, *increase* and *double*. The *increase* function adds 1 to an integer value while the *double* function doubles the integer value given to it. The Test application then first applies the *increase* function to the Applicative Functor and then applies both the *increase* and *double* functions to the Applicative Functor. Finally the Test application illustrates the use of the pure operation.

The results of running this application are shown below:

```
List(2, 3)
List(4, 6)
IntListAppFunctor(List(23),0)
```

37.9 Pros and Cons

The benefit of the Applicative Functor is that it adds the pure and apply methods to the basic Functor concept. It is thus possible to create (pure) an Applicative Functor from some objects. It also allows functions to be applied to the objects held in the context of the Applicative Functor.

The drawback of the Applicative Functor is that it is only a small step up from the basic Functor concept and thus this can be confusing.

37.10 Related Patterns

Functor An Applicative Functor is a type of Functor.

Monad A Monad is also a type of Applicative Functor.

Factory Operation The pure method of the IntListAppFunctor object essentially implements the factory operation pattern.

Immutable The Applicative Functor as written in the example presented here is essentially an immutable object. It could therefore also implement the Immutable trait and is thus an example of the Immutable pattern.

Chapter 38
Monoid Pattern

38.1 Introduction

The term *Monoid* is one that you will come across repeatedly within the field of Functional Programming and also within abstract algebra and group theory. The pattern described in this chapter is derived from these concepts but is applied to Scala. Within the field of abstract algebra, a branch of mathematics, a monoid is an algebraic structure with a single associative binary operation and an identity element. In general the monoid concept captures the idea of function composition within a set.

In terms of patterns, the Monoid Pattern defines a set of objects and an operation for combining them together (plus a unique identity value which can be combined with any object to return that object).

You can see the Monoid behaviour in several well-known types:

- Integer numbers where 0 is the identity and you can combine them together to from new numbers
- Lists that can be concatenated together (where Nil or the empty list [] is the identity)
- Strings that can be appended (and where the empty string or "" is the identity)

The identity of the Monoid is often referred to as the "no-op" element in that it has no effect when combined with something else in the set of values.

Finally, the operation that combines objects together in the Monoid must be associative. That is the order in which the values are combined must not be significant. For example, adding 5 to 3 or adding 3 to 5 both result in the value 8 being generated.

There are numerous concrete examples of the Monoid Pattern in Scala. These include String and Int on which the examples in this chapter are based. They also include other numeric sets (such as Doubles), Lists, Sequences and other collection classes etc.

J. Hunt, *Scala Design Patterns: Patterns for Practical Reuse and Design*,
DOI 10.1007/978-3-319-02192-8_38, © Springer International Publishing Switzerland 2013

38.2 Pattern Classification

Functional

38.3 Intent

To allow two objects to be combined together

38.4 Context

The Monoid Pattern is useful in two contexts. It is usual in any scenario where you have a group of values/objects that you wish to be able to combine together and for which you wish to have a *no-op* identity element. Such scenarios are common whenever you are creating data structure like types. The other context for a Monoid is that it is a stepping-stone towards the Monad pattern.

It is also useful to note that if you have a Monoid that it is possible to reduce a set of values in the Monoid down to a single value by repeatedly applying the append operator to each value . For example, if I have a list of integers, then I can use the Monoid Pattern to define a type that can append each value to the preceding value to generate a single integer value (which might be the sum of all the integers depending on the operation of the com).

38.5 Forces/Motivation

The need for a standardised way to combine together objects in a set such that the combination order is not important.

38.6 Constituent Parts

The constituent parts of the Monoid Pattern are a type 'T', an operation to combine them (typically called 'append') and a value identity. There are two rules associated with the Monoid Pattern:

- Append must be associative such that append(x, y) == append(y, x)
- Identity must be an identity for that append function such that append (identity, x) == x

38.7 Implementation Issues

A decision must be made regarding the objects to which the Monoid functionality is applied. In the example in the next section the objects are contained within the Monoid type. However, another approach would be to hold the objects in a separate list and implement a Monoid type that defined a set of functions that took the List (that is the context) and applied the Monoid functionality to the objects in the list.

38.8 Concrete Example

The following example illustrates how the Monoid Pattern can be implemented in Scala. We will first define a trait Monoid to represent the Monoid concept. This trait is a generic trait that works with objects of type T. The append method takes two objects of type T and returns a new object of type T. This new object represents the result of appending the two objects together. The result of this append operation will depend on the types involved. For example, if you append together two integers then the result might be the total of the two integers, where as appending two strings together might be the concatenation of the two strings etc..

```
trait Monoid[T] {
  def append(m1: T, m2: T): T
  val identity: T
}
```

This trait can be mixed into classes, objects or extended by other traits as required. In this example we will look at mixing the trait into a case class and an object. The case class defines a concrete implementation of the Trait Pattern for Strings. The StringMonoid is presented below:

```
case class StringMonoid extends Monoid[String] {
  def append(s1: String, s2: String) = s1 + s2
  val identity = ""
}
```

The StringMonoid is a parameterized class that sets the type T for the Monoid trait to String. The append method thus combines string together (using string concatenation). The identity value is also set to the empty string literal "".

This StringMonoid can be used as shown below:

```
val stringMonoid = StringMonoid()
println(stringMonoid.append(stringMonoid.identity, "John"))
println(stringMonoid.append("John", "Hunt"))
```

This example appends a string with the StringMonoid identity value and also appends two strings together. The output from this code is shown below:

```
John
JohnHunt
```

As a second example, an object IntMonoid has also been defined. This creates a Monoid for Int values and illustrates that the trait representing the Monoid Pattern can be mixed into different types:

```
object IntMonoid extends Monoid[Int] {
  def append(x: Int, y: Int) = x + y
  val identity = 0
}
```

In this case the append method adds the two integers together and returns a new integer as the result. The identity value is also set to Zero (which again acts as the no-op operator). An example of using the IntMonoid is presented below:

```
println(IntMonoid.append(IntMonoid.identity, 1))
println(IntMonoid.append(1, 2))
println(IntMonoid.append(2, 1))
```

This example adds the Int identity value (0) to the value 1. It also appends 1 and 2 together and 2 and 1 together. The end result is shown below:

```
1
3
3
```

This illustrates the associative nature of the Monoid Pattern.

38.9 Pros and Cons

The advantages of the Monoid Pattern include:

- A standardised approach to how values may be combined in a particular domain.
- The guarantee of associativity ensures that the behaviour associated with function combinations is defined.

The drawbacks are that

- Not all sets can easily be made transitive. For example, strictly speaking the String Monoid as implemented falls down on this point as concatenating two strings together may result in a different result depending on the ordering of the strings.

38.10 Related Patterns

Monad A Monad can be viewed as a type of Monoid.

Chapter 39
Monad Pattern

39.1 Introduction

As with Monoids, Monads are a recurring theme in the Scala and Functional Programming world. This chapter presents a design pattern based on the concept of a Monad. In pure functional programming a monad is a structure that represents computations on a set of objects.

The Monad Pattern takes the concepts behind the monad structure and defines how these can be used to create a container type that handles the creation and combination of Monads, the application of functions to members of that container, how pipelines of functions may be applied to the contents of the container and how multiple containers can be flattened into a single container.

The Monad Pattern identifies a container of type T that provides a set of operations that can be grouped together as follows:

Functor like operations

- Possesses a unique identity value to which applying the functions in the Monad has no affect
- The ability to apply a function to every object in the container (via a function fmap) returning a new container of the same type.
- Functional combination applicability. That is combining two functions together and applying the combined function has the same effect as applying one function followed by a second function.

Applicative Functor like operations

- The *pure* operation. This operation places objects in a context (or container).
- The *apply* operation. This operation takes one or more functions, already in a context (such as a List) and applies them to the objects already in the context. The result that is generated is also in the context.

J. Hunt, *Scala Design Patterns: Patterns for Practical Reuse and Design*,
DOI 10.1007/978-3-319-02192-8_39, © Springer International Publishing Switzerland 2013

Monoid like operations

- A combination (append) operation that combines the elements of the set together.

With the additional of

- An operation that takes multiple sets of values and combined them into a single set of values, often referred to as *join*.

From this description you can see that a Monad is actually the combination of the Monoid pattern with the Applicative Functor (and thus Functor) patterns. Or to put it another way a Monad is an Applicative Functor and it is a Monoid (combined together). The one addition made by the Monad Pattern itself is the addition of a single operation *join*.

Many of the collection classes in the Scala language are examples of the Monad Pattern.

39.2 Pattern Classification

Functional

39.3 Intent

To allow for the creation of object containers with a default set of operations that allow for the composition of the containers and the application of functions to the contents of the containers.

39.4 Context

Containers (or more generically contexts) for a group of objects that is generally useful. Standardising the way this is done brings major benefits in comprehension, (human) reusability and consistency.

39.5 Forces/Motivation

Many data structures represent common behaviour that when understood allow a new data structure to be quickly and effectively adopted. These recurring themes can be identified as concrete implementations of the Monad Pattern. By explicitly identifying these behaviours and standardising them both consistency and clarity benefit.

39.6 Constituent Parts

The constituent parts of the Monad Pattern are the container for the types being contained, plus the operations inherited from the Functor, ApplicativeFunctor and Monoid patterns. The final component is the *join* operation provided by the Monad itself.

39.7 Implementation Issues

Consideration must be given to the style of Monad required. The approach taken in the next section assumes one in which the Monad is the container for the objects and for the functionality that can be applied to the objects. However, many other examples will assume that the Monad functionality is separate from the container of the objects (for example where a List is used as the context and a separate type provides the Monad functionality).

39.8 Concrete Example

The example implementation used in this section represents the very nature of the Monad; that is it is:

- a Functor,
- an Applicative Functor and
- a Monoid

combined together. Thus the types involved in the implementation of the Monad Pattern include these concepts plus the type to be placed into content (i.e. the type of the container). These are illustrated in Fig. 39.1.

The end result is that the Monad trait, as illustrated in this diagram, merely combines together the Monoid and Applicative Functor traits. The four traits involved in this implementation are described below.

The Functor and Applicative Functor traits define the *identity*, *fmap* and *apply* features of the Monad. The Functor and Applicative Functor traits are essentially those described in previous chapters.

```
trait Functor[T[_], A] {
  def fmap(func: A => A): Functor[T, A]
  val identity: T[A]
}

trait ApplicativeFunctor[T[_], A] extends Functor[T, A] {
  def apply(functions: T[A => A]): ApplicativeFunctor[T, A]
}
```

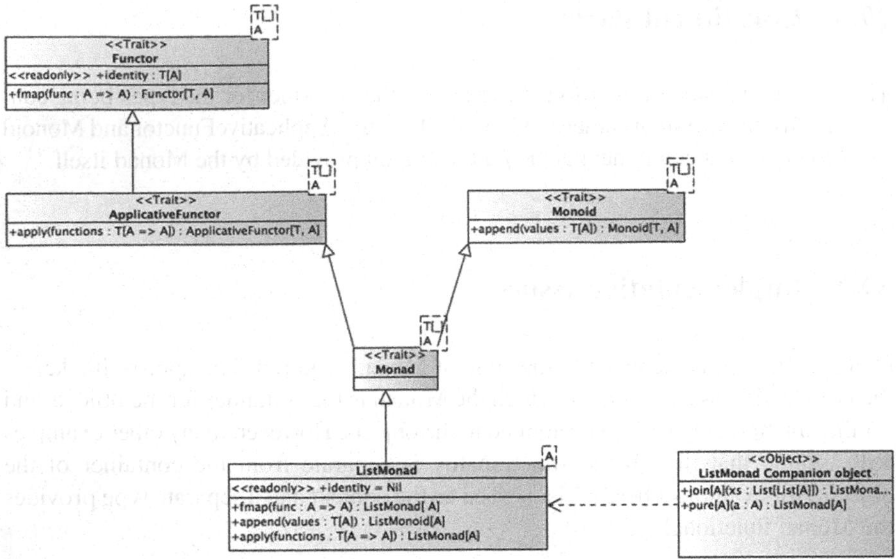

Fig. 39.1 Types used in the Monad example

Similarly the Monoid trait is essentially that presented in the last chapter with the exception that the identity property has not been included here as it will be inherited from the Functor trait:

```
trait Monoid[T[_], A] {
  def append(values: T[A]): Monoid[T, A]
}
```

The Monad trait is then merely the association of the Applicative Functor with the Monoid trait:

```
trait Monad[T[_], A] extends Monoid[T, A] with ApplicativeFunctor[T, A]
```

This very neatly highlights that a Monad is the combination of Monoid with an Applicative Functor.

The concrete class used to implement the Monad trait in this case uses the List collection type to hold the values within the Monad container:

```
case class ListMonad[A](val list: List[A]) extends Monad[List, A] {
  val identity = Nil

  def fmap(f: A => A): ListMonad[A] = ListMonad(list.map(f))
  def apply(tf: List[A => A]): ListMonad[A] = {
    var l: List[A] = list
    tf.foreach(f => l = l.map(f))
    return ListMonad(l)
  }
  def append(l: List[A]) = ListMonad(list ++ l)
}
```

The case class ListMonad mixes in the Monad and provides a definition for the *identity* read only property (in this case the empty list *Nil*) and implementations for the *fmap*, *apply* and *append* methods.

The implementation of the *fmap* operation exploits the built-in map function of the underlying List implementation.

The implementation of the *apply* operation takes each function and applies it in turn. The first function is applied the objects held by the Applicative Functor in the list. Subsequent functions are applied to the results returned by the previous function.

Finally the append method takes a list of values and concatenates them with the list of values already held and returns a new List Monad that contains the result of the concatenation.

The *pure* and *join* operations are not defined within the class itself, instead these are defined in a companion object as they are effective factory methods used to create List Monads for the values passed to them:

```
object ListMonad {
  def join[A](xs: List[ListMonad[A]]): ListMonad[A] = {
    val buffer = ListBuffer[A]()
    xs.foldLeft(buffer)((x, y) => x ++= y.list)
    ListMonad(buffer.toList)
  }
  def pure[A](a: A) = ListMonad(List(a))
}
```

The *pure* method takes a single object and returns that object wrapped in a ListMonad. The *join* method takes a list of ListMonads and returns a single ListMonad that represents the concatenation of the multiple ListMonads passed in.

The following Test application illustrates some examples of using this List Monad class for a set of Ints.

```
object Test extends App {
  val monad = ListMonad[Int](List(1, 2))
  println(monad)
  println(monad append List(6, 7))
  println(monad fmap (_ + 1))

  val increase = (x: Int) => x + 1
  val double = (x: Int) => x * 2
  println(monad apply (List(increase)))
  println(monad apply (List(increase, double)))

  val l1 = List(ListMonad(List(1, 2)), ListMonad(List(5, 6)))
  println(ListMonad join l1)

  println(ListMonad pure 4)
}
```

This Test application illustrates creating a List Monad and appending a list to it and mapping a function to the elements in the List Monad. It then defines two functions (increase and decrease) that can be placed in a list and applied in sequence to the List Monad. Finally, the example joins to List Monads together and illustrating using the pure method to create a new List Monad.

The output from this application is shown below:

```
ListMonad(List(1, 2))
ListMonad(List(1, 2, 6, 7))
ListMonad(List(2, 3))
ListMonad(List(2, 3))
ListMonad(List(4, 6))
ListMonad(List(1, 2, 5, 6))
ListMonad(List(4))
```

39.9 Pros and Cons

The primary advantage of the Monad Pattern is that it is a standardised building block for a large set of function oriented data structures within Scala (and within your own applications).

The primary drawback of the pattern is that the terms used with the pattern may be confusing for those not familiar with Functional Programming (or the design pattern) and may therefore result in less comprehensible applications.

39.10 Related Patterns

Functor A Monad is a type of Functor.
Applicative Functor A Monad is also a type of Applicative Functor.
Monoid A Monad is also a type of Monoid.

Chapter 40
Foldable

40.1 Introduction

When representing sets of objects, a common requirement is to want to reduce that set down to a single object by applying a function. This object represents the final result of applying the given function to the first two elements, then taking the result of that application and applying it to the next in the sequence and so on until all elements are processed.

For example, given the set of integers 1, 2, 3, 4 we could apply the function '+' to the set such as we obtain the result 10 which is equivalent to $(((1+2)+3)+4)$. We have thus folded (or reduced) the set down to a single element.

The Foldable pattern presents a standard design pattern for applying such a reduction to a set. It is also sometimes known as *Reduce*.

40.2 Pattern Classification

Function Design Pattern

40.3 Intent

To reduce a set of objects of type T to a single object of type T.

J. Hunt, *Scala Design Patterns: Patterns for Practical Reuse and Design*,
DOI 10.1007/978-3-319-02192-8_40, © Springer International Publishing Switzerland 2013

40.4 Context

Given a set of objects it may be necessary to produce a single object that represents the result of applying a function to each element in the set. A simple integer example is shown above. Another example might be a set of Strings that are to be concatenated together to form a single string. Rather than iterate over the whole set, requiring the creation of a temporary variable to hold the result, we can *fold* the set into a single resultant object.

40.5 Forces/Motivation

The Foldable Pattern can be used when

- A set of objects of type T are held in some context (such as a List).
- A function can be applied to these objects to construct a single object of type T.

40.6 Constituent Parts

The constituent parts of the Foldable pattern are a type 'T', a set of objects of type T held in some context, an operation that can combine these objects together and a function that can take the operation and return a single result of type T

40.7 Implementation Issues

The foldable operation may be intrinsic to the context in which the objects are held or extrinsic to it. That is, if a set of objects is held in MyContainer (the context) then the fold operation may be part of the container or may be external to that container.

It is also necessary to decide in which direction the fold operation is applied. That is, is it applied left to right or right to left? In some cases the decision on the direction may be delegated to the client code by the provision of a *foldRight* and a *foldLeft* operation (see the List class in Scala).

40.8 Concrete Example

As an example of a container that implements the Foldable pattern we will explore a simple generic class.

The Foldable trait defines the key abstract fold method. This method takes a two parameter operation and returns a single result. The Foldable trait is generic and can be parameterized to held a container (T[_]) and a type A. For convenience an *identity* read only property is also abstractly defined (although this is not required it is a useful feature)

```
trait Foldable[T[_],A] {
  val identity: A
  def fold(op: (A, A) => A): A
}
```

The abstract class FoldableList (defined in the package foldable) applies the Foldable trait to a class which will use a List as the container to hold the set of objects. The type remains generic with the type of the elements of the list being specified by the generic type A. Note private[foldable] means that the list val is visible within the package foldable but private to anything outside the package.

```
abstract class FoldableList[A] extends Foldable[List,A] {
  private[foldable] val list: List[A]
  def fold(op: (A, A) => A): A = list.foldRight(identity)(op)
}
```

As the container for the set of objects is a List we can use the build in function *foldRight* to implement our fold method. The identity is used for the initial (starting value) used with *foldRight*. This is why the abstract *identify* property was defined in the Foldable trait. Note that at this point we have still not said what the identity value is nor what the type contained in the List will be.

Two concrete FoldableList classes are defined, one to hold Integers and one to hold Strings:

```
case class FoldableIntList(val list: List[Int])
                          extends FoldableList[Int] {
  val identity = 0
}

case class FoldableStringList(val list: List[String])
                            extends FoldableList[String] {
  val identity = ""
}
```

Both classes define a constructor argument list that will meet the requirement of providing a concrete implementation of the list property (that overrides the abstract definition defined in the FoldableList class). In the first case it is a List of Integers that will be required and in the second it is a List of Strings. Both classes also define what the identity (or no op value) for that class will be. In the case of integers it is Zero and for Strings it is the empty string "".

The following code illustrates how these two Foldable classes are used. The first example illustrates the creation of a FoldableIntList containing the integers 1, 2, 3 and 4. The function + is then applied the members of the FoldableIntList (note we have used the implicit parameter placeholder format in this example):

```
val foldable = FoldableIntList(List(1, 2, 3, 4))
println(foldable.fold(_ + _))
```

The result of executing these lines of code is that the number '10' is printed out.

The second example illustrates the use of the FoldableStringList class:

```
val strings = FoldableStringList(List("A", "B", "C"))
println(strings.fold(_ + _))
```

The result of applying the string concatenation operator to the three strings "A", "B" and "C" is the string "ABC".

40.9 Pros and Cons

The advantages of the Foldable Pattern are:

- A standard approach to the reduction of a set of objects to a single resultant object.
- Different functions can be applied to the set of objects held in the container thus allowing different resultant objects to be created.

The drawbacks of the Foldable Pattern include:

- It must be possible to combine the objects in the container together in some way. For example a set of Person objects may not be able to be reduced in this way.

40.10 Related Patterns

Monoid A Monoid is a container that holds a set of objects and allows functions to be applied to the elements in the set. It is not uncommon to find that a particular implementation of a Monoid is also an implementation of the Foldable pattern.

Chapter 41
Zipper

41.1 Introduction

The Zipper pattern is oriented around the traversal and possible *mutation* of immutable data structures such as trees. Within the Zipper pattern the *focus* is on a particular node in a structure. The Zipper therefore acts like an index or pointer into the structure. It is then possible to move around the structure with respect to the *focus* point. For example to move forward to backward, or up and down depending upon the semantics of the structure. In general it is also possible to insert before or after (or the left or right) of the current *focus* point as well as delete the element at the point of focus. Assuming the structure is immutable; the result of these operations will be the generation of a copy of the original structure but with the modification applied to the copy.

41.2 Pattern Classification

Functional Pattern

41.3 Intent

To capture the potential movement within a list or tree like structure.

41.4 Context

If you are working with a list or tree like structure there are certain *movement* style operations that you might reasonable expect to be able to perform, such as the ability to move to the next node in the structure or to the previous node in that

J. Hunt, *Scala Design Patterns: Patterns for Practical Reuse and Design*,
DOI 10.1007/978-3-319-02192-8_41, © Springer International Publishing Switzerland 2013

structure. You may also be expect to be able to modify the structure in certain ways, such as inserting nodes before or after the current reference point (or focus point) within the structure and the deletion of the current focus. The Zipper pattern formalises such functionality.

41.5 Forces/Motivation

The Zipper Pattern can be used when

- An order structure is used to maintain a group of objects.
- It should be possible to move through this ordered structure.
- It may be possible to modify the structure by inserting or deleting nodes within the structure relative to a specific point in the structure.

41.6 Constituent Parts

The constituent parts of the Zipper pattern are the structure used to hold the objects, a focus point which indicates the current position within the structure and a set of operations that can be applied to the structure to move around that structure, insert new elements to the structure and delete the current (focussed upon) node.

41.7 Implementation Issues

The key decision to make with the Zipper pattern is exactly what the semantics of the Zipper should be. For example should terms like *previous* and *next* be used in a tree like structure? Additionally should the structure be *mutable* or *immutable*? If the structure is immutable are operations such as *insert* and *delete* included at all? If they should be included then they should return a modified copy of the structure.

41.8 Concrete Example

The key element on this example is the Zipper trait. This trait defines the core operations of the Zipper pattern, such as *next* and *prev* as well as some useful additional operations such as *atStart* and atEnd which help to allow clients to determine if they are at the start of the structure of at the end of the structure. The trait also records the element that is current the *focus* of the Zipper and elements that are to the left or right of the Zipper.

```
trait Zipper[A] {
  val focus: A
  val left: Seq[A]
  val right: Seq[A]

  def next: Option[Zipper[A]] = right match {
    case Nil => None
    case _ => Some(zipper(left :+ focus, right.head, right.tail))
  }
  def prev: Option[Zipper[A]] = left match {
    case Nil => None
    case _ => Some(zipper(left.init, left.last, focus +: right))
  }
  def insert(a: A): Zipper[A] = zipper(left :+ focus, a, right)
  def delete: Option[Zipper[A]] = right match {
    case Nil => None
    case _ => Some(left match {
      case Nil => zipper(Nil, right.head, right.tail)
      case _ => zipper(left.init, left.last, right)
    })
  }
  def atStart: Boolean = left.isEmpty
  def atEnd: Boolean = right.isEmpty
  override def toString = "Zipper: " +
                          focus +
                          " (left: " + left +
                          ") (right: " + right + ")"
}
```

Notice that the Zipper itself is an immutable concept. When the user moves the Zipper to the left or the right a new Zipper is created. This new Zipper represents the new position. It is thus impossible to inadvertently move a zipper in one piece of code and adversely affect another piece of code referencing the same Zipper. We have also made extensive use of the head, tail, init and last features of the Seq class to move the position of the Zipper around the underlying structure. These aspects would change depending upon that underlying structure, for example in a tree structure they would relate to the operations available to traverse the tree.

This Zipper trait is used with a simple Anonymous class to provide a set of values for the focus, left and right properties. This is created by the zipper method defined on the package object:

```
package object zipper {
  def zipper[A](ls: Seq[A], a: A, rs: Seq[A]): Zipper[A] = new Zipper[A] {
   val focus = a
   val left = ls
   val right = rs
  }
}
```

This method creates an anonymous class that extends the Zipper trait and is instantiated to create a Zipper object.

```
object Test extends App {
  val data = Seq("John", "Denise", "Phoebe", "Adam")
  var zip = zipper[String](Nil, data.head, data.tail)
  println(zip)
  println(zip.atStart)
  zip = zip.next.get
  println(zip)
  println(zip.atStart)
  zip = zip.prev.get
  println(zip)
  println(zip.atStart)
}
```

The test application that illustrates the use of the Zipper trait is shown above. This simple Test harness creates a Seq to hold a group of objects in order. A Zipper is then created based on the Seq. Note that the left side of the Zipper is Nil, the Focus is the first string "John" and the right hand side of the Zipper is the Seq "Denise", "Phoebe" and "Adam".

The test application then prints out the zip and checks to see if it thinks it is at the start of the underlying structure. The application then moves to the next element in the structure and again prints out the contents of the zipper returned and checks to see if we are at the start of the structure. It finally moves to the previous element and repeats the printout. Note that each time we move the zipper we restore the reference to the returned zipper.

The output from this program is shown below:

```
Zipper: John (left: List()) (right: List(Denise, Phoebe, Adam))
true
Zipper: Denise (left: List(John)) (right: List(Phoebe, Adam))
false
Zipper: John (left: List()) (right: List(Denise, Phoebe, Adam))
true
```

41.9 Pros and Cons

The advantages of the Zipper Pattern are:

- It makes explicit the semantics of traversal and modification of an ordered structure.

The drawbacks of the Zipper Pattern include:

- Not all structures are ordered.

41.10 Related Patterns

Views Provide an alternative View onto a structure where as a Zipper provides a perspective on the structure from a given focus point.

Chapter 42
Lens Pattern

42.1 Introduction

Lenses provide a managed (and semantically clear) way to handle updates to immutable objects. They allow you to change a value held by an immutable object by creating a copy of the object containing the updated data.

A Lens is an object that contains two function; *get* and *set*. The *get* function takes a container and returns a value from that container, while a *set* takes a container and a value and returns a *new* container that is the union of the original container and the value. This can be represented as:

```
get(a: A): B
set(a: A, b: B): A
```

That is the type b is a value contained within the *container* A. A may be a collection or some other type that holds values of type B.

Get retrieves the value (of type B) from the container A while Set takes a container and updates the value B in that container return a new container (containing the update).

In many implementations get is aliased to apply:

```
def apply(a: A) = get(a)
```

42.2 Pattern Classification

Functional Design Pattern

J. Hunt, *Scala Design Patterns: Patterns for Practical Reuse and Design*,
DOI 10.1007/978-3-319-02192-8_42, © Springer International Publishing Switzerland 2013

42.3 Intent

To enable updates to immutable data.

42.4 Context

Scala has a presumption of immutability; that is objects should be immutable unless there is a good reason for them not to be immutable. In general this makes for simpler, cleaner code. However, what happens if the data being processed is immutable but you need to update it? In many cases developers construct their own strategies for handling these situations which involve operations such as copying the object but resetting a value, or making a new instance of an object and copying values across etc.

However, the resultant code may become convoluted and is spread throughout the client code base (and as such becomes the client's responsibility to handle).

Lenses provide a clean, controlled approach to such situations where the meaning of the operation being performed is clear (provided an updated copy of the immutable object) and the responsibility for creating the appropriate lenses can remain with the provider of the immutable type.

42.5 Forces/Motivation

The Lens Pattern can be used when

- The state of an immutable object must be updated.

42.6 Constituent Parts

There are two main roles within the Lens Pattern, the Immutable Object and the Lens itself:

Immutable Object This is the container that is to be updated by some value.
Lens This is the operation that will create a copy of the original immutable object but containing the updated value.

42.7 Implementation Issues

A key idea when implementing lenses to consider is the *focus* of the lens. In general we want Lenses to be as *focussed* as possible. This means that the lenses should only update members that are direct children of the container and not children, of children, of children of the container. If this is required then a hierarchy of lenses should be constructed to allow each level in the parent–child hierarchy to be updated appropriately.

42.8 Concrete Example

The simple application defines a Lens trait containing the two methods *set* and *get* and a concrete case class that can provide a Lens onto a List.

The Lens trait is a generic type that is parameterized with a type T that contains elements of type A and the type A. The *get* method takes containers of type T and returns a value of type A. The setter method takes containers of type T and a new element of type A and returns a new copy of the container type T updated with the element a.

```
trait Lens[T[A],A] {
  def get(t: T[A]): A
  def set(t: T[A], a: A): T[A]
}
```

The class ListLens mixes in the Lens trait and specifies that the container involved is a List. However, the type of the elements held within the container is still represented by the generic type T.

```
case class ListLens[A] extends Lens[List,A] {
  def get(list: List[A]): A = list head
  def set(list: List[A], b: A): List[A] = list :+ b
}
```

The ListLens class defines the *get* method as retrieving the head of the list and the set method using the :+ operator that creates a new List with the value held in b appended to the end of the list (note this is an O(n) operation).

The ListLens is used in the following example to illustrate how it might be used with an immutable list.

```
object Test extends App {
  var l = List(1,2)
  val lens = new ListLens[Int]()

  println(lens.get(l))

  l = lens.set(l, 3)
  println(l)
}
```

In this simple application a List object is created containing the Integers 1 and 2. List in Scala is an immutable type (its mutable equivalent is ListBuffer). The ListLens is instantiated with Int being specified as the type contained with the lists that ListLens will operate on. The ListLens is used to obtain an element within the list and to print this out. It is then used to set a new value (3) into the list. Note that this line of code stores the reference returned by the set method into the variable '*l*'. The new value is printed out. The result of executing this application is shown below:

```
1
List(1, 2, 3)
```

42.9 Pros and Cons

The advantages of the Lens Pattern are:

- Simplifies the client code of immutable objects when they need to be updated.
- Makes explicit the semantics of the update operation.

The drawbacks of the Lens Pattern include:

- May appear trivially simple but when used appropriately can greatly simplify a code base.

42.10 Related Patterns

View A View provides a lazily constructed *view* of a collection while a Lens allows for update of immutable objects (whether collections or not).

Chapter 43
View Pattern

43.1 Introduction

A view represents a transformation of an underlying collection. That is a view provides another way to view the contents of a collection. For example, a collection may be inherently unordered, where as a view onto that collection may be ordered.

Such views are lazily loaded (with data from the underlying collection) rather than being eagerly populated as with normal collections. Views are constructed by applying a function to the collection which (logically) results in a new collection being created. However, each value in the view of the collection is generated dynamically when accessed (rather than being stored in a new collection). This avoids the need to copy these underlying objects (which may represent an expensive operation).

A view can be seen as a special kind of collection that represents some base collection, but implements all transformers lazily.

43.2 Pattern Classification

Functional Design Pattern

43.3 Intent

To provide a different way to represent a (underlying) data structure.

J. Hunt, *Scala Design Patterns: Patterns for Practical Reuse and Design*,
DOI 10.1007/978-3-319-02192-8_43, © Springer International Publishing Switzerland 2013

43.4 Context

Views can have advantages over the use of collection as:

- Views can represent a subset of the data contained in a collection; consequently, a view can limit the degree of exposure of the underlying collection to client code.
- Views can hide the complexity of data; for example a view on all Sales could appear as Sales for 2010 or Sales for 2011, transparently partitioning the actual underlying collection.
- Views take very little space to store; the environment contains only the definition of a view (i.e. the function used to generate the view), not a copy of all the data that it presents.

43.5 Forces/Motivation

The View Pattern can be used when

- You wish to represent an existing data structure in a different way, but without duplicating the underlying structure.
- When the *content* of the view can be determined dynamically on demand rather than eagerly (as with normal collections).
- Where a lazily populated collection is required.
- Where due to performance a view is preferred as the switch to a view avoids the construction of intermediate objects (thus resulting in few object instantiations and reducing the need for garbage collection).
- A view can be used to apply changes only to those objects accessible via the view rather than to all objects in the underlying collection.

43.6 Constituent Parts

There are two main roles within the View Pattern, the Underlier and the View. In addition there must be some mechanism for generating the view from the underlier.

Underlier This role indicates the collection holding the actual data.

View Generator This role represents the function used to generate the view based on a collection.

View The view provides a version or transformation of the data held in the underlier based on some function.

43.7 Implementation Issues

The primary question to consider when implementing the view is how the *function* to be applied to the underlier, to generate the view, is defined. It could be provided dynamically as part of the view generation operation or could be provided as part of a view trait etc. In the Scala library transformers such as *map* or *filter* generate an appropriate *view* of the underlying data collection (for example if you apply a view with a filter to a Seq you get a SeqView defined by that filter).

43.8 Concrete Example

All the collection classes in Scala directly support the concepts of views. In this section a few examples of views in these classes will be given.

As a first example of why views are very useful consider the following code:

```
object Test extends App {
   val r = (1 to 1000000000).filter(_%2==0).take(10).toList
   println(r)
}
```

This code looks reasonable, however if you run it then you get an out of memory error:

```
Exception in thread "main" java.lang.OutOfMemoryError: Java heap space
        at scala.collection.immutable.VectorPointer$class.gotoNextBlockStartWritable(Vector.scala:886)
        at scala.collection.immutable.VectorBuilder.gotoNextBlockStartWritable(Vector.scala:692)
        at scala.collection.immutable.VectorBuilder.$plus$eq(Vector.scala:706)
        at scala.collection.immutable.VectorBuilder.$plus$eq(Vector.scala:692)
        at scala.collection.TraversableLike$$anonfun$filter$1.apply(TraversableLike.scala:264)
```

However, the following code works without any problem (and generates a result much quicker than the previous one generated an error):

```
object Test extends App {
   val r = (1 to 1000000000).view.filter(_%2==0).take(10).toList
   println(r)
}
```

The output of this code is:

```
List(2, 4, 6, 8, 10, 12, 14, 16, 18, 20)
```

How is it that one of the above throws an error and the other executes quickly? The key difference is the call to *view* before the *filter* in the second example. In this case the view causes the filtered collection to be produced lazily. That is, calls to filter do not evaluate every element in the collection. Elements are only evaluated once they are explicitly accessed.

Another example of the lazy nature of views is to apply a *map* function to generate the view. In this example we will place a print out of the value being considered in the map function:

```
val xs = List(3, 2, 3, 4, 5)
val ys = xs.view map { x => println(x); x * x }
```

However, if you execute this code no values are printed out. This is because the *map* function is not executed until the SeqView is accessed. If we attempt to access the head of this sequence then we will get the following output:

```
1//the result of the println
```

And the value returned will be

```
9//the result of x * x
```

43.9 Pros and Cons

The advantages of the View Pattern are:

- It avoids the generation of additional objects.
- It lazily generates the view data on demand.
- Can be used where some type T must be viewed as some type S in order to be used with client code.

The drawbacks of the View Pattern include:

- The view is generated lazily based on the underlying data collection and thus there may be access time performance implications.

43.10 Related Patterns

Lens An adapter *delegates* some of its behaviour to an *adaptee* object, however the semantics of the adapter pattern differ from the delegate pattern.

Chapter 44
Arrow Pattern

44.1 Introduction

Arrows are actually are a generalization of Monads and as such all Monads are also Arrows (although not all Arrows are Monads). As formally defined "arrows provide a referentially transparent way of expressing relationships between *logical* steps in a computation" (Hughes 2000). In terms of data structures, Arrows provide set of behaviours that can be applied to a container. These behaviours can be summarised as

Having an identity (no op) value

And a set of functions, one to *combine* two arrows together,

```
compose(arrow(b, c), arrow(c, d)) = arrow(b, d)
```

Plus two others that take an arrow between two types and convert it into arrow between two tuples (where one version create the tuples from the inputs and an unaltered element and the second creates the tuples from the unaltered element and the inputs). These functions are often referred to as first and second:

```
first(arrow s t) = arrow(s, u) (t, u)
second(arrow s t) = arrow (u, s) (u, t)
```

A merge operator may also be defined such that two arrows, possibly with different input and output types can be joined together into one arrow between two tuples (note that the merge operator is *not* necessarily commutative):

```
merge(arrow(s, t), arrow(u, v)) = arrow(s,u)(t,v)
```

J. Hunt, *Scala Design Patterns: Patterns for Practical Reuse and Design*,
DOI 10.1007/978-3-319-02192-8_44, © Springer International Publishing Switzerland 2013

Associated with the Arrow pattern are some arrow related laws, such as Arrows must always preserve all types' identities, that is

```
arrow(id) = id
```

And composition should be distributed over the compositions from the left, thus

```
arrow(compose(f, g)) == compose(arrow(f), arrow(g))
```

The pattern presented in this chapter is based on the Functional Programming arrows concepts.

44.2 Pattern Classification

Functional Pattern

44.3 Intent

To encapsulate functions as arrows that can be combined and manipulated.

44.4 Context

In function-oriented applications it may be useful to combine together functions, to split functions apart and to manage those functions in an ordered manner. The Arrow pattern provides a way to handle such functions, to combine them into larger functions and to split them as required.

44.5 Forces/Motivation

The Arrow Pattern can be used when

- The allowed side effects of a Monad are undesirable.

44.6 Constituent Parts

The constituent parts of the Arrow are made up of the Arrow type itself and the functions to be composed / manipulated.

44.7 Implementation Issues

Exactly how the arrows are combined and the effects of operations such as first and second need to be determined for the type of arrow you are creating.

44.8 Concrete Example

In the sample application presented in this section we first define a trait that encapsulates the Arrow abstraction. This defines a constructor operation arrow that builds an arrow from a function. A compose method that combines two arrows together and the first and second functions that create new arrows from existing arrows.

```
trait Arrow[A[-_, +_]] {
  def arrow[B, C](f: B => C): A[B, C]

  def compose[B, C, D](a1: A[B, C], a2: A[C, D]): A[B, D]

  def first[B, C, D](a: A[B, C]): A[(B, D), (C, D)]

  def second[B, C, D](a: A[B, C]): A[(D, B), (D, C)]
}
```

This trait is used to create an Anonymous class that extends the Arrow trait and specifies the type created by the arrow is Function1. Thus the value returned from the arrow construction method is a Function1 that maps from an input to an output as specified by the function provided.

```
object Arrow {
  val Function1Arrow = new Arrow[Function1] {
    def arrow[B, C](f: B => C) = f

    def compose[B, C, D](a1: B => C, a2: C => D) =
      a2 compose a1

    def first[B, C, D](a: B => C) =
      (bd: (B, D)) => (a(bd._1), bd._2)

    def second[B, C, D](a: B => C) =
      (db: (D, B)) => (db._1, a(db._2))
  }
}
```

The use of this Function1Arrow implementation is shown in the Test harness below:

```
object test extends App {
  import Arrow._
  val f1 = (x: Int) => x / 2
  val a1 = Function1Arrow.arrow(f1)
  println(a1)
  println(a1(4))

  val f2 = (x: Int) => x * 3 + 1
  val a2 = Function1Arrow.arrow(f2)
  println(a2)
  println(a2(4))

  val a3 = Function1Arrow.compose(a1, a2)
  println(a3)
  println(a3(4))

}
```

Note that the result of the composed arrows a1 and a2 is the result of dividing 4 by 2 (to get 2) and the multiplying 2 by 3 and adding 1 (giving 7), see below:

```
<function1>
2
<function1>
13
<function1>
7
<function1>
```

44.9 Pros and Cons

The advantages of the Arrows Pattern are:

- Arrows generalize much of the complex function passing that can occur in heavily function-oriented applications.

The drawbacks of the Arrows Pattern include:

- There is some confusion between Monads (a subset of Arrows) and arrows themselves.
- Strictly adhering to the Arrow laws can result in more complex implementations, where as the Arrow pattern is a looser interpretation of those laws.

44.10 Related Patterns

Monads A Monad is an Arrow but not all Arrows are Monads. As Monads are easily to implement than Arrows it is often preferable to use a Monad.

Reference

Hughes, J. (2000, May). Generalising monads to arrow. *Science of Computer Programming* (Elsevier), *37*(1–3), 67–111. 0167–6423.